The Great Smokies

The Great Smokies

From Natural Habitat to National Park

Daniel S. Pierce

The University of Tennessee Press / Knoxville

An earlier version of chapter 6 was published as "The Barbarism of the Huns," *Tennessee Historical Quarterly* 57, no. 1 (1998): 62–79.

The paper used in this book meets the minimum requirements of ANSI/ NISO Z39.48-1992 (R 1997) (Permanence of Paper). The binding materials have been chosen for strength and durability. Printed on recycled paper.

Frontis: Clouds in valleys of the Great Smoky Mountains, 1920s. Photo by Jim Thompson.

Library of Congress Cataloging-in-Publication Data

Pierce, Daniel S.
The Great Smokies : from natural habitat to national park / Daniel S. Pierce.— 1st ed.
        p. cm.
Includes bibliographical references and index.
ISBN 1-57233-076-7 (cl.: alk. paper)
ISBN 1-57233-079-1 (pbk.: alk. paper)
1. Great Smoky Mountains National Park (N.C. and Tenn.)—History.
2. Natural history—Great Smoky Mountains National Park (N.C. and Tenn.). 3. Human ecology—Great Smoky Mountains National Park (N.C. and Tenn.). 4. Great Smoky Mountains National Park (N.C. and Tenn.)—Environmental conditions. I. Title.
F443.G7 P54 2000
976.8'89—dc21   99-050464

To Mom,
Archie Smith Pierce,
and in memory of Dad,
Rev. C. R. Pierce, Jr.

Contents

Figures

Maps

Acknowledgments

This book would not be complete if I did not acknowledge the debt I owe to individuals and institutions who have supported and sustained me during the more than five years required for the completion of this project. I am greatly indebted to the institutions which employed me and supported my research during this period: the University of Tennessee at Knoxville and its Bernadotte Schmidt Research Fellowships, Mars Hill College, Western Carolina University, Warren Wilson College, and the University of North Carolina at Asheville. Special thanks go to Max Williams of Western Carolina University, who read a draft of this work and suggested the addition of much of the material in chapter 2. I am also grateful to graduate school colleagues who inspired and encouraged my work: Margaret Stair, who gave me the idea for the project; Dan Jansen, who provided invaluable guidance for research in the National Archives and who opened his apartment to me on two extended research trips; Jenny Brooks; Connie Lester; Bren Martin; and Craig Pascoe. Durwood Dunn and Gordon McKinney read the work, made helpful suggestions, and were most kind in their overall assessment.

I have been blessed over the years with wonderfully gifted, insightful, and supportive mentors. At the University of Alabama, Grady McWhiney encouraged my research and writing. Forrest McDonald helped me overcome many of my writing deficiencies and will never know the importance of his "damn well written" on a draft of my master's thesis. James C. Cobb nurtured my love for the New South, helped me navigate the maze of researching and writing a dissertation, taught me the invaluable lesson that "historians are first and foremost humanists," and will always serve as an inspiration in my life as both teacher and researcher. Most importantly, I must thank Paul Bergeron. In the process of helping me turn a dissertation into a book, he became not only a mentor but also a dear friend. I will always cherish Paul's four-page, single-spaced, chapter-by-chapter critique of the first draft of this book, complete with his "if we're still friends, then. . . ." We are; indeed, every individual should have a friend such as Paul, who cares enough about him or her to tell the truth.

This book would not have been possible without the assistance of dedicated professionals at the archives and special collections where I did my research and at the University of Tennessee Press. I am indebted to George Frizzell, special collections librarian at Western Carolina University, and to Jimmy Rush at the National Archives. Fortunately for me, the bulk of the research for this project was done in the park library and archives of the Great Smoky Mountains National Park. Kitty Manscill and Annette Hartigan have created a wonderful research environment there. I cannot thank them enough for their kindness and support. Jennifer Siler, director of UT Press, encouraged my work even before it became a dissertation. She, along with Managing Editor Stan Ivester, freelance copyeditor Mavis Bryant, and many others at UT Press made the process of turning a dissertation into a book a very smooth and enjoyable one.

Many friends and family members also helped to make this book possible. I must thank the people of West Asheville, North Carolina, and the members of Grace Baptist Church, who were so instrumental in my growth and development, for their love and support over the years. I am especially indebted to one of those church members who helped raise me, Marie Clontz. She proofread countless drafts of this book and should be credited for anything in it that is grammatically correct. I am grateful to two brothers, David and Jon, who know all my faults yet remain wonderfully supportive. My children—Anna Clare, Taylor, Sullivan, and Coulter—have been true blessings throughout this long process. They will never know the value of their hugs and unconditional love in sustaining me through these long years of research and writing. My wife, Lydia, has remained patient, supportive, and loving through five changes of residence, two pregnancies, and my frequent absences. I never would have made it through the long process of researching, writing, and publication without her. Indeed, this book is a product of her sacrifice and hard work as much as of mine.

Finally, I must thank my parents, Archie and C. R. Pierce, to whom this book is dedicated. I will always treasure the two summers I spent in their basement revising this book, especially the precious time I spent with my dad the summer he died of cancer. Throughout my life, my parents have taught me the qualities that made this book possible: the value of hard work, the importance of dreams, and the power of prayer.

Introduction

I first glimpsed the Great Smoky Mountains in the summer of 1959, in the midst of a family move from Lake Village, Arkansas, to Asheville, North Carolina. I don't remember much about the experience, except for the bear we saw digging in a trash can (this was before bear-proof trash cans relegated most of these animals to the backcountry) and the small stuffed bear my parents bought me in Cherokee, North Carolina.

Spending the greater part of my lifetime in either Western North Carolina or East Tennessee, however, has enabled me to make countless visits into the Smokies since that first trip. The opportunity to experience nature, seemingly undisturbed by humanity, draws me back time and again. I treasure my close encounters with deer, wild turkeys, grouse, brook trout, and even bear; the solitude and majesty of old-growth forests in Albright Grove, Greenbriar, and Cataloochee; the clear, aquamarine headwaters of the Pigeon, Little, Oconoluftee, and Little Tennessee rivers rushing around, through, and over massive boulders; fall leaves, spring wildflowers, wondrous displays of rhododendron and flame azalea; and, perhaps most important, views from practically every high place in the Smokies. Here one can look for miles and see no evidence of the hand of man.

It is the experience of wilderness that draws people—even those visitors who never stray far from their cars—to the Smokies. Michael Frome, in *Strangers in High Places,* describes the Smokies as most people see them: "Eight hundred square miles, much of it an unspoiled wilderness of singing mountain streams feeding their clear waters democratically to a fantastic variety of flowering shrubs, small herbs, and tall trees." In the same work, Frome comments, "Happily, in a world where nothing remains static, the Great Smoky Mountains provide the prescription to ward off ills and evils born of super-civilization. A single day spent in the Smokies away from the works of man is therapy to last a year."[1] We Americans have come to see the Smokies as a place somehow separate from human civilization, a place that is controlled by "natural," nonhuman forces, a place to escape human influences. We see these mountains as the proper and natural habitat not of humans but of denizens of the wilderness—black bear, winter wren, brook trout, northern flying squirrel, and pileated woodpecker. Few places in this nation, especially east of the Mississippi River, better embody our vision of undisturbed wilderness.

Indeed, the Great Smoky Mountains National Park contains by far the largest areas of old-growth forest in the East. The park also harbors amazing biodiversity, including 125 species of native trees, 125 species of shrubs, 1,500 species of vascular plants, 60 ferns and fern allies, 280 mosses, 250 species of lichens, 200 species of birds, 40 reptiles, 40 amphibians, 80 species of fish, 50 mammals, and uncounted species of insects and other arthropods. Recent estimates of one measure of wilderness—the presence and success of black bears—have placed the population at over 700 animals—the highest level in the twentieth century.[2]

Upon closer examination of the park, however, we realize that a trip into the Smokies is a voyage not "away from the works of man," but rather into a very human place. For at least eight thousand years, the Smokies have been the "natural" habitat of human beings fully as much of the black bear.[3] During those millennia, human civilization has shaped and molded the Smokies just as surely as tectonic forces or the erosive action of wind and rain. No creature or natural force has had a greater impact on the environment of the Smokies in the last eight thousand years than human beings. During that time, human use of the Smokies has run the gamut from wise to shockingly wasteful.

As an environmental historian, my intention in writing this book is not to explore what God and nature have done in the Great Smoky Mountains; countless books do that. Rather, I want to examine what *people* have done in the mountains and to them. I am concerned especially with the men and women behind the movement to establish a national park in the Great Smoky Mountains in the 1920s and 1930s. How has this particular human use of the mountains shaped, and how does it continue to shape, these mountains?

Looking at the Smokies in this way gives us a totally new (and much more useful) perspective on nature and wilderness. Historian William Cronon has been at the forefront of a movement, controversial in some circles, that encourages this new view of the "natural" world. Cronon recently commented:

> Far from being the one place on earth that stands apart from humanity, it [wilderness] is quite profoundly a human creation— indeed, the creation of very particular human cultures at very particular moments in human history. It is not a pristine sanctuary where the last remnant of an untouched, endangered, but still transcendent nature can for at least a little while longer be encountered without the contaminating taint of civilization. Instead, it is a product of that civilization, and could hardly be contaminated by the very stuff of which it is made.
>
> Wilderness hides its unnaturalness behind a mask that is all the more beguiling because it seems so natural. As we gaze into the mirror it holds up for us, we too easily imagine that what we behold is Nature when in fact we see the reflection of our own unexamined longings and desires.[4]

The story of the Great Smoky Mountains for the past eight thousand years, then, is as much a story of the people of Western North Carolina and East Tennessee, who helped shape this land, as it is the story of the geology, flora, and fauna that make it a unique landscape. For much of human history, Native Americans left their imprint on the land through their subsistence practices, as they hunted, farmed, and burned the land. Although their touch may have been light by modern industrial standards, nevertheless they manipulated and changed the environment to suit their purposes and lifestyles. The arrival of Europeans and their domesticated animals broadened the scope of human impact on the environment. Their expansion of farming into even the most remote coves, and their burning and clearing to produce better forage for their animals, represented a new and more aggressive form of subsistence. Loggers, railroad builders, and miners came to the Smokies in the late nineteenth and early twentieth centuries, driven by the desire for commercial profit. They made an unmistakable impact on the land, leaving in their wake a denuded and eroded landscape, ravaging wildfires, and silt-laden streams.

Reacting to the devastation wrought in the Smokies by large-scale logging, a new group of people in the region, aided by a small group of influential outsiders, began to exert an influence on the land as they called for a new use for this territory, as a national park. These individuals, ironically based in the more urbanized sections of the region, were a particularly optimistic and energetic group of human beings, active during a particularly optimistic period in the region's history. Their desire to segregate the land from most forms of human use reflected not so much love of the

GREAT SMOKY MOUNTAINS

U.S. TO SEVIERVILLE AND KNOXVILLE

TO MARYVILLE AND KNOXVILLE

WEAR COVE

COVE MTN.

U.S. 129

KINZEL SPRINGS

73 TOWNSEND

PARK HEADQUARTERS

LAUREL LAKE

LAUREL FALLS

TUCKALEECHEE COVE

SINKS

RICH MTN. ROAD

LITTLE RIVER ROAD

SUGARLAND VISITOR CENTER

CHILHOWEE MOUNTAINS

WHITE OAK SINK

ELKMONT

LOOK ROCK

ABRAMS FALLS

RICH MTN.

MIDDLE PRONG

HAPPY VALLEY

CADES COVE

TREMONT

DAVIS RIDGE

ABRAMS CREEK

SPENCE FIELD

APPALACHIAN T.

HANNAH MOUNTAIN

THUNDERHEAD

MOUNT DAVIS

SILERS BALD

CHILHOWEE LAKE

DOE KNOB

MOUNT SQUIRES

TENN. N.C.

GREAT SMOKY MOUNTAINS

HAZEL CREEK

FORNEY CREEK

GREGORY BALD

CALDERWOOD DAM

SHUCKSTACK

HIGH ROCKS

DEALS GAP

TAPOCA

TENN. N.C.

U.S. 129

CHEOAH RIVER

FONTANA DAM

FONTANA RESERVOIR

Great Smoky Mountains National Park.

NATIONAL PARK

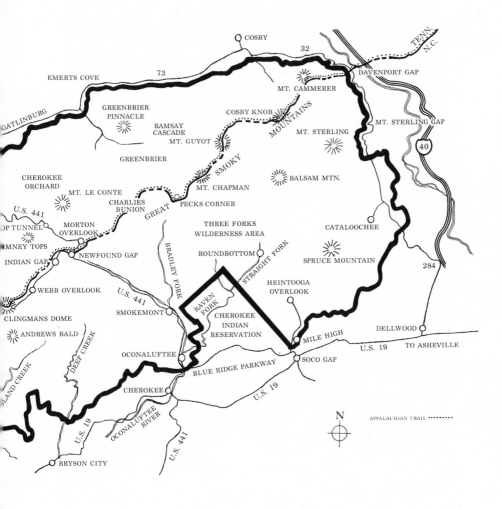

COSBY

32

TENN.
N.C.

EMERTS COVE   73

DAVENPORT GAP

MT. CAMMERER

GATLINBURG

GREENBRIER
PINNACLE

COSBY KNOB

MOUNTAINS

MT. STERLING GAP

RAMSAY
CASCADE

MT. STERLING

40

MT. GUYOT

GREENBRIER

SMOKY

BALSAM MTN.

CHEROKEE
ORCHARD

MT. LE CONTE

MT. CHAPMAN

CHARLIES
BUNION

PECKS CORNER

GREAT

U.S. 441

OP TUNNEL

MORTON
OVERLOOK

THREE FORKS
WILDERNESS AREA

CATALOOCHEE

MNEY TOPS

INDIAN GAP

NEWFOUND GAP

ROUNDBOTTOM

STRAIGHT FORK

SPRUCE MOUNTAIN

284

WEBB OVERLOOK

U.S. 441

BRADLEY FORK

HEINTOOGA
OVERLOOK

CLINGMANS DOME

SMOKEMONT

RAVEN FORK

CHEROKEE
INDIAN
RESERVATION

DELLWOOD

ANDREWS BALD

MILE HIGH

TO ASHEVILLE

OCONALUFTEE

SOCO GAP

U.S. 19

DEEP CREEK

BLUE RIDGE PARKWAY

LAND CREEK

U.S. 19

CHEROKEE

U.S. 19

OCONALUFTEE
RIVER

U.S. 441

N

APPALACHIAN TRAIL ·········

BRYSON CITY

land as a desire to see the regional economy grow and finally become part of the national economic mainstream. Most of the park boosters saw the establishment of a national park in the Smokies as a means of attracting millions of tourists ready to deposit money on the doorsteps of the region's residents. Although modern environmentalists may consider their motives impure, these individuals battled against huge odds to convince the people of the region of the advantages of a national park, persuade the National Park Service and the United States Congress that the land was worthy of selection, raise most of the money to purchase the land, buy the land from unwilling sellers, and turn the land over to the Park Service so that the federal government could develop it as a national park.

While this story is primarily about the boosters who made the park a reality, it also deals with other people who consider this land, this park, "theirs." Indeed, this story would be incomplete without telling the tragic tale of the thousands of individuals who called the Smokies home before the coming of the park. Their removal to transform the land into a national park still causes pain to those who were uprooted and to their descendants.

This book also traces the activities of a small group of individuals who helped to turn the Smokies into a unique type of national park—one devoid of the skyline drives, grand lodges, and other tourist developments characteristic of most of the larger and more popular national parks. The park's current form dramatically reflects the influence of this small but influential group of wilderness advocates.

Indeed, looking out over the Great Smoky Mountains from Newfound Gap, Clingman's Dome, Mount Cammerer, Shuckstack, Gregory Bald, Mount Sterling, or thousands of other high places, one sees spread out below not only a "wonderment of mountains," but also a wonderment of human action.[5] The Smokies stand as a tribute to, and in some cases a condemnation of, the varied people who have lived in East Tennessee and Western North Carolina for the past eight thousand years. Look closely at these mountains, and you can read the story of a people and their land. For more than sixty years, that story has been one of a people and their park. At various turns, this story delights and disgusts; recounts triumphs and tragedies; and, most important, teaches us lessons about who we are and who we can be.

1.

"Evils Born of Super-Civilization"

Approximately eight thousand years ago, humans first entered the land now known as the Great Smoky Mountains National Park. Although we can only make educated guesses about what the land looked like at that time, we do know that, as people came in, the land began to change. Despite Michael Frome's assertion to the contrary, since that time, the landscape of the Great Smoky Mountains has been anything but "static." Indeed, a parade of humanity has transformed this mountainous landscape to varying degrees. Native American hunter-gatherers were succeeded by their settled agriculturist descendants, just as European hunters and traders were succeeded by their pastoralist and settled agriculturist descendants. The late nineteenth and early twentieth centuries brought miners, timbermen, and finally tourists. All left their legacy on the land, shaping it in accord with their own needs, desires, and self-images.

With each new group of people, however, the human impact seemed to increase, becoming more destructive and changing the land more dramatically. Although Native Americans definitely altered the Smokies with their hunting and horticultural practices, after 7,500 years of their use, much of the characteristic vegetation of the Smokies remained, and its animal populations were relatively stable. With the coming of European farmers and their domestic animals, change became more apparent, as grass balds were enlarged and created on the high ridges and agriculture expanded into previously untilled bottomland. Many animals disappeared from the mountains, most notably such predators as the gray wolf and the mountain lion, which these settlers exterminated in order to protect their cattle and hogs.

Despite these changes, parts of the Smokies remained as remote and inaccessible as any area east of the Mississippi until late in the nineteenth century. As the United States became more "civilized," however, degradation of the environment in the Smokies accelerated. The later nineteenth and early twentieth centuries saw a level of destruction unimagined by earlier inhabitants of the region. Enormous logging operations blanketed these mountains, as railroad lines penetrated to even the remotest watersheds. In their wake, the loggers left a denuded landscape, massive erosion, streams clogged with silt, and debris that ignited devastating forest fires. Amid this onslaught, it appeared that little would remain in the Smokies that could be considered wilderness.

For most of the past eight thousand years, Native Americans inhabited, used, and shaped the landscape of the Great Smoky Mountains. Our popular culture, and even some historians, would lead us to believe that Native Americans made little impact on the environment, that they were not only the "first people" but the first environmentalists. One Sierra Club publication argues that "Indians moved over the face of the land and when they left you could not tell they had ever been there."[1] Supreme Court Justice William O. Douglas, an environmentalist, once asserted, "Although Indians took their living from the wilderness, they left that wilderness virtually intact."[2] Archaeologists and historians have demonstrated that this view is not only inaccurate, but condescending in its disregard of Indian life and culture. Indeed, the Smokies offer clear evidence of the varied ways in which Native Americans shaped and molded this particular environment.

In an extensive archaeological survey conducted in the Smokies in the mid-1970s, archaeologists discovered tools and pottery characteristic of every cultural period since approximately 6,000 B.C., including Archaic, Woodland, Mississippian, and Historic. The survey also found archaeological evidence of prehistoric human use in all sections and landforms within the Great Smoky Mountains National Park. Artifacts recovered from these sites indicate that prehistoric Indians used the Smokies primarily as hunting and gathering sites, or, as archaeologist Quentin Bass argues, "as a peripheral area of exploitation for populations based in the lower drainages of the Little Tennessee and Pigeon rivers."[3]

Humans of the Archaic and Woodland periods utilized a variety of landscapes and ecosystems in order to survive. Lacking horticulture, these hunter-gatherers moved from site to site throughout the year, gathering roots, seeds, leaves, and fruits of plants such as persimmon, maypop, grape, black cherry, and sumpweed. They hunted deer, elk, bear, raccoon, beaver, and turkey and constructed weirs to catch fish in the creeks and rivers.[4] As a matter of survival, these individuals had to possess an intimate knowledge of the ecology of their environment, including the life cycles of plants and the habits of animals.[5] The Smokies provided an excellent setting for such a lifestyle, as short moves up or down the mountainside enabled the people to take advantage of varied microenvironments, each with its associated plant and animal populations.[6]

For these prehistoric hunter-gatherers, the fall season was a time of bounty. They moved to the summit areas of the Smokies to hunt for deer and elk and to gather chestnuts and acorns, apparently choosing to set up camp in a high gap with relatively easy access, a nearby spring, and enough flat land to accommodate the group.[7] Fall was an ideal time to hunt deer, a major component of the Indian diet. Feeding on acorns and chestnuts that had fallen, the deer reached their largest size at this time of year and herded together in specific areas of major mast production. In addition, during the fall rutting season, the bucks became much more aggressive and less cautious, thus becoming easier to hunt.[8] While the men hunted, the women gathered chestnuts, acorns, and hickory nuts, commodities easily stored for winter consumption.

These prehistoric Indians, like their Cherokee descendants, gathered a wide variety of medicinal herbs in the Smokies. According to Cherokee myth, animals created disease to exact revenge for the actions of the growing populations of humans, who crowded them out, stepped on them, and overhunted them. The animals became so angry at humans that, "had not their invention finally failed them[,] not one of the human race would have been able to survive." The plants, however, "who were friendly to man, . . . agreed to furnish a remedy for some of the diseases named [by the animals]." As James Mooney recorded the Cherokee legend: "Thus did medicine originate, and the plants, every one of which has its use if we only knew it, furnish the antidote to counteract the evil wrought by the revengeful animals. When the doctor is in doubt what treatment to apply for the relief of a patient, the spirit of the plant suggests to him the proper remedy."[9]

Mooney listed twenty medicinal plants used by the Cherokee, most found in the Smokies, with some growing only at higher elevations. This fact suggests a trade in these plants with Cherokee in lower areas. Black snakeroot was blown on patients for fever, chewed and spit on snakebites, and placed in a hollow tooth for toothache. The Indians made vetch into a decoction and drank it for back pain, rubbed it on their stomachs for cramps, and applied it to ballplayers to toughen their muscles. The roots of ginseng were made into a decoction for headache, cramps, and "female problems." The Cherokee also used a number of other plants found in the Smokies for medicinal purposes; among these were maidenhair fern, tassel flower, ladyslipper, cone flower, Solomon seal, and shield fern.[10]

In the Middle and Late Woodland periods (from the time of Christ until about 1,000 A.D.), land use by prehistoric Indians in the Smokies began to change. Horticulture gradually was introduced. In the early stages of this development, the Indians domesticated indigenous plants such as Iva or sumpweed, storing the seeds for later use. They discovered that the plants grew best in disturbed soil in the floodplains of streams and rivers.[11] Archaeological evidence indicates a resultant shift toward a more sedentary lifestyle, with habitation tending to concentrate in the floodplains at lower elevations. Many of these places were outside the current park boundaries. Although it remained significant, use of the summit areas diminished.[12]

The move toward a more settled and sedentary lifestyle intensified during the Pisgah Phase (1000 A.D. up to the arrival of Europeans), when these prehistoric Indians adopted the use of more tropical crops, especially the so-called "three sisters"—maize, beans, and squash. The introduction of the eastern flint variety of maize, well adapted to the moist soil and cool climate of the mountain region, helped facilitate this change.[13] Indians of the Pisgah Phase practiced a type of agriculture referred to as "riverine," most often burning and clearing streamside canebrakes. The presence of river cane provided a clear indication of soil well suited for the cultivation of maize. Soils in such areas were tilled easily with basic tools available to the Indians (primarily the hoe) and recovered their fertility with only a short fallow period. If the fields contained trees, they were girdled with stone axes and left standing in the field to rot and then burned when they fell.[14]

During the Pisgah and later Qualla phases (the Qualla Phase dates from the European arrival up to the Cherokee removal), women assumed most of the burden of agricultural production. They used a system of "intercropping" (planting maize and beans in the same hill and gourds, squashes, sunflowers, and pumpkins between the rows). Although to Europeans this type of agriculture looked crowded and disorganized, it actually made highly efficient use of the limited bottomland of the Smokies. Beans and maize, planted together, make an ideal pair, as the maize stalks provide poles for the beans to run up, while the beans replenish at least part of the nitrogen removed from the soil by the maize. In addition, while maize is a good source of vegetable protein, it lacks the amino acid lysine, which most beans provide in abundance. The vines of gourds, squash, and pumpkins covered the ground between the rows of maize, preventing erosion and crowding out weeds, freeing Indian women from the task of weeding and allowing them to gather wild plant foods once the crops began to mature.[15]

Although horticulture was important to Indians of the Great Smoky Mountains, they continued to use the more mountainous areas much as their hunter-gatherer ancestors had—hunting deer and other game and gathering wild plant foods. This practice provided these Indians with what William Cronon has called an "ecological safety net." If one area of subsistence was limited in some fashion, another area could be exploited more intensively.[16] In other words, if a shortage of mast adversely affected the deer and bear populations, then the Indians could intensify their agricultural activities and their gathering of other wild plant foods. On the other hand, if a drought caused a poor harvest, the Indians could intensify hunting activities. However, the Cherokee tried to avoid overhunting, as they believed the deer would retaliate by sending sickness.[17] By the time Europeans appeared, exploiting the great variety of plants and animals found in the Smokies, coupled with the efficient practice of horticulture, had enabled the Cherokee to achieve sizable numbers, particularly in the surrounding river basins.[18]

While the Cherokee and their Indian ancestors impacted the environment of the Smokies in relatively minor ways through their hunting, gathering, and horticultural activities, anthropogenic fire produced the most dramatic change in the environment. Although it is impossible to calculate the full extent and impact of Indian burning in the Great Smoky Mountains, fire "literally made the world habitable."[19]

The Indians used fire in numerous ways. Fire was the most efficient means, both initially and annually, of clearing the floodplain to create fields for horticulture. Fire not only eliminated competing vegetation, but also enriched the soil with mineralized nitrogen contained in ashes.[20] Moreover, the Indians managed the forest environment by using low-intensity fires in the woods. Fires set in early spring burned off undergrowth and forest litter that had accumulated. This process promoted the growth of grasses and the sprouting of hardwoods (foods favored by deer and turkeys), while making it easier to travel and spot both game and enemies in the more open forest. Fall fires were used to drive game, particularly deer, to waiting hunters and made it easier to locate and collect acorns and chestnuts.

Fire served a variety of other useful purposes for the Indians, too. Burning the forest around villages and campsites consumed forest litter and reduced the likelihood of wildfire. Light burns around village sites helped control plant diseases and reduced the numbers of insect pests, particularly fleas, that often plagued Indians. Periodic burning favored the so-called "sprout hardwoods," such as chestnut, oak, and hickory, which helped to create a forest dominated by these mast-producing species. Burning around blackberry and blueberry gathering sites improved production of these important foods.[21] Indeed, for the Cherokee and their ancestors, fire was a beneficent, even a sacred, force: "The Cherokees maintained a great reverence for fire, considering it equal to water in importance, the 'giver of good things,' and the focal point of power and life."[22]

Perhaps one of the most significant effects of Indian burning was the creation, or at least the expansion, of the famous grass balds of the Smokies. Over the years, scholars have engaged in intense debate concerning the origin of mountain balds in the Southern Appalachian region, and it is likely that the mystery never will be solved conclusively. Nevertheless, at least a strong possibility exists that Indian land use played some role in the process. Cherokee legends recorded by James Mooney in the 1890s give credence to the notion that at least some of the balds existed prior to European settlement—including Gregory Bald in the Smokies, which was known as *Tsistu'yi,* or Rabbit Place. According to legend, the deer-sized chief of the rabbits, the Great Rabbit, held council in his townhouse, located on the bald.[23] Although some observers argue that these legends came into being after Europeans created the balds as pasturage for their domesticated animals, there is no evidence to support this contention.[24]

A reasonable, although admittedly speculative, hypothesis concerning bald formation is that some natural force, such as lightning fires, high winds, or other natural conditions, caused openings in the high forests. Noticing that these open areas served to attract deer, turkeys, and other game, the Indians sought to maintain these conditions by the use of fire. Mary Lindsay, who has made the most intensive study of the balds, thinks that "it seems unlikely" that the balds are of Indian origin, as "there was ample game for their needs in the valleys." The land-use patterns uncovered by archaeologists in the Smokies, as well as current knowledge of deer migration, however, seem to support the use of the summit areas near the balds as fall hunting camps. Archaeologists Quentin Bass, C. R. McCollough, and Charles Faulkner also dispute the notion of Indian origin of the balds, pointing to the lack of artifacts and the scant evidence of hunting camps on the balds.[25] However, the absence of a dependable water supply on most of these balds, the desire to maintain the areas as game attractors and not scare the game away by human occupation, and the better protection from the elements offered by gaps argue for the placement of hunting camps in the gaps, which do yield abundant evidence of human occupation.[26] In any case, evidence of Indian land use patterns in the Smokies suggests that the Indians were responsible for at least a thinning of the forest on the summit areas, and that Europeans later cleared these more thoroughly and expanded them by burning, clearing, and grazing domestic animals.

Bald formation aside, we know that the Great Smoky Mountains encountered by Europeans, while remote, had been changed dramatically by human action over thousands of years. The notion of a landscape characterized by "pristine" mountains or "virgin" forest when Europeans came flies in the face of what we know of human land use in the Smokies. As Michael Williams has observed:

> The Indians were a potent, if not crucial[,] ecological factor in the distribution and composition of the forest. Their activities through millennia make the concept of "natural vegetation" a difficult one to uphold. This does not mean that there was no untouched forest, or even fluctuations of climate; but the idea of the forest as being in some pristine state of equilibrium with nature, awaiting the arrival of the transforming hand of the Europeans, has been all too readily accepted as a comforting generalization and as a benchmark [by which] to measure all subsequent change. When the Europeans came to North America the forest had already been changed radically."[27]

Early explorers and naturalists who visited the area often commented on the parklike appearance of the open forests. The De Soto Expedition, which skirted either the eastern end (through the Pigeon River gorge) or western end (through the Little Tennessee gorge) of the Smokies, had no problems moving its six hundred men and accompanying horses and hogs through the area.[28]

Perhaps the best account of what the landscape of the Great Smoky

Mountains actually looked like before extensive European occupation comes from naturalist William Bartram's travels in the region in 1775. Although Bartram did not enter the park's present area, he got as far as the Nantahala Gorge, traveled through terrain very similar to that in the Smokies, and actually came within sight of the Smokies. Even as Bartram recorded his impressions of "scenes of primitive and unmodified nature," his comments reveal a forest obviously shaped by millennia of human use. Near the Jore village, located between the present-day towns of Franklin and Bryson City, North Carolina, Bartram noticed an obvious human impact on the forest—a grove of casine yaupon, a plant native to the coastal plains of North and South Carolina. The Cherokee referred to this as the "beloved tree" and kept the trees pruned and cultivated, making a strong-tasting medicinal drink out of the leaves, buds, and stems. As Bartram passed through a mile-long "elevated plain" (a grass bald, perhaps?) in the Nantahala Mountains, he described the view, probably of the Smokies, from the top of a mountain: "An expansive prospect, exhibiting scenes of mountainous landscape, westward, vast and varied, perhaps not to be exceeded anywhere." Although Bartram recorded this observation as evidence of the primeval nature of the landscape, the fact that he had a panoramic view from this mountaintop provides evidence of some sort of human clearing.[29]

Bartram also observed what William Cronon has called the "mosaic quality" of the forest, where the abandonment of fields no longer fertile and the burning of woods had created "forests in many different stages of ecological succession."[30] Bartram commented on "grassy, open forests" and "grassy vales, or lawns," and told of "proceeding through . . . spacious high forests and flowery lawns." At one point, he "came near the banks of a large creek or river, where . . . the trees became more scattered and insensibly united with a grassy glade or lawn bordering on the river," probably the site of an Indian "oldfield."[31]

With the coming of Europeans to the Great Smoky Mountains, the landscape faced even more significant changes. Although numbers of Europeans, especially Indian traders, visited the Smokies in the eighteenth century, white settlement in the Smokies came slowly, primarily because the terrain was rugged and treaties with the Cherokee prevented occupation. However, the presence of Europeans in the surrounding region changed Cherokee land use even before European settlement reached the Smokies. First, the trade in deer skins and other hides by Cherokee desiring European products increased hunting pressure on animals in the Smokies. Well before the first Europeans settled in the Smokies, this fur trade produced a marked decline in deer populations, the extirpation of elk, and the near extirpation of river otters and beavers. Second, for most Cherokee, life became even more sedentary. As they sought to demonstrate to those in authority that they were just as "civilized" as the white settlers who were encroaching on their lands, the Indians spent more of their time and energy in agriculture, including the use of European domesticated animals.[32]

A series of treaties in the late eighteenth century and early nineteenth century culminated in the Treaty of Calhoun in 1819, which eliminated all Cherokee claims in the Smokies. These treaties gradually opened up the coves and river valleys of the Smokies to white settlement.[33] John Jacob Mingus and Felix Walker, the first white settlers within the current boundaries of Great Smoky Mountains National Park, established permanent homesites in the 1790s, in the area around the Oconoluftee River, just north of present-day Cherokee, North Carolina.[34]

Europeans soon occupied other areas of the Smokies as well. John and Lucretia Oliver moved into Cades Cove in 1818, followed by the Tiptons, Jobes, Davises, and Cables.[35] Although no permanent settlers moved into the Cataloochee area until 1839, when James and Levi Caldwell, William Noland, and Evan Hannah moved into the area, whites in the early part of the century began using the valley for hunting and for seasonal ranging of livestock. In 1825, a group living in the Jonathan Creek section of Haywood County, North Carolina, widened an ancient Indian trail for driving livestock in and out of the area, called it the "Catalooch Turnpike," and began collecting tolls. Tollgate attendants charged drovers 18-3/4 cents for a man and horse, 6-1/2 cents for an extra pack horse, 1 cent per hog, and 2 cents for every head of cattle.[36]

By the late 1830s and early 1840s, whites had settled in nearly all the major stream valleys of the Smokies. The Ogles, Huskeys, and Whaleys moved into the watershed of the Little Pigeon River in Tennessee, starting the Greenbriar and Sugarland communities. Arthur and Brice McFalls, Wiley King, and Alexander McKenzie settled on Little River and formed the Little Greenbriar community. Cables, Crisps, Gunters, Myerses, Proctors, and Welches moved up Deep, Noland, Forney, Hazel, and Eagle Creeks and their tributaries to form the communities of Jackson, Wayside, Dorsey, and Hubbard.[37]

For these early settlers, life and land use differed little from those of the former Cherokee inhabitants. For these early farmers, the primary goal in life was subsistence. They farmed the bottomlands, oftentimes the "oldfields" once used by the Cherokee for the same purpose, growing crops similar to the ones grown by the Indians and using farm implements little more advanced than the Cherokee hoe. They hunted game in the woods and collected chestnuts, hickory nuts, blueberries, and blackberries for food.[38]

These early white settlers learned the uses of other plants for medicinal purposes from their Cherokee neighbors. Dorie Cope, born in the Oconoluftee River area in the 1890s, remembered many of the medicinal plants used by whites in the Smokies: "We gathered cockleburs to be boiled into a cough syrup for winter colds. Tansy was a fern-like plant used as tea for upset stomachs and headaches. Boneset and catnip were brewed into tea for fretful babies and nervous disorders. Sassafras was a good blood builder. Spignet root was kidney medicine. Crushed ragweed was rubbed on skin blistery from poison ivy and oak."[39] Durwood Dunn has asserted that nearly everyone in Cades Cove kept a copy of *Gunn's Domestic Medicine* to guide them in using herbal remedies found in the nearby mountains.[40]

The major early difference in land use by white settlers came as they introduced domesticated livestock to the Smokies. Influenced by terrain and the culture of the largest ethnic group to settle in the Smokies (the Scotch-Irish), settlers quickly adapted to a new environment the traditional methods of upland grazing of cattle and other livestock used in Scotland and Ireland. Ranging livestock in the woods and on the peaks of the Smokies soon became one of the most important components of life in the area. Throughout the nineteenth century, and in some cases well into the twentieth, the law allowed individuals to free-range their cattle, sheep, and hogs on others' property. Each farmer simply marked his or her animals with some special mark, usually a distinctive notch on one ear, although the Myers family of Cades Cove used brass rings in the ears of their cattle, and some in later years used tattoos. Each farmer then would register his or her special mark with the county "range master," who settled disputes over ownership.[41]

Throughout the nineteenth and early twentieth centuries, thousands of head of cattle ranged in the Smokies. Because of the difficulties of preservation, settlers themselves rarely ate beef. Cattle were a market commodity, perhaps the most important one for inhabitants of the Smokies, and one of their few sources of cash. After spending several summers mapping and observing the Southern Appalachian region, geographer Arnold Guyot noted the importance of cattle to the mountain economy: "The great resource of Haywood County [North Carolina], as in most of the mountain region, is the raising of cattle, which find an abundant and rich grazing ground in the surrounding mountains and forests, and are eagerly bought by Virginia and Tennessee traders, to find a ready market in northern cities. I have been told that the County, the boundaries of which coincide with this [Big Pigeon River] basin, sells alone 3,000 head a year."[42]

Due to the shortage of bottomland, which was used for the cultivation of crops, cattle were ranged in the high mountains, particularly on the balds, beginning in April and lasting until September or October. Herders stayed near the cattle in small cabins, protecting them from predators, marking newborn calves, searching for strays, and putting out salt so that the cattle would stay nearby. Owners attached bells to some of the cattle so that they would be easier to track.[43] In Cades Cove, Russell Gregory was "famous for his method of calling cattle. Using a large blowing horn, he summoned them to the top of Gregory Bald from miles around in order to salt them. The sight and sounds of hundreds of cattle converging on him with their bells jingling remained for many years one of the cove's most memorable spectacles."[44]

In early fall, the owners rounded up their cattle into temporary holding pens and separated them by mark, usually a three- or four-day process. Women and children combed the surrounding forest and collected chestnuts, which they both consumed and sold in area markets.

For these mountaineers, as for the Cherokee before them, the fall was a time of bounty and celebration, as friends and family thronged to the mountain balds to help out. The large numbers gathered and the festive occasion warranted the slaughter and barbecuing of one or more yearlings ("yerlins," in mountain parlance). This was one of the few times that these people consumed beef. A party ensued, with eating, music, dancing, and the consumption of corn liquor, a product often produced by herders in their spare time.[45]

After the roundup, the cattle, horses, and mules were driven down to the coves and valleys, where most were sold to drovers. On occasion, the owners themselves drove the animals to market, sometimes as far away as Charleston and Savannah. William Holland Thomas of Quallatown (now Cherokee, North Carolina) was a store owner, land speculator, politician, and friend and "white chief" of the Cherokee. Thomas regularly hired drovers to drive his own cattle and those that he had bought or traded for from his neighbors to Augusta and Charleston.[46] Drovers in Tennessee most often took their cattle to Knoxville, although some were driven over the mountains through Indian Gap or over the turnpike that was built between Big Creek and Cataloochee in the 1850s. Through the winter, the owners fed their breeding stock on hay grown in the bottomlands.[47]

Hogs also ranged throughout the Smokies, thriving on acorns, chestnuts, roots, and almost anything they could swallow. Horace Kephart, in his classic work *Our Southern Highlanders*, gave one of the best descriptions of the half-domesticated hog of the Smokies and its high value for mountain settlers:

> The wild pig, roaming foot-loose and free over hill and dale, picks up his own living at all seasons and requires no attention at all. He is the cheapest possible source of meat and yields the quickest return.... Shaped in front like a thin wedge, he can go through laurel thickets like a bear. Armored with tough hide cushioned by bristles, he despises thorns, bramble, and rattlesnakes alike. His extravagantly long snout can scent like a cat's, and yet burrow, uproot, overturn, as if made of metal. The long legs, thin flanks, pliant hoofs, fit him to run like a deer and climb like a goat. In courage and sagacity he outranks all other beasts. A warrior born, he is also a strategist of the first order.

The inhabitants of the Smokies had only to mark the ears of the young and castrate the males in the spring, and to round up and slaughter those needed for meat or sale to drovers in the fall.[48]

The ranging of cattle, sheep, horses, and mules in the Smokies dramatically altered the landscape. New balds were created and older ones enlarged. According to oral tradition, early settlers cleared the timber and regularly burned Russell Field and Spence Field, in the western end of the park, to create better grazing conditions. Whites greatly enlarged Gregory Bald, considered pre-European in origin, through similar means. Herders also grazed cattle on Parson Bald, Little Bald, Thunderhead, Silers Bald, High Springs Bald, Mount Buckley, Anders (now Andrews) Bald, Mount Sterling, Hemphill Bald, and numerous other smaller cleared areas in the gaps, swags, and saddles of the Smokies.[49]

Although Indian land-use practices may have resulted in the partial clearing of some of the summit area, cattle grazing produced marked changes in the landscape of the Smokies. As Mary Lindsay observed, "In using the balds as stock ranges, people gradually enlarged them. The herders and hunters who came up in the winter cut many trees for firewood. More trees were cut near the balds to make pens to hold livestock when they were rounded up and sorted in the fall. The trampling and browsing of the stock prevented trees from reproducing themselves, and the forest around the balds had very widely spaced trees with no undergrowth except grass. If grazing had continued until the youngest of the trees originally present around the balds died, the whole state line ridge west of Newfound Gap would probably be bald."[50]

The mountain oat grass (*Danthonia compressa*) that replaced trees and shrubs on these balds made excellent forage for the cattle, sheep, horses, and mules, attracting drovers from as far away as Knoxville. Herdsmen drove hundreds of animals to the high peaks of the Smokies for summer ranging. Indeed, the very process of driving the animals to and from the mountain summits also had an impact on the landscape, as the trails became deeply rutted and eroded from repeated use.[51]

Sheep grazing on one of the unique grass balds of the Great Smoky Mountains. Photo by Jim Thompson.

Although the changes were less noticeable, hogs also helped to transform the landscape of the Smokies. These prolific animals consumed large amounts of native plants and so had a negative impact on native animal species who consumed the same plants. The hogs' rooting also disturbed the soil and opened many areas to invasion by non-native plant species brought to the region by Europeans. In addition, their rooting and wallowing caused erosion and muddied streams.[52]

Just as the Indians had burned the woods to improve habitat for deer and other game, white settlers burned the woods to foster the growth of grasses and shoots for their domesticated animals. In the early 1980s, Mark Harmon conducted an extensive study of the fire history of the extreme western end of the park. His examination of trees and soil indicated regular burning of the woods in that area since white inhabitants came to the region.[53] Stephen Pyne and others have argued that burning of woods remained part of the southern cultural landscape long after the practice had ceased in other regions of the country.[54] Burning, plus intensive grazing by livestock, gave the forests of the Great Smoky Mountains (especially those on the peaks in the western end of the park) a much more open prospect than they have today.

The importance of livestock raising to the white inhabitants of the Smokies resulted in another important change in the landscape, the virtual elimination of predators in the mountains. At the insistence of herders, both North Carolina and Tennessee issued bounties on gray wolves (*Canis lupus*) in the early nineteenth century. Cades Cove residents Robert Burchfield, John Jones, and James Shields collected bounties on seven wolf scalps between 1834 and 1840; and William H. Thomas recorded the killing of eighteen wolves by the Quallatown Cherokee in 1844. Although wolf populations increased during the Civil War as hunting pressure decreased, an all-out war on wolves, launched by herders in the postwar period, virtually eliminated the species from the Smokies.[55] The last reported wolf killing in the Smokies occurred in the Cataloochee area in 1890, although wolf sightings continued in the area up until 1910.[56]

Herders and hunters also extirpated the mountain lion (*Felis concolor*), known to mountain residents as a panther or "painter," from the Smokies. Naturalist C. H. Merriam asserted in 1888 that the panther was "unknown" in the Smokies, although hunters killed one near Fontana Village in 1920. Individuals have reported a number of sightings of the elusive cat since this time (the last being in 1967), but no scientific evidence has been collected to confirm the presence of panthers in the Smokies since the early years of the twentieth century.[57] By the time of the establishment of the Great Smoky Mountains National Park, bounties, herders, and the destruction of habitat by lumber companies had silenced the once-common howl of the gray wolf and scream of the panther, perhaps forever.

Although bears occasionally fed on cattle, sheep, or hogs (one report credited a bear with killing thirty-five sheep in one night on Porters Flat) and mountain men loved the sport of bear hunting, bears maintained a tenuous hold on life in the most remote and rugged areas of the Smokies until they came under the protection of the National Park Service.[58]

While most of the early white inhabitants of the Smokies lived a subsistence lifestyle, selling cattle to raise the little cash they needed for taxes, coffee, and sugar, others were attracted to the region by the commercial opportunities offered by the natural bounty of the Smokies in the burgeoning market economy of the nineteenth century. By the time of white settlement, deer populations had declined markedly in the Smokies and their surrounding region, as the demand for deer hides and the attractiveness of European consumer goods caused the Cherokee to overhunt the deer.[59] During the nineteenth century, the Smokies saw the founding of a number of commercial enterprises which further altered the landscape.

The ledger books of Quallatown merchant and entrepreneur William Holland Thomas from the 1830s, 1840s, and 1850s document the types of trade commodities coming out of the Smokies in the nineteenth century. As one would expect, Thomas, who also operated a tannery at Quallatown, recorded a steady trade in deer, cow, and hog hides. He traded in the skins of bears, panthers, wildcats, raccoons, muskrats, minks, and otters, too. Thomas took in considerable amounts of butter (2,400 pounds in a year and a half in the 1830s), beeswax, tallow, lard, bacon and hams, wool, and balsam. He traded in timber and apparently invested in several small-scale sawmills in the area. He also traded in large amounts of corn, which he used to feed cattle before driving them to market.[60]

Thomas did a surprisingly large trade in medicinal herbs, the bulk of it in snakeroot, pinkroot, and ginseng. At one point, Thomas sent a wagonload of twelve hundred pounds of pinkroot (*Spigella marilandia*), used at this time as a cure for parasitic worms, to Augusta. In 1834, Thomas processed over 4,300 pounds of ginseng, most of which he sent to Dr. Isaac Heylin in Philadelphia, who exported it to Asian markets. Long prized in China as an aphrodisiac and cure-all, ginseng prices skyrocketed in the nineteenth century, due to China's overharvesting of wild plants, believed to be more potent. Both Cherokee and whites began to scour the mountainsides seeking the precious root.[61] To take advantage of this market, Thomas built a special "sang" house for drying and processing the root near his Quallatown store. Nimrod Jarrett and Bacchus Smith, merchants on Jonathan Creek, also did extensive trade in ginseng. "Sangin'" soon became an important commercial and cultural pursuit for the people of the Smokies, until the plant almost vanished from the wild in the early twentieth century due to overcollecting.[62]

In the first half of the nineteenth century, a surprising quantity of pig iron came from the Smokies. Thomas often sent wagonloads of iron, produced at his own bloomery forges or at ones scattered around Western North Carolina, to markets in Georgia and South Carolina.[63] Daniel Foute built a bloomery forge in Cades Cove in 1827 and operated it for twenty years. However, the low grade of iron ore found in the Smokies, the cost of charcoal to operate the forges, and improvements in transportation elsewhere that increased the availability of cheaper and higher-quality iron led to a dramatic decline in the mining of iron ore and the production of pig iron in the region by the late 1840s.[64]

In the 1850s, prospectors flooded the Smokies searching for gold and silver after the discovery of significant gold deposits in North Georgia. The lack of marketable deposits disappointed prospectors, however, and they soon moved on, leaving behind signs of their digging and incongruous place names like "Eldorado" on Rich Mountain above Cades Cove. One legend from the gold-prospecting days of the Smokies has persisted, however. Folks in the area still tell stories of Perry Shults, who allegedly discovered gold and silver in the headwaters of Porters Creek in the Greenbriar section. Observers testified that Shults would come out of the mountains loaded with the precious ores. In 1867, Shults and several partners received a corporate charter for the Sevier County Silver, Copper, Lead, and Zinc Company. Unfortunately, Shults never told anyone the location of the mine, not even his wife, whom he took with him into the mountains but left sitting on a rock while he worked his claim. Although the Shults story lends some romance and excitement to mining days in the Smokies, extensive mining surveys conducted over the years found only negligible traces of silver and gold inside park boundaries.[65]

One of the more interesting mining episodes in the history of the Smokies involves one of the park's most famous topographical features:

Alum Cave, on the slopes of Mount Le Conte. In 1838, Ephraim Mingus, Robert Collins, and George Hayes, all from the Oconoluftee River area of North Carolina, bought Alum Cave and the land surrounding it and formed the Epsom Salts Manufacturing Company. The company constructed a camp at the base of the bluff and built hoppers and vats for processing the salts. They hauled their product to market in Knoxville on horseback. The owners seem to have operated the mine only sporadically, and in 1854 they sold it to a group of East Tennessee investors. Abraham Mingus wrote to his brother John, explaining the sale: "If the mine was situated favorable it would be perhaps worth double but pent up against cloud caped mountains . . . greatly depreciates its value." Mining operations resumed at Alum Cave during the Civil War, when Confederate troops seized it because of the presence of saltpeter, a necessary component of gunpowder. Late in the war, William H. Thomas and the Cherokee troops under his command operated the mine, digging out saltpeter, alum, and magnesium for medicines. Attempts at mining continued at Alum Cave in the postwar period, but the lack of roads and the difficulty of accessing the site frustrated all attempts to make it a profitable enterprise.[66]

The most successful mining operations conducted within or near the current park boundary were copper mining operations in the far southwestern corner of the park, in the Fontana Lake–Hazel Creek area. Miners conducted small-scale copper mining operations on Hazel Creek, near Silers Bald, and on Eagle Creek in the late nineteenth and early twentieth centuries. With the coming of the railroad, in conjunction with large-scale timber operations and the development of smelting operations in nearby Ducktown, Tennessee, mining corporations developed sizable mines at the Fontana Mine (now under the waters of Fontana Lake) and the Adams or Everett Mine on the Little Fork of Sugar Fork in the headwaters of Hazel Creek. Between 1926 and 1942, the Fontana Mine produced over half a million tons of ore and refined it into over eighty million pounds of copper. The Everett Mine also had the potential to produce high-grade ore, and local people contend that the mine holds one of the richest copper deposits anywhere. Mining operations ceased from 1917 to 1943, however, while the courts sorted out competing claims to the mine. In one year of operation (1943), the Everett Mine produced 350 tons of ore, but the expense and difficulty of transporting the ore caused the mine's owners to sell it to the National Park Service. Legends notwithstanding, extensive investigations by geologists over the years indicate that no commercially viable mining sites exist within the current boundaries of the park.[67]

In order to facilitate commerce in the mountains, entrepreneurs launched a number of road construction projects in the Smokies. William H. Thomas and Daniel Foute played a pivotal role in the development of roads there. Foute built a turnpike—later known as the Cooper Road—that connected Cades Cove with Knoxville by way of Maryville and his resort at Montvale Springs. He also helped promote the development of roads connecting Cades Cove to other communities.[68] Thomas had a passion for road building and spearheaded the construction of the Oconoluftee Turnpike, which ran from Quallatown to the Tennessee line near Indian Gap. However, the builders of the road never effectively coordinated with interests in Tennessee; on that side of the line, the road remained little more than a trail well into the twentieth century.

Thomas also served as president of the most successful road-building project in the Smokies in the nineteenth century: the Jonathan's Creek and Tennessee Mountains Turnpike. Its path is now followed by North Carolina Highway 284. The turnpike company sold $22,000 in stock to over one hundred subscribers in the 1850s, including $5,000 worth to the State of North Carolina. The road, connecting Big Creek with Jonathan's Creek and running through Cataloochee, took nine years to build and finally was completed in October 1860. The purpose of this road, like most of the others, was to attempt to capitalize on the stock-driving business.[69]

Although roads and trails of varying quality (most were little more than stock trails) crisscrossed the Smokies by the middle of the nineteenth century, the region remained the remotest area east of the Mississippi River. Professor Arnold Guyot of Princeton University spent the summer of 1859 in the Smokies, guided by Robert Collins of the Oconoluftee River area, in order to map the region and calculate the elevation of its peaks. He referred to the Smokies as the "master chain of the Appalachian system" due to "the general elevation of its peaks and crests, by its perfect continuity, its great roughness and difficulty of approach."[70] Guyot remarked especially on the rugged character of the terrain and the lack of human habitation on the summit area between the Big Pigeon River and Indian Gap, an area including Mount Cammerer, Inadu Knob, Mount Guyot, Mount Kephart, and Mount Le Conte: "The top of these ridges is usually sharp and rocky, deeply indented, and winding considerably, covered with a dense growth of Laurels and high trees, which make travel over them extremely difficult and almost impracticable. Neither the White man nor the Indian hunter venture in this wilderness." Guyot also referred to the Hazelnut (Hazel) Creek and Eagle Creek area—indeed, the entire eastern slope of the Smokies—as "still a wilderness, little frequented," although a few white families had settled in this area at least ten years before Guyot's visit.[71]

The rugged character, remote location, and inaccessibility that plagued road builders and miners in the Smokies proved advantageous to some mountain residents. Most of the Cherokee who became the Eastern Band already had settled in Quallatown on land owned by William H. Thomas, and the accounts of hiding out by the Cherokee are greatly exaggerated by legend and by the outdoor drama *Unto These Hills*. Nevertheless, the Smokies did provide refuge for some of the Cherokee who attempted to escape deportation to Oklahoma over the "Trail of Tears" in 1838. As many as two hundred were able to escape removal by hiding out in the mountains until the War Department gave up on catching them, as they were considered "not worth the trouble and expense to move." This group included a band led by Euchella, who were allowed to join the Quallatown Cherokee when they aided in the capture and execution of the fugitive Tsali and his sons, who had killed two soldiers and wounded another in their resistance to removal. The lack of quality bottomland and the rough terrain of the area they inhabited also helped protect them, as "whites seemed little concerned about the Cherokee remnant that remained on the periphery of their day-to-day existence."[72]

Remote sections of the Smokies also provided hiding places for individuals sympathetic to one or the other side during the Civil War. The presence of large numbers of pro-Union sympathizers in Western North Carolina and East Tennessee made the Smokies one of the most hotly contested areas of the South. It became, as historian John Finger has argued, "a land of famine and fear." Mountain residents suffered at the hands of raiders, or bushwhackers, from both sides, who used the mountains as a base of operations from which to prey on the inhabitants of the Smokies. Cades Cove suffered greatly from Confederate bushwhackers who came over the mountains on herding trails from North Carolina and stole food and livestock from the pro-Union inhabitants of the cove.[73] In return, the Quallatown Cherokee, who sided with the Confederacy, suffered the attacks of Union troops and Unionist bushwhackers who came over the mountains through Cades Cove. Both sides suffered terribly from food shortages created by war, bushwhacking, and the absence of male labor. Late in the war, the situation became particularly acute for some communities. In 1864, William H. Thomas begged Confederate authorities for food aid as the Cherokee of Quallatown were "now in a starving condition."[74]

The Smokies also provided a haven for individuals who deserted or were attempting to escape conscription into the Confederate army. As the war progressed and the need for replacement troops increased, however, Confederate officials intensified efforts to capture and punish deserters and "outliers," many of whom had become bushwhackers. Late in the war, Capt. Albert Teague of the Confederate Home Guards hid out in the Big Creek area to capture some notorious "outliers" who had used the Smokies as an effective hideout and base of bushwhacking operations. Teague rounded up George and Anderson Grooms and another man named Caldwell. His men bound the men and marched them over the turnpike toward Waynesville. Just past Sterling Gap, the group stopped. Teague told Anderson Grooms to play a final tune on the fiddle he had brought along. Grooms complied, playing "Bonaparte's Retreat"—for years thereafter known in the mountains as "Grooms's Tune." At the completion of the tune, the soldiers gunned down the three men and left their bodies in the ditch.[75]

The remoteness of the Smokies was an advantage for those who pursued one of the most important commercial activities in the Smokies in the late nineteenth and early twentieth centuries: the production of moonshine, or blockade, whiskey. As one of Horace Kephart's respondents argued, "The main reason for this 'moonshining,' as you-uns call it, is bad roads." He continued, "The only farm produce we-uns can sell is corn. You see for yourself that corn can't be shipped outen hyar. We can trade hit for store credit—that's all. Corn juice is about all we can tote around over the country and git cash money for. Why man, that's the only way some folks has o' payin' their taxes."[76]

The legal distilling of alcoholic beverages long had been part of life and culture among the white settlers of the Smokies. The ledgers of William H. Thomas indicate that residents of the Smokies often traded corn whiskey for store goods.[77] Before the war, Julius Gregg operated a legal distillery in Cades Cove, making corn whiskey and apple brandy. After the war, George Powell, also of the Cades Cove area, built probably the largest distillery in Blount County, "maintaining an orchard of several hundred fruit trees and manufacturing fine brandies."[78]

In the 1870s, however, the federal government changed the economics and geography of distilling, as it imposed a tax of 90 cents a gallon on whiskey, increased in 1894 to $1.10. This tax immediately made the Smokies and other remote mountainous regions likely places for the manufacture of illegal whiskey. With the introduction of large-scale timber cutting came improvements in transportation, population growth, and the increased availability of cash; these and the advent of regional and national Prohibition only increased the incentives. Many sections of the Smokies, such as Hazel Creek, Cosby, Sugarlands, and Chestnut Flats, became legendary for their moonshine, although residents of all sections participated in this activity.[79]

For most residents of the Smokies, manufacturing blockade whiskey did not conflict with fundamentalist religious beliefs or with community mores. Those who made the whiskey, for the most part, drank little of their own product. As Horace Kephart, a serious imbiber himself, observed, "Comparatively few highlanders see liquor oftener than once or twice a month. The lumberjacks and townspeople get most of the output; for they can pay the price."[80]

As local-color authors such as Horace Kephart and Robert Lindsay Mason told tales of their experiences in the Smokies in the late nineteenth and early twentieth centuries, many of the most notorious and colorful moonshiners took on the status of folk heroes. Exaggerated yarns of the exploits of Black Bill Walker, Quill Rose, George Powell, and Sam Burchfield formed the backbone of many popular national images of the "typical" mountaineer. Cades Cove farmer, postmaster, and Primitive Baptist preacher John Oliver complained about this image: "All these men are public outlaws, and were never recognized as true, loyal mountaineers, or as true American citizens, by the rank and file of the mountain people."[81]

By the beginning of the twentieth century, an unusually high birth rate among mountain residents, and resultant population growth, increased the stress on the land. The practice of dividing land equally among male children decreased the size of farms that barely had supported a family before. Farmers moved up from the exhausted bottomlands and began farming the thin soil of the mountainsides. The soil on these hillsides soon lost its fertility and eroded.[82] Horace Kephart discussed this situation with a neighbor on Hazel Creek:

"Thar, I've cl'ared me a patch and grubbed hit out—now I can raise me two or three severe craps!"

"Then what?" I asked.

"When corn won't grow no more I can turn the field into grass a couple o' years."

"Then you'll rotate, and grow more corn again?"

"La, no! By that time the land will be so poor hit wouldn't raise a cuss fight."

"But then you must move, and begin all over again. This continual moving must be a great nuisance."

"Huk-uk; when I move, all I haffter do is put out the fire and call the dog."[83]

Increasingly, however, the scarcity of good farmland, declining crop and livestock prices, and the overall impossibility of subsisting on smaller and poorer mountain farms caused mountain families to make some hard decisions. Many moved out of the mountains and tried their luck in the textile mills of the Piedmont. Others flocked to the coal mines of East Tennessee, eastern Kentucky, western Virginia, and West Virginia and to timber camps scattered throughout the mountain region.[84]

Kephart pointed to another important environmental effect of the increased population pressures in the Smokies: the virtual disappearance of mountain wildlife by the early part of the twentieth century. "A stranger in these mountains," he wrote, "will be surprised at the apparent scarcity of game animals. It is not unusual for one to hunt all day in an absolute wilderness, where he sees never a fresh track of man, and not get a shot at anything fit to eat." Kephart noted that deer and turkey had been almost "exterminated," "even squirrels" were "rather scarce," and trout had disappeared from every stream except those that were stocked or ran through old-growth forests.[85]

Less than one hundred years of white settlement in the Smokies had produced a number of dramatic changes in the landscape of the region. The more intensive use of farm and range land had exhausted soil fertility in many areas, increased erosion, and clouded once-clear streams with sediment. Mountain balds had been either created or greatly expanded along much of the state-line range. Scattered mining sites pockmarked the region, and Indian trails had been widened to form stock trails or even turnpikes. Much of the native wildlife of the mountains had disappeared.

Despite these changes, the landscape of the Smokies still retained much

By the late nineteenth century, population growth and soil exhaustion pushed Southern Appalachian farmers onto increasingly marginal land. Photo courtesy of Great Smoky Mountains National Park.

of its characteristic forest cover. That would change in the early twentieth century, as highly capitalized and mechanized large-scale timber cutting came to the region. It would produce the most obvious, dramatic, and environmentally destructive change in the history of human use of the Smokies.

Residents and regional entrepreneurs had logged parts of the Smokies throughout the nineteenth century. Most of the larger mills that were built in the Smokies in the nineteenth century, such as the Mingus Mill in the

Oconoluftee area and the Shields and Cable mills in Cades Cove, operated sash saws as well as grinding stones, a fact reflected in the growing number of frame houses and weatherboarded cabins in the area.[86] These operations involved selective cutting of the most valuable and accessible timber, usually poplar, cherry, and ash. Their lack of capitalization, small scale, and overall "slow tempo" meant that the forest had an opportunity to regenerate. Although in some cases their activities were harmful to the landscape and the environment, they had not done damage that could not be easily rectified.[87]

The coming of the large timber and pulp companies, with their railroads that penetrated practically every watershed, their steam-powered skidders and log loaders, their log flumes, splash dams, and incline, or "Sarah Parker," railways, made change inevitable. As Robert Lambert observed, "The cutting of the later period brought with it the seeds of the virtual annihilation of the forest."[88]

The first large-scale logging operations in the Smokies were conducted in the Big Creek area. Indicative of the economic risks involved in such

Industrial logging, which brought railroads and steam log loaders to the Smokies, produced major changes in the landscape. Photo courtesy of Great Smoky Mountains National Park.

operations, at least six different corporations logged in the Big Creek area from the 1880s until the 1920s. The Scottish Carolina Timber Company, which owned a mill in Newport, Tennessee, began operations in the late 1880s. Loggers floated trees cut in the Big Creek watershed down Big Creek and into the Pigeon River to the mill at Newport. The first railroad into the Smokies was built in the early years of the twentieth century, when the North Carolina Land and Timber Company built a standard-gauge railroad from Newport to Waterville. Its successor company, the Cataloochee Lumber Company, extended the railroad three miles up Big Creek and constructed a large mill at Crestmont. When the Cataloochee Company went bankrupt in 1904, the Pigeon River Company bought it out, extended the railroad ten miles further up Big Creek, and added to the mill a drying kiln and a double bandsaw with a capacity of eighty thousand board feet a day.[89] In 1911, Pigeon River went bankrupt and sold out to Champion Lumber Company. Within six years, Champion had cut most of the watershed all the way to the top of Mount Guyot and the Mount Sterling Divide. In 1917, Champion Lumber, a subsidiary of Champion Fibre, went bankrupt and sold to Suncrest Lumber Company, which concentrated on cutting spruce on the higher ridges and peaks; this was used for making airplanes during World War I. In 1918, Suncrest suddenly moved its operations to Sunburst, leaving thousands of cut spruce trees behind to rot.[90]

In the early twentieth century, similar situations occurred in almost every watershed in the Smokies. Timber tracts changed hands constantly; the names of lumber and pulp companies, such as Parsons, Whitmer-Parsons, Harris-Woodbury, Eversole, Norwood, W. M. Ritter, Montvale, Kichen, Swaggerty and Eubanks, and the largest of them all, Little River Lumber Company, became part of the history and lore of the Smokies. These companies built railroads into the watersheds, standard-gauge when they could, narrow-gauge using geared Shay locomotives on steeper sections, and incline railways where even a Shay could not go. The Appalachian, Oconolufty, Smoky Mountain, and Little River railroads penetrated farther and farther into the heart of the mountains. New place names, too, appeared on maps of the Smokies, as the companies built mills and timber camps to access the timber. Mills at Ravensford, Smokemont, Proctor, Fontana, Twentymile, Townsend, Tremont, and Elkmont turned out an estimated two billion board feet of lumber in the early part of the twentieth century. Dozens of temporary timber camps, or "stringtowns," of portable housing lined the logging railroads and housed the thousands of individuals who came out of the mountain coves or from far away for steady wages of sixty-five cents to a dollar a day and a break from the uncertainties of farming.[91]

Loggers initially went after only the most valuable hardwoods: poplar, white oak, ash, and cherry. This meant that the wetter, north-facing coves were primary early targets. As transportation improved and lumber demand and prices increased, the loggers took an increasing number of other hardwoods, such as basswood, birch, buckeye, peawood, and maple. New tanning operations in the region increased the demand for the acid woods—chestnut oak, hemlock, and chestnut. With the establishment of the Champion Fibre Company's pulp mill at Canton, North Carolina, in 1905, the demand for hemlock and especially red spruce, used

The development of overhead skidders allowed loggers access to even the steepest slopes in the Smokies. Photo courtesy of Great Smoky Mountains National Park.

in the sulfite process of paper manufacturing, expanded. The market for red spruce also boomed during World War I, as the trees provided an important source of light wood for airplanes.[92]

The financial pressures of such highly capitalized enterprises, and the common practice of "cut and run" timber operations, caused the lumber companies to use the quickest yet most destructive methods to remove the timber. Early on, to get the timber to the mill, logging operations used destructive methods such as "ballhooting," or simply letting huge poplars and oaks roll down the mountainside. Companies also constructed wooden dams, known as splashdams, in many watersheds. These dams created ponds, and loggers filled the ponds with logs. Then the loggers dynamited the dam, releasing a torrent of water and logs downstream, gouging out stream banks and destroying aquatic life as they went.[93]

As operations became more mechanized, the companies utilized more efficient, steam-powered cable-pulley systems, known as skidders, to bring the timber to the railroad tracks. The skidders dragged poplars, chestnuts,

Logging devastation and "stringtown" of portable worker housing at Little River Lumber Company Camp No. 18, at Three Forks above Elkmont. Photo courtesy of Great Smoky Mountains National Park.

and oaks as large as twenty-five to thirty feet in circumference down the steep slopes, leaving devastation in their wake. Clyde overhead skidders enabled loggers to bring timber in from as far away as 3,500 feet and helped facilitate the logging of the highest peaks in the Smokies, including Clingman's Dome and Mount Guyot. The use of skidders produced devastating effects on the steep mountainsides of the Smokies. Skidding pulled up underbrush, scoured the forest floor, and uprooted young trees, creating a huge accumulation of debris, known to loggers as slash.[94]

The logging operations, with this practice of massive clearcutting, had a number of other negative environmental effects. The cutting itself destroyed huge amounts of wildlife habitat; along with increased hunting pressure, the cutting depleted wildlife populations in the Smokies. Clearcutting on the steep slopes left nothing to hold the soil and caused massive erosion. It clogged streams with silt and slash, contributed to the massive flooding problems of this period, and destroyed countless numbers of fish and other aquatic life.[95]

The all-too-common aftermath of logging in the early twentieth century. In 1922, the Blanket Mountain fire burned out of control for weeks. Photo courtesy of Great Smoky Mountains National Park.

Aside from the cutting itself, the most devastating environmental effects came with the massive wildfires that burned over many of the major logging areas in the second and third decades of the twentieth century. Robert Lambert has documented major fires in every area of the Smokies where logging operators employed skidders. Indeed, almost every major fire in the Smokies during this period occurred when sparks from locomotives and skidders ignited fires in the slash. In the heyday of the logging era, fires raged up the slopes of Silers Bald, Clingman's Dome, and Mount Guyot. One series of fires reportedly burned for two months in the Jakes Creek and Fish Camp Prong watersheds, logged by the Little River Lumber Company.[96]

The environmental effects on the Great Smoky Mountains caused by logging are nowhere more apparent than at one of the park's great "natural" scenic attractions, Charlie's Bunion. One of the most popular scenic sites in the park, this unusual rock outcropping was produced by the combined efforts of humans and nature. In 1925, a devastating fire, ignited in the slash, swept up the Kephart Prong watershed (an area clear-cut using overhead skidders by Champion Lumber Company) and crossed the divide into Tennessee. The fire burned so hot that it consumed green trees and all of the groundcover, completely denuding the steep slopes and sterilizing the soil. Four years later, "torrential rains washed over this barren area, removing all the soil and laying bare the rock beneath," creating Charlie's Bunion.[97]

In conjunction with the heavy logging activity of the early twentieth century, the forest of the Smokies faced another heavy blow: chestnut blight, which wiped out the "monarch" tree of the Great Smoky Mountains. Chestnuts once had dominated the forests of the Smokies, growing as large as thirty-three feet in circumference and comprising 30 to 40 percent of the forest cover, up to an elevation of 5,500 feet. Like so many of the other ecological changes in the Smokies, the chestnut blight resulted from human action. First noticed in 1904 in New York, the blight probably came from Chinese chestnuts imported as nursery stock. The blight quickly spread to American chestnuts, arriving in the Great Smoky Mountains around 1925 and killing most of the chestnuts in the Smokies in the late twenties and early thirties. One park forester estimated that 85 percent of the chestnuts had died by 1938. Surviving trees at higher elevations died out by the early forties.[98]

The blight dramatically changed ecological relationships in the Smokies, opening up the forest canopy for chestnut oaks, northern red

One of the largest chestnut trees in the Smokies, located just below Tremont Falls. Photo courtesy of Great Smoky Mountains National Park.

oak, white oak, black oak, sourgum, red maple, tulip tree, and various hickories. Animals (including deer, bear, and turkeys) whose diet was heavy in chestnuts and who already were under intense pressure from overhunting and habitat destruction, had to adjust their diets and rely more upon acorns, which are more subject to shortfalls than chestnuts. Humans suffered as well; they lost the most valuable tree in the forest. The chestnut had yielded rot-resistant wood for cabins, split-rail fences, and household implements; tannin for tanning hides; and chestnuts for both consumption and sale.[99]

In little more than thirty years, that most distinctive aspect of the Great Smoky Mountains, its forests, had been completely transformed by human action, either direct or indirect. The Smokies had lost two-thirds of its original forest cover. Old-growth forest remained only in the spruce-fir forest on the highest peaks in the eastern half of the park, particularly the area between Mount Le Conte and Mount Guyot; the far western end of the park, which was owned by the Morton-Butler Lumber Company but was never logged; the northeastern upper slopes of the state-line range, which had been held by Champion as reserve; and the upper sections of Deep and Noland creeks, where the railroad never had penetrated. At the same time, the chestnuts, once the dominant trees of the forest, stood as bare monuments to their glorious past or lay slowly rotting on the forest floor. By the mid-1920s, the Smokies would not have been recognized by inhabitants of only a generation earlier, much less the Cherokee and their ancestors who had hunted and gathered in these forests for millennia.[100]

The cloud placed over the Smokies by these "evils born of super-civilization" contained a silver lining, though—the increasing popularity and profitability of tourism, direct results of the improved access brought to the region by the logging railroads. The scenic beauty of the Smokies had been praised by observers and had attracted elite tourists and health enthusiasts

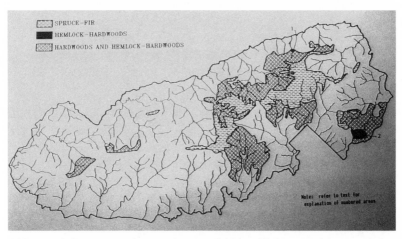

Old-growth forest remaining on the eve of the establishment of the national park. Courtesy of Great Smoky Mountains National Park.

throughout the nineteenth century. Noted traveler and journalist Charles Lanman, who visited Alum Cave in the late 1840s, waxed poetic about the spectacular scenery: "To gaze upon this prospect at the sunset hour, when the mountains were tinged with a rosy hue, and the immense hollow before me was filled with a purple atmosphere, and I could see the rocky ledge basking in the sunlight like a huge monster on the placid bosom of a lake, was to me one of the most remarkable and impressive scenes that I have ever witnessed. . . . It was a glorious picture, indeed, and would have amply repaid one for a pilgrimage from the remotest corner of the earth."[101] Even as Lanman wrote these words, tourists started to make their way to the Smokies. Cades Cove resident Daniel Foute built one of the first tourist hotels in the region, at Montvale Springs, in the 1840s. The Montvale Springs resort attracted the elite from all over the South. One visitor was poet and author Sidney Lanier, whose grandfather managed the hotel for many years.[102] Other resorts and tourist hotels cropped up on the edges of the Smokies, but the difficulty of travel strictly limited the industry.

On holidays and weekends, the Little River Railroad took tourists into the Smokies. Younger passengers enjoyed riding in the open "observation car." Photo courtesy of Great Smoky Mountains National Park.

With the coming of the logging companies, however, the accessibility of the region to tourists improved significantly. Railroads built to transport timber out of the Smokies soon began to carry tourists into the mountains. The construction of the Little River Railroad created a tourist boom along the banks of Little River, as resort hotels sprang up at Kinzel Springs, Sunshine, and Elkmont. The railroad added several passenger cars on the weekends, and many Knoxvillians regularly took day trips through the scenic Little River Gorge to Elkmont.[103] The elite of Knoxville also organized two resort clubs near Elkmont on land purchased from the Little River Lumber Company: the Appalachian Club in 1910, and the Wonderland Club in 1914. Both clubs contained summer cottages, clubhouses, and hotel and recreation facilities. These facilities attracted thousands of tourists to the Smokies in the teens and twenties.[104] In 1916, Andy Huff built the Mountain View Hotel in Gatlinburg; and John Oliver began renting out tourist cabins in Cades Cove in 1924.[105] Railroad development attracted growing numbers of tourists to Bryson City and the Cherokee Indian Reservation on the North Carolina side of the Smokies. Logging railroads in North Carolina also put on passenger cars on weekends and took tourists into the upper reaches of the Smokies.

The combination of intensive logging in the Smokies, increasing numbers of tourists, and the profitability of the regional tourist industry helped to produce an important change in attitude within the region. Regional boosters and entrepreneurs began to realize that, while logging brought needed short-term economic gain to the region, that gain was, in fact, short-term. Once the companies had logged the forest, the logging companies, along with their jobs and their capital, would be gone. Preserving the scenery to attract tourists, however, could make the Smokies an endlessly productive economic resource. The problem was how to stop the timber companies, who now owned most of the land in the Smokies and showed no inclination to sell it. The attitudes of area boosters dovetailed perfectly with the rise of the national park movement, a new idea of land use embraced by increasing numbers of Americans and extremely profitable to the communities surrounding national parks.

The combination of regional boosters and national park advocates would produce land-use changes in the Smokies as revolutionary as those brought by woods burners, stock grazers, railroads, and timber companies.

2.

National Parks:
"For Pleasure And Profit"

On 25 August 1916, with the stroke of a pen, United States President Woodrow Wilson created the National Park Service (NPS). This was perhaps the most important step in laying the foundation for establishment of a national park in the Great Smoky Mountains. Under the leadership of the first NPS director, Stephen Mather, and Assistant Director Horace Albright, the few national parks in existence captured the attention and the imagination of a sizable segment of the American population, quickly acquiring the status of national treasures. This promotional effort, undertaken by NPS in concert with the western railroads, along with war in Europe, combined to make the national parks of the West favored travel destinations for elite Americans in the latter part of the second decade of the twentieth century. Indeed, "the lure of Yellowstone, Yosemite, Glacier, and the Grand Canyon transformed the passenger train into a magic carpet, a means to a larger and more exciting end."[1]

Between 1916 and 1922, the number of annual visitors to America's national parks increased from 356,097 to 1,280,886.[2] The popularity of the parks in the West, and especially the economic benefits that accrued to communities near them, made civic boosters around the nation take notice of the economic potential of preserving land. By the early 1920s, a strong, popular, and politically powerful national park movement caused many parts of the nation—including the Southern Appalachian region and especially the region surrounding the Great Smoky Mountains—to welcome, covet, and even demand the establishment of national parks in their area.

The popular fascination of Americans with the national parks in the teens and twenties was a relatively new phenomenon. Indeed, the elevated position enjoyed by the national parks was the culmination of almost one hundred years of struggle to persuade the American people of the value of preserving land and scenery.

The national park movement was born out of the virtual destruction of one of the nation's great scenic treasures, Niagara Falls. As early as the 1830s, developers and hucksters began to descend on the falls, fencing off the best overlooks, setting up tacky souvenir sheds, and harnessing its immense water power. Particularly galling to Americans was criticism by Europeans who traveled to the falls and recorded their observations. Alexis de Tocqueville visited in 1831 and wrote to a friend, telling him to hurry to the site before American enterprise had completely spoiled its beauty: "Already the forest round about is being cleared. . . . I don't give the Americans ten years to establish a saw or flour mill at the base of the cataract."

Sir Richard Henry Bonnycastle visited in 1849 and took Americans to task for the sights that awaited him at Niagara: "The Yankees put an ugly shot tower on the brink of the Horseshoe and they are about to consummate the barbarism by throwing a wire bridge . . . over the river just below the American Falls. . . . What they will not do next in their freaks it is difficult to surmise, but it requires very little more to show that patriotism, taste, and self-esteem, are not the leading features in the character of the inhabitants of this part of the world." Stung by these criticisms, many Americans became determined to prevent similar degradation of other scenic treasures.[3]

The discovery of monumental scenery in the West boggled the minds and imaginations of both Americans and Europeans. This gave Americans the opportunity to redeem themselves after the Niagara Falls fiasco and protect these symbols of American greatness. White Americans' discovery of such sites as the Yosemite Valley, Yellowstone, and the Grand Canyon, and their immortalization by American artists, photographers, and writers, gave Americans a source of pride that the rest of the world, particularly the European nations, could not match. Upon seeing the Yosemite Valley in 1859, Horace Greeley called it "the most unique and majestic of nature's marvels." The Reverend Thomas Starr King, in an article on Yosemite in the *Boston Evening Standard,* argued that "nowhere among the Alps, in no pass of the Andes, and in no canyon of the mighty Oregon range is there such stupendous rock scenery [as in Yosemite]." Nathaniel Pitt Langford commented on his visit to Yellowstone in 1870: "A grander scene than the lower cataract of the Yellowstone was never witnessed by mortal eyes. It is a sheer, compact, solid, perpendicular sheet, faultless in all the elements of grandeur and picturesque beauties." On seeing the geysers and mudpots of Yellowstone, Langford further proclaimed, "Taken as an aggregate, the Firehole Basin surpasses all other great wonders of the continent." John Burroughs argued that the Grand Canyon suggests "a far-off, half-sacred antiquity, some greater Jerusalem, Egypt, Babylon, or India. We speak of it as a scene; it is more like a vision, so foreign is it to all other terrestrial spectacles, and so surpassingly beautiful."[4]

Yosemite, the most accessible of the western wonders, first drew the attention of scenic preservationists in 1864. By this point, developers had begun to move into the Yosemite Valley, setting up businesses to take advantage of the growing numbers of affluent tourists who came by railroad, then by stage, then on muleback to see the spectacular rock formations and waterfalls. Concerned individuals could see the potential for another Niagara Falls in the near future if the government did not step in to protect the valley. The threat posed by loggers to the uniquely American Sierra redwoods in the nearby Mariposa Grove also prompted calls for some sort of preservation. In 1864, at the urging of a small group of Californians, United States Sen. John Conness of California introduced legislation calling for the protection of the valley and the preservation of a grove of the Sierra redwoods. Amid the Civil War, Congress approved the bill, and President Abraham Lincoln signed it on 30 June 1864. The bill created two sections of the park, a northern unit composed of forty square miles, including the Yosemite Valley and the surrounding peaks; and a southern unit of four square miles, containing the Mariposa Grove of Sierra redwoods. The bill called for the State of California to hold these lands "inalienable for all time." Because the bill turned these areas over to California for administration, many have argued that this was not the first national park. However, Alfred Runte has asserted that, as Yosemite first fulfilled the idea of a style of preservation embodied in the national park ideal, it was the first "in fact, therefore, if not in name."[5]

Congress followed up on the preservation of Yosemite with the Yellowstone Park Act, signed by President Ulysses S. Grant in 1872. The positive documentation of the geysers, mudpots, waterfalls, and canyons of Yellowstone had taken place only in 1869 and 1870, with a series of expeditions to the region. As early as 1871, however, individuals were staking claim to these sites of scenic wonder and preparing to fence out any nonpaying customers. In a memorial to Congress, Dr. Ferdinand Vandiveer Hayden, who led the first scholarly expedition into Yellowstone, reminded Congress of the problems at Niagara Falls and argued that it would be an abomination to "fence in these rare wonders so as to charge visitors a fee, as is now done at Niagara Falls, for the sight of that which ought to be as free as the air and water."[6] Congress agreed, and 3,300 square miles of the Yellowstone region were "dedicated and set apart as a public park or pleasuring ground for the benefit and enjoyment of the people." The bill also called on the secretary of the interior to maintain the timber, resources, and "natural curiosities . . . in their natural condition." The huge size of the park, particularly in comparison with Yosemite, represented more the concern that Yellowstone might contain other "natural curiosities" than any notion of preserving an entire ecosystem.[7]

As Congress established Yosemite and Yellowstone and added additional parks at General Grant and Sequoia in the California Sierras, and as the national park concept became increasingly popular, individuals began to consider the idea of parks in the Southern Appalachian region. The first documented suggestion that Congress establish a national park in the area came in a paper delivered by Dr. Henry O. Marcy of Boston to the American Academy of Medicine on 29 October 1885. In supporting the idea of a national park in the mountains of Western North Carolina, Dr. Marcy argued: "The pure air, water and climate hold out a hopeful helpfulness to invalids from every land. The wise legislator, seeking far-reaching results, would do well to consider the advisability of securing, under state control, a large reservation of the higher ranges as a park. Its cost, at present, would be merely nominal. Like the peaks and glaciers of Switzerland, its sanitary advantages would be of value incalculable to millions yet unborn."[8]

Although this proposal had more to do with the precedent set by Congress in 1832 of reserving Hot Springs, Arkansas, for its medicinal value and had little to do with prevailing notions of monumentalism, it does reflect the nineteenth-century preoccupation with outdoing the Europeans.[9]

Other proposals soon followed, and in the early 1890s the idea of a national park in the Southern Appalachian region received its first attention from a state legislature. In February 1893, the North Carolina Legislature passed a resolution "requesting our Senators and Representatives in Congress to use their influence for the establishment of a national park in Western North Carolina."[10] The "interests of science" provided the primary impetus for this resolution. In April of the same year, the North Carolina Press Association adopted a memorial to the United States Congress, urging that it give the national park matter serious consideration. Later in the year, U.S. Rep. John S. Henderson of Salisbury introduced the memorial in the House. However, nothing tangible came from this flurry of activity, and the idea of a national park in the region lay dormant for five more years.[11]

Even as the national park idea gained in popularity, Congress was not quite sure what to do with the parks, and their management was haphazard at best. Vandalism and poaching soon became major problems in Yellowstone, until Congress sent the U.S. Cavalry to protect the area in 1886. Herders disregarded regulations keeping sheep out of Yosemite, Sequoia, and General Grant, and their "hooved locusts" (as John Muir referred to them) denuded the steep slopes of fragile vegetation. State management of the Yosemite Valley proved ineffectual, with little control over use of the land. The valley went the way of Niagara Falls, becoming a hodgepodge of hotels, bars, and stables. For one Yosemite hotel owner, the words "inalienable for all time," contained in the Yosemite Park Bill, took on an unusual meaning, as he "cut a swath through the trees to provide his barroom with an unobstructed view of Yosemite Falls."[12]

The most serious challenge to the preservation of land and the national park idea, however, came with the rise of utilitarian conservation. Utilitarians believed in the wise, managed use of natural resources, under the direction of scientifically trained experts. They opposed "locking up" resources in national parks and valued management over preservation. Under the leadership of a new class of foresters, hydrologists, and civil engineers, these conservationists sought to improve upon nature and harness it for more efficient human use. They believed that forests should be managed effectively to prevent fires and diseases, to promote the promulgation of "desirable" species, and to produce an endless supply of lumber. Rivers should be harnessed to generate electricity, their waters channeled to irrigation projects in the dry West, and their flow controlled to prevent flooding.[13]

No individual promoted this idea better, or stands as a stronger symbol of utilitarianism, than Gifford Pinchot. Trained in the forestry schools of Germany and France, Pinchot began his professional career managing the forests of the Vanderbilt family at its massive Biltmore Estate in Western

North Carolina. Pinchot helped turn the Biltmore forest, ravaged by cut-and-run logging and forest fires, into one of the first managed forests in the nation. The energetic and charismatic Pinchot, a politician at heart, soon captured the attention of officials in Washington. In 1898, he received appointment as the head of the forestry division of the Department of Agriculture. Pinchot gained tremendous power and influence in Washington when his good friend, Theodore Roosevelt, became president of the United States, upon the assassination of William McKinley. In speaking of Pinchot, Roosevelt commented, "I have one friend . . . in whose integrity I believe as I do my own."[14]

With this enhanced political influence, Pinchot and the forestry division began to exercise control over more and more of the millions of acres set aside as forest reserves. Congress had passed the Forest Reserve Act with little fanfare in 1891, during a lame-duck session. The act allowed the president, without any congressional oversight, to designate areas of the public domain as forest reserves. Under the provisions of this act, Presidents Benjamin Harrison, Grover Cleveland, and William McKinley set aside almost 46 million acres, and Theodore Roosevelt designated 100 million acres under the act before Congress revoked this power in 1908. Although initially hailed by preservationists as a first step toward establishing new national parks, the forest reserves increasingly came under the control of the utilitarian-minded forestry division. In 1905, Pinchot and other utilitarians successfully lobbied for the establishment of the U.S. Forest Service under the Department of Agriculture, gained control of most of the forest reserves, and designated them as national forests.

The rise of the utilitarians caused confusion within the national park movement and clouded the issue for many Americans. Few understood the important differences between national parks and forest reserves, and the press often used the terms interchangeably. Pinchot and other utilitarians, intentionally or not, encouraged this confusion, as they sought to have the national parks placed under their administration. Given the lack of an administrative voice in Washington and the fact that they "had no recognized 'use' of their own" for lands in the public domain, preservationists quickly lost ground to the utilitarians. The former lost favor with the American public, too, due to their failure to "counter the objections of those who considered scenic preservation an extravagance."[15]

In 1904, Congress demonstrated the growing utilitarian influence when it deleted 542 acres of land in Yosemite because of the timber, grazing, and mining potential of the area. Acts passed during this period providing for establishment of two major national parks, Glacier and Rocky Mountain, kept the door open for utilitarian use of the parks, should such a need arise. The Glacier National Park Bill, passed in 1910, allowed the Reclamation Service to dam streams "which may be necessary for the development and maintenance of a government reclamation project" and allowed the secretary of the interior to "sell and permit the removal of such matured, or dead or down timbers as he may deem necessary or advisable for the protection or improvement of the park." The 1915 act establishing Rocky Mountain National Park opened the door for railroads, mines, and dams, if the resources in the park were needed for development.[16]

The confusion over preservation and utilitarian land use and the increasing power of utilitarians became apparent in the first major movement to establish a national park in the Southern Appalachian region. Dr. Chase Ambler of Asheville, North Carolina, spearheaded this early movement. On a fishing trip in the mountains of Western North Carolina in June 1899, Ambler, with the help of his friend, Judge William R. Day, developed a plan to start an organized drive to establish a national park in North Carolina. Enlisting the aid of A. H. McQuilkin, publisher of the magazine *Southern Pictures and Pencilings*, Ambler successfully lobbied the Asheville Board of Trade to form a Parks and Forestry Committee to promote the park idea. This committee organized a mass meeting, held in Asheville in November 1899, to broadcast the advantages of a park in the area and invited leaders from all over the Southern Appalachian region to participate. The notables who attended included Locke Craig, future governor of North Carolina; U.S. Sen. Marion Butler of North Carolina; U.S. Rep. W. T. Crawford of North Carolina; Moses Cone of the Cone family of textile magnates; Josephus Daniels, editor of the *Raleigh (N.C.) News and Observer;* Charles A. Webb, editor of the *Asheville Citizen-Times;* M. V. Richards, land and industrial agent for the Southern Railroad; N. G. Gonzales, editor of the *Columbia (S.C.) State;* and Pleasant Stovall, editor of the *Savannah (Ga.) Press.*[17]

The speeches given at the meeting reflected a new motivation for national park development and a common concern throughout the South that, while the region had the scenery to qualify for national park status, it had failed to get its fair share from the federal government. Locke Craig argued: "It has been the policy of the government to establish parks from time to time, and it is remarkable that this mountain region of the South has heretofore been overlooked; for above all other sections it is an ideal country for a park.... It would be reckless stupidity, negligence of the grossest kind, if a portion of this grand and picturesque region be not preserved in its original, natural condition for the enjoyment of the people.... Other sections have their parks, why not the South?"[18] Craig also asserted that the establishment of a national park in the South would symbolize the reconciliation of Civil War divisions between North and South. Senator Butler echoed Craig's thoughts: "If the government is going to have parks for all of us, then there should be one laid here.... The next park should be established in the east, and there is no place in the Appalachian range where you can find such a favorite region."[19]

The meeting resulted in the establishment of a permanent organization, the Appalachian National Park Association, to continue to promote the park idea. The group elected retired Asheville businessman George Powell president of the organization and Chase Ambler secretary-treasurer. In its first

Organizational meeting of the Appalachian National Park Association, Asheville, North Carolina, November 1899. Front row notables include Pleasant Stovall, editor, *Savannah Press* (fourth from left), and Dr. Chase Ambler (eighth), meeting organizer. Back row: N. G. Gonzales, convention president and editor, *Columbia (S.C.) State* (fourth); Josephus Daniels, editor, *Raleigh News and Observer* (sixth); A. H. McQuilkin, publisher, *Southern Pictures and Pencilings* (eighth); Sen. Marion Butler (twelfth); Rep. W. T. Crawford (sixteenth); and Carl Schenck, founder of Biltmore Forest School of Forestry (twenty-second). Photo courtesy of Great Smoky Mountains National Park.

official action, the group sent a memorial to Congress, requesting the establishment of a park in the region. The memorial contained a variety of arguments asserting the need for a national park in the area: "The rare natural beauty of the southern Appalachian region; the necessity of preserving the headwaters of many rivers rising in these mountains; the healthfulness of the region; the climate is fine the whole year; the location is central; the eastern states are entitled to a national park; the title to the land can be easily acquired."[20] In an argument that foreshadowed the future direction of the Appalachian National Park Committee and the confusion concerning national parks caused by utilitarians, the memorial also argued that the park would produce a profit as a forest reserve.[21]

Despite the early enthusiasm of the participants in this meeting, the movement for an Appalachian national park quickly ran out of steam. During the next two years, congressmen and senators from the region introduced several bills related to the establishment of national parks in the area. One bill did result in a thorough survey of the region by the Forestry Bureau in the summer of 1900, and another bill requesting an appropriation of $5 million to establish a forest reserve in the Southern Appalachians passed the Senate in 1901. Still, Congress took no substantive action.[22] In addition, the local movement experienced a great deal of difficulty in raising funds and generating interest in the project outside the immediate area. Increasingly, lumber groups and utilitarian conservationists began to dominate the organization. In recognition of this fact, the group in 1901 changed its name to the Appalachian Forest Reserve Association. By 1905, the movement had run its course. On 2 December of that year, the Appalachian Forest Reserve Association turned over its membership rolls to the American Forestry Association, because "we have exhausted our resources in time, energy, and money."[23]

Despite its national, rather than regional, focus, the Appalachian Forest Reserve Association in 1911, after a long fight, pushed through Congress the Weeks Law, which allowed the U.S. Forest Service to purchase lands in the East for forest reserves. The passage of this act almost altered the pattern of land use in the Smokies drastically, when the Forest Service established the Smoky Mountain Purchase Unit. Between 1912 and 1916, the Forest Service received options to purchase 61,350 acres from the Little River Lumber Company. However, in 1916, with lumber prices rising due to World War I and land titles in the area tangled, Little River voided the deal, and the Forest Service moved on to more fruitful enterprises.[24]

Scenic preservationists soon realized that they needed to take a stand against the utilitarians or risk the demise of the national park ideal of preservation. A crisis in the conflict occurred over the proposed damming of the Tuolumne River and the flooding of the Hetch Hetchy Valley in Yosemite National Park. Allowing such use of a national park would undermine the very foundation of the national park idea of preservation and threaten the very existence of national parks.

As early as 1903, the City of San Francisco had petitioned the federal government for permission to flood the valley in order to create a much-needed reservoir. Rebuffed on several occasions, the city increased its demands, especially after the devastating earthquake and fire of 1906. Leading utilitarian conservationists like Gifford Pinchot favored the plan, as did the majority of politicians in the region. Under Pinchot's mathematical formula for land use ("the greatest good of the greatest number in the long run"), the Hetch Hetchy Valley, visited by a few thousand individuals annually, stood little chance against the water needs of five hundred thousand San Franciscans.[25] Besides, as Pinchot and other utilitarians argued, inundating the Hetch Hetchy Valley would turn a "somewhat unusable mosquito-infested meadow floor" into a "lake of rare beauty."[26]

Scenic preservationists, led by John Muir and the Sierra Club; Robert Underwood Johnson, editor of the nationally circulated magazine *Century*; and J. Horace McFarland, president of the influential American Civic Association, organized a spirited defense of the valley. Reflecting the aesthetic arguments often used by scenic preservationists of this time, John Muir asserted in the conclusion of a book on Yosemite: "These temple destroyers, devotees of ravaging commercialism, seem to have a perfect contempt for Nature, and instead of lifting their eyes to the God of the mountains, lift them to the almighty dollar. Dam Hetch Hetchy! As well dam for water-tanks the people's cathedrals and churches, for no holier temple has ever been consecrated by the heart of man."[27]

While Muir's words inspired many and helped to unite the scenic preservation movement, they demonstrated a basic flaw in the arguments most often relied upon by preservationists. What measurable value would accrue to the American public if Hetch Hetchy were not dammed, and how would that value compare with the water needs of five hundred thousand San Franciscans? Preservationists had few answers to such questions. Congress approved the San Francisco petition, and President Woodrow Wilson signed it in 1913. The damming and flooding of the valley proceeded.[28]

While the Hetch Hetchy defeat came as a damaging blow to scenic preservationists and threatened the safety and very existence of the national park system, preservationists hoped that something good could come from the defeat. John Muir asserted that, "in spite of Satan & Co. (Pinchot and the utilitarians), some sort of compensation must surely come out of this dark damn-dam-damnation."[29] That compensation came in the form of a renewed commitment among many to broaden the rationale for scenic preservation beyond aesthetics, to expand the movement's appeal beyond the well-to-do, to push harder for legislation clarifying the purpose of the national parks, and to place the management of the national parks under a single government bureau.[30]

Even before the Hetch Hetchy defeat, the problems of administration in the national parks had become evident to many scenic preservationists. J. Horace McFarland complained that Washington contained "not a single desk or a single individual who worked full time" administering and protecting the national parks.[31] Scenic preservationists had no real voice in Washington, no strong entity with which to combat the powerful utilitarians, whose voices were heard through the Forest Service and Reclamation Service. Indeed, administration of the national parks was split among a hodgepodge of federal agencies. While the Department of the Interior ostensibly administered the national parks, the U.S. Army patrolled and protected Yellowstone, Yosemite, Sequoia, and General Grant from vandalism, poaching, and illegal grazing. Road building in the parks fell to the U.S. Army Corps of Engineers. To complicate matters further, Congress had passed legislation in 1906 allowing the president to designate as national monuments public lands that contained "man-made wonders and scientific curiosities." By 1911, Presidents Theodore Roosevelt and William Howard Taft had designated twenty-eight sites as national monuments, including Devils' Tower, the Petrified Forest, Lassen Peak, and eight hundred thousand acres of the Grand Canyon and its surrounding area.[32] In the 1906 act, Congress had assigned administration of the monuments to the agency that originally had administered the land. This action left thirteen of the twenty-eight national monuments in 1911, including Grand Canyon, under the administration of the Forest Service—a frightening prospect, in view of the Hetch Hetchy decision.[33]

As early as 1910, J. Horace McFarland and the American Civic Association launched a campaign to place all national parks and monuments under the administration of a single bureaucratic agency within the Department of the Interior. McFarland proved an able and energetic, albeit extremely unlikely, advocate of national parks and wilderness. The owner of a printing company in Harrisburg, Pennsylvania, that specialized in gardening publications, McFarland felt much more at home in his extensive rose gardens than in a national park. As Stephen Fox has argued, "He was more repulsed by cities than attracted to nature."[34] Attempting to broaden the appeal of national parks and give them a more utilitarian and less aesthetic focus, McFarland argued, "The park now serves the people, the park decreases the demand on the forces for keeping order, the park is the direct competitor in the United States of the courts, of the jail, of the cemetery, and a very efficient competitor with all of them."[35]

Utilitarians, as usual led by Gifford Pinchot, responded that the Forest Service could best manage the national parks. Most of the national parks either adjoined or were surrounded by national forest lands. Setting up a new government agency would be inefficient, a waste of taxpayer money, and "a needless duplication of effort."[36]

The response of scenic preservationists marked an important turning point for the movement. Confronting the utilitarians, they advanced a powerful utilitarian argument of their own: the most efficient use of America's scenic wonders lay in preserving them so that tourists would visit, providing a steady, never-ending source of income for local residents and the nation. In a 1909 magazine article, J. Horace McFarland combined this economic argument with patriotism: "Are we to proceed with the conservation of all our God-given resources but the beauty which has created our love of country[, so] that the generation to come will spend, in beauty travel to wiser Europe, the millions they have accumulated here, being driven away from what was once a very Eden of loveliness by our careless disregard for appearance?"[37]

McFarland's colleague at the American Civic Association, Richard B. Watrous, urged scenic preservationists to advertise "the direct material returns that will accrue to the railroads, to the concessionaires, and to the various sections of the country that will benefit by increased travel."[38] In a further stab at utilitarians, Enos Mills, the father of Rocky Mountain National Park, argued, "Using land for its scenic attractiveness is perhaps putting it to its highest and greatest use; this is real conservation."[39]

By lobbying Congress repeatedly, supporters of the national park bureau eventually got their message through. The House Committee on Public Lands held hearings on the issue in 1912 and 1914, and bills calling for the establishment of a National Park Service were introduced, but voted down, in both sessions. By 1916, supporters had answers to most of their opponents' objections and had enlisted new and important allies.

Perhaps no man had more influence on the establishment of the National Park Service and the subsequent success of the national parks than Stephen Mather, a wealthy Chicagoan who had made his fortune in the borax industry. Mather brought both an enthusiasm for nature and a desire to sell scenic preservation to the American people, much as he earlier had sold them "Twenty Mule Team Borax." A long-time supporter of the national parks, Mather had visited most of them, had organized opposition in the Midwest to the flooding of the Hetch Hetchy Valley, and actively had criticized the management and administration of the parks and monuments. In 1915, Secretary of the Interior Franklin K. Lane, tired of hearing complaints about the operation of the national parks, challenged Mather: "If you don't like the way the national parks are being run, come on down to Washington and run them yourself." Although he expected to remain in government service only a few years, Mather accepted and threw the weight of the Department of the Interior into the campaign to create a National Park Service.[40]

While lobbying Congress to establish a Park Service, Mather also busied himself revamping and revitalizing the national parks and their administration. In both the national parks and his division of the Department of the Interior, he replaced most of the park superintendents and other political appointees with able young men, "imbuing them with a distinctive esprit de corps and a firm dedication to the cause of natural beauty."[41] Mather also chose a young lawyer named Horace Albright to serve as his right-hand man. Together these two began the task of solidifying the place of the national parks within the government and in the minds of the American people. Mather's most important task was to broaden the appeal of the national parks and convince the American public that parks could produce economic, as well as aesthetic, benefits.[42] In accepting the job, Mather argued, "Secretary Lane has asked me for a business administration. This I understand to mean an administration which shall develop to the highest possible degree of efficiency the resources of the national parks both for the pleasure and the profit of their owners, the people."[43]

To accomplish this task, Mather began an ambitious campaign to popularize and even romanticize the national parks. He persuaded Robert

Sterling Yard—a former colleague at the *New York Sun* and former editor of the *Century Magazine,* the Sunday *New York Herald,* and the Sunday *New York Times*—to become publicity director for the parks. In an unusual arrangement, Mather paid Yard out of his own pocket. With a war going on in Europe, Mather saw this as a perfect time to promote park visitation, particularly by elite Americans: "A hundred thousand people used the national parks last year. A million Americans should play in them every summer. Our national parks are practically lying fallow, and only await proper development to bring them into their own."[44] Soon most of the leading magazines in the nation, including the *Saturday Evening Post* and *National Geographic,* ran articles extolling the beauties of America's national parks. Yard also wrote the immensely popular *National Parks Portfolio,* a book filled with photographs documenting the wonders of the national parks. Scribners published the book, but western railroads financed it and distributed copies free of charge to 275,000 leading Americans, including every member of Congress.[45]

Not only did the western railroads aid in the promotion of *National Parks Portfolio,* but also they launched their own highly successful advertising campaign promoting travel to the western national parks. Employing the patriotic theme of "See America First," the railroad campaign helped create the romantic image of both American national parks and the western railroads that many Americans retain to this day. The railroads also built luxury accommodations in and near national parks and monuments to attract the elite tourist of the time. In 1904, the Santa Fe Railroad built El Tovar on the rim of the Grand Canyon; the Northern Pacific Railroad built a number of lodges in Yellowstone; and the Great Northern Railroad built lodges and chalets, including the monumental Glacier Park Lodge, in Glacier National Park.[46]

In 1916, McFarland's persistence and Mather's promotion paid off. Despite the active opposition of the Forest Service and its parent agency, the U.S. Department of Agriculture, Congress created the National Park Service. Stephen Mather became its first director. When Woodrow Wilson signed the National Park Service Act into law, the national parks attained not only a much-needed administrative advocate in Washington, but also at least a general idea of how land in the national parks would be used. According to the act, the purpose of the national parks "is to conserve the scenery and the natural and historic objects and the wild life therein and to provide for the enjoyment of the same in such manner as will leave them unimpaired for the enjoyment of future generations." While clarifying some issues, particularly ones related to utilitarian uses of the parks, the clause also presented the National Park Service with sometimes contradictory tasks. It was to provide for the American public's "enjoyment" of the parks, while at the same time seeking to "conserve" and leave "unimpaired" "the scenery and the natural and historic objects and the wild life therein."[47]

The combination of the promotion of the national parks and the professionalization of the National Park Service made both the parks and the new agency overnight successes. The National Park Service quickly gained a reputation within the federal government for efficiency, enthusiasm, and dedication.[48] As the number of visitors to national parks skyrocketed, congressional appropriations for the parks also increased—from $498,647 in 1916 to $1,823,330 in 1922.[49]

The success of the western parks in attracting visitors and their dollars stirred the interest of civic boosters in every region of the nation, but especially in the Southern Appalachian region, already eager to have a park in its own backyard. For the first time in many years, Congress, "confronted with evidence the parks were capable of paying economic as well as emotional dividends," began to look for ways to expand the national park system rather than destroy it.[50] Statistics published by the National Park Service on the millions of dollars spent by park visitors in surrounding communities especially attracted the attention of southern boosters, always on the lookout for ways to stimulate regional economic growth. In addition, most of the sites outside the West that measured up to "national park standards" of monumentalism and scenic beauty were located in the South, and particularly in the Southern Appalachian region.

Southerners' enthusiasm for national parks meshed neatly with Stephen Mather's desire to win the support of southern representatives and senators. Despite the early success of the National Park Service, Mather harbored no illusions about the long-term staying power of the agency. He knew that he would have to continue to solidify his agency's position within the federal government in the face of new battles for congressional funding of existing parks and new parks, as well as ongoing conflict with utilitarian conservationists in the Forest Service.

The cause of southern park boosters was enhanced as, within Congress, the power of southern representatives and senators increased dramatically at the time the National Park Service was created. That power began growing rapidly in the late teens and early twenties, as southern states returned the same men to Washington year after year. Political scientist V. O. Key examined this phenomenon in his classic work, *Southern Politics in State and Nation:* "The re-election of individual Senators and Representatives over long periods wins a special advantage for the South through the workings of the seniority principle. Southern voters have a keen awareness of the benefit accruing from long congressional service and the challenger of an elder statesman cannot easily persuade the electorate that young blood is preferable to seniority on committees and in congressional leadership."[51] Southern representatives and senators also were more cohesive in their voting than any other group in Congress at the time. Although this unity related primarily to issues concerning the racial status quo in the South, it made southerners a group worth wooing.[52]

Stephen Mather recognized this reality early on, as southern representatives and senators often had provided key opposition to legislation relating to federal involvement in conservation issues. Some southerners opposed the acquisition of land by the federal government for any purpose, seeing it as a violation of states' rights. Rep. Charles L. Bartlett, in a 1908 House Judiciary Committee hearing, argued that setting aside land in the Appalachian and White mountains for federal forest reserves signaled the death of federalism and broke down all barriers to congressional power. If Congress approved this action, "the old American idea of the sovereign State with independent and sovereign duties to be performed by its own citizens, has become but a dream of past generations."[53]

Southern Democrats frequently allied with midwestern and western Republicans against conservation legislation, based on the issues of property rights and potential economic damage to affected areas. In considering the same issue as the House Judiciary Committee in 1909, five members of the House Agriculture Committee—three Republicans from the Midwest and West, and two southern Democrats—issued a minority report protesting committee approval of the bill: "The very best that can be said in support for the federal purchase of these lands is that as a result of such purchase the impairment of navigable streams may possibly be diminished or retarded. But will this vague general possibility, or probability, of a distant and shadowy good offset the immediate and certain evil of driving large numbers of people away from homes which in many instances have been occupied for generations, of reducing the productivity of large areas, and of [removing] large amounts of property from local tax rolls?"[54]

The best example of the impact of southern representatives and senators on issues directly related to the national parks concerned the Hetch Hetchy bill. In both the House and the Senate, the decisive votes in favor of allowing the City of San Francisco to flood the valley came from southerners.[55] These votes reflected not so much hostility to the idea of national parks, however, but a profound indifference. What good did national parks, the vast majority of them located in western states, do them or their constituents? The comments of Sen. James A. Reed of Missouri best reflected the attitudes of many southerners in Congress when he observed during the Hetch Hetchy debate:

> It seems to me that if this is not a case of "much ado about nothing," it surely is a case of much ado about little. The Senate of the United States has devoted a full week of time to discussing the disposition of about 2 square miles of land located at a point remote from civilization in the very heart of the Sierra Nevada Mountains, and possessing an intrinsic value of probably not to exceed four or five hundred dollars. The great national park in which the paltry 2 square miles is embraced contains, I am informed, over 1,100 square miles of territory. It is merely proposed to put water on these 2 square miles. Over that trivial matter the business of the country is halted, the Senate goes into profound debate, the country is thrown into a condition of hysteria, and one would imagine that chaos and old night were about to descend upon the land.[56]

To Mather and the National Park Service, it seemed that the establishment of national parks in the South would help turn apathetic or even hostile southern representatives and senators into supporters of the fledgling agency.

Mather also knew that, to solidify the position of the national parks in the hearts and minds of the American people, new parks would have to be more accessible. As late as the early 1920s, only the wealthy could afford the time and expense of trips to national parks in the West. Parks in the Southern Appalachian region would be a day's drive away from two-thirds of the nation's population.

By the summer of 1923, Mather and the Park Service's promotion had created a national park mania in the South among both people and politicians. Without any consultation with the National Park Service, bills calling for the establishment of national parks in the region flooded the House and Senate. In the first half of 1923 alone, legislators submitted bills for the creation of an Appalachia National Park in Virginia and a Lincoln National Park in Kentucky, Tennessee, and Virginia.[57] In preceding years, congressmen had introduced bills to establish parks at Mammoth Cave in Kentucky and at Grandfather Mountain in North Carolina.[58]

While the pressure to establish new parks increased, Mather faced pointed criticism from his old friend and former National Park Service publicist, Robert Sterling Yard. Yard had left the National Park Service in 1918, when new government regulations had forced Mather to end the practice of privately paying Yard his $5,000 annual salary. With Mather's financial support, Yard had established the National Parks Association, dedicated to defending "the National Parks and National Monuments fearlessly against the assaults of private interests and aggressive commercialism."[59]

As executive secretary of the National Parks Association, Yard became a zealous—some would say overzealous—defender of his particular view of "national park standards." Yard feared that, if the Park Service lowered its standards, every senator or representative would jump on the band wagon to gain a national park for her or his constituency. This flood of new parks would divert crucial funds from parks already established. Yard warned that a "National Park Pork Barrel would be the final degradation." On the question of national parks in the East, he said: "One argument for these gift-enterprise parks is that we should have National Parks in the East. We should indeed! Until our System represents also the supreme magnificence of our eastern landscape, it will be incomplete. Several National Parks should represent the glory of our Appalachians; but in magnificence of included scenery, in variety, in scientific importance and in ample spaciousness, these parks must do justice to the National Parks System. None but the noblest examples, painstakingly chosen, must be admitted."[60] Yard and the National Parks Association became highly critical of any parks project that they believed compromised the high standards of scenic monumentalism upon which the national park system had been established.[61]

In order to gain control over this chaotic situation and to maintain some sort of standard, other than political pressure, for national park selection, Mather made a significant announcement in 1923. On the fourteenth page of the annual report of the director of the National Park Service, Mather declared, "I should like to see additional national parks established east of the Mississippi, but just how this can be accomplished is not clear."[62] In making this statement, Mather for the first time made the establishment of a national park in the Great Smoky Mountains a serious possibility. At the same time, however, he recognized that, in attempting to establish parks east of the Mississippi, the National Park Service was entering territory largely uncharted and fraught with pitfalls. Mount Desert Island—now part of Acadia National Park—was the only national park in the East. However, its small size (six thousand acres) and the fact that it was donated in one piece by wealthy eastern philanthropists gave Mather and the National Park Service little guidance in acquiring larger areas owned by thousands of individuals and large corporations who were unwilling to sell, or in energizing an entire region to contribute the needed land, or funds to buy the land, that Congress required.[63]

In late 1923, Mather began discussions with Secretary of the Interior Hubert Work about the best way to approach the problem. On 2 January 1924, Work issued a press release giving a first glimpse into his and Mather's proposed solution: "The existing National Park system is the finest in the world. In making any additions to it sites should be chosen that will be in every respect up to the standard, dignity, and prestige of the existing National Parks and National Monuments. A thorough study, therefore, will be necessary before any definite conclusion may be reached."[64] In further discussions, Mather and Work decided to create a special investigating committee to examine possible national park sites. They also decreed that this investigation would involve exclusively the Southern Appalachian region and would extend only as far north as the southern border of Pennsylvania.[65]

By February 1924, plans began to crystallize, as Mather and Work contacted individuals best capable of conducting such a study. To avoid accusations of favoritism that might taint recommendations made by the committee, they decided that the group would include no southerners. Rep. Henry W. Temple of Pennsylvania, a former professor of history and political science at Washington and Jefferson College and an avid preservationist, agreed to chair the committee. Mather also received permission from the U.S. Geological Survey to allow a topographical engineer, Col. Glenn S. Smith, to serve on the committee because of his familiarity with the region.[66] Maj. W. A. Welch, general manager and chief engineer of the Palisades Interstate Park Commission of New York, was added to the group because of his experience with state parks and his contacts with eastern philanthropists. Work asked the Council on National Parks, Forests and Wild Life—an umbrella

organization composed of representatives of the leading conservation organizations in the East—to choose two of its members to round out the committee. The council chose New Jersey railroad-car manufacturer and long-
time national park supporter William C. Gregg, and Harlan P. Kelsey of
Massachusetts, a former president of the Appalachian Mountain Club, one
of the oldest preservation groups in the nation.[67]

The committee held its first meeting at the Department of the Interior
on 26–27 March 1924. Secretary Work welcomed the committee, thanked
its members for their willingness to serve, and challenged them to "undertake a thorough study of the Southern Appalachian Mountains for the purpose of selecting the most worthy site in that range as a national park, in order
to conserve the scenery and the plant and animal life under the established
national park policies for the use and education of the people."[68]

The committee immediately went to work, first addressing the issue of
how to respond to letters, already pouring in, asking the committee to inspect a particular site. To collect as much data as possible before they conducted field visits, the committee decided to prepare a form letter and questionnaire to send to prospective communities. The questionnaire asked for
information on natural boundaries of the proposed park; minimum and
maximum altitude; special features such as mountain peaks, cliffs, gorges,
waterfalls, and caverns, and varieties of plant and animal life; improvements
to the area, such as towns, factories, mines, farms, quarries, and hydroelectric dams; size of holdings in the area; extent of area that had been lumbered
or burned over; and the amount of assistance that might be expected from
gifts. The committee also decided to send out a circular entitled "A Policy
for National and State Parks, Forests, and Game Refuges," giving the general qualifications for inclusion in the national park system. Next the committee tackled the issue of officially naming the committee. The group unani-
mously agreed on "Southern Appalachian National Park Committee." They
also approved a resolution that, as a matter of policy, at least a subcommit-
tee of the main committee would visit each proposed site. In a final ironic
action, Harlan Kelsey offered to send each member of the committee a copy
of Horace Kephart's book, *Our Southern Highlanders* (erroneously recorded
in the minutes as *Our Southerland Highlanders*). Kelsey argued that the book
"contained the truest description of this area available."[69]

The establishment of the committee elicited a variety of responses, including a somewhat hostile reaction from the utilitarian conservationists in
the Department of Agriculture. Secretary of Agriculture Henry C. Wallace

wrote a lengthy letter to Sen. George Norris, chair of the Senate Committee on Agriculture and Forestry, defending his turf and explaining that, in his opinion, the Southern Appalachian region did not meet national park standards. In his view, "The region is totally different from that in which the National Park System was conceived and developed. It has been extensively lumbered and the remaining areas of virgin forest are for the most part small and scattered. It is a region of relatively large industrial development maintained by the use of forest products. It is a region in which other uses of the mountains for such purposes as municipal water supply, power development and the like are relatively common and increasing in normal and necessary demand. Local mountain settlements, even in the more rugged portions, are numerous."[70] Wallace argued that the Forest Service could easily protect the "dozens of small areas of special interest, beauty or adaptability to recreational use," such as Mount Mitchell, Grandfather Mountain, Linville Gorge, or the Pink Beds in North Carolina, the crests of the Smokies in Tennessee and North Carolina, and the Toccoa Basin of North Georgia. In an obvious dig at the National Park Service, he further asserted that "the National Forest system of protection with varied use seems better adapted to the situation herein set forth than the National Park system of preservation coupled with prohibition of all but museum use."[71]

Communities in the Southern Appalachian region, however, responded much more enthusiastically than Wallace and the Forest Service. The Department of the Interior received letters touting potential national park sites from groups in Jonesboro, Chattanooga, Elizabethton, Johnson City, Knoxville, and Cleveland in Tennessee; Louisville, Mammoth Cave, and Clay City, Kentucky; Asheville, Linville, Bakersville, and Wilmington in North Carolina; Staunton, Wise County, Big Knob, and Harrisonburg in Virginia; Morganton, Berkeley Springs, and Canaan Valley in West Virginia; and Atlanta and Tallulah Park in Georgia.[72]

Perhaps nothing better testified to the success of Mather's promotion of the national parks than this outpouring of letters. Under his leadership as director of the National Park Service, Mather had taken the national parks from the post–Hetch-Hetchy period, when the parks faced a tenuous and uncertain future, to a point where practically every community and every politician wanted one in their backyard. This conversion had come about not because the American public had become appreciably more environmentally sensitive, but because of the twofold purpose that Mather envisioned for the parks: pleasure and profit. He effectively sold the nation the idea that national parks were fascinating and fun places to visit. Indeed, during Mather's heyday, the terms "national playgrounds" and "pleasuring grounds" became commonly used synonyms for national parks. At the same time, Mather convinced politicians and federal bureaucrats that the nation needed more parks, especially ones nearer the nation's population centers. These parks not only would provide the American people with valuable recreational opportunities, but also would enrich the surrounding communities.

Mather's message resonated throughout Western North Carolina and East Tennessee (indeed, throughout the Southern Appalachian region), as boosters sought to attract the attention of the Southern Appalachian National Park Committee. Always alert to ways to improve the economy of one of the poorest regions of the nation, boosters latched onto the idea of putting the surrounding mountain land to a new use, one they hoped would prove much more profitable than grazing cattle, hard-scrabble farming, hunting ginseng, or even cutting timber. As many regional boosters saw it, Stephen Mather had given them the map to an El Dorado they always had known lay hidden in their mountains.

3.

"God-Fearing, Hustling, Successful, Two-Fisted Regular Guys"

The seeds of the national park idea found their most fertile ground not in individuals who lived in and loved the Great Smoky Mountains in an intimate way, but in the civic boosters of the region, particularly the men and women of Knoxville, Tennessee, and Asheville, North Carolina. Perhaps no group of individuals better fit the description given by George F. Babbitt (the quintessential 1920s man in Sinclair Lewis's novel) of the "ideal of American manhood and culture": a "God-fearing, hustling, successful, two-fisted Regular Guy, who belongs to some church with pep and piety to it, who belongs to the Boosters or the Rotarians or the Kiwanis, to the Elks or Moose or Red Men or Knights of Columbus or any one of a score of organizations of good, jolly, kidding, laughing, sweating, upstanding, lend-a-handing Royal Good Fellows, who plays hard and works hard, and whose answer to his critics is a square-toed boot that'll teach the grouches and smart alecks to respect the He-man and get out and root for Uncle Samuel, U.S.A.!"[1]

These men and women had come of age during the Progressive Era and possessed both a strong sense of civic duty and an intense optimism that they could change their world. They were also infused with the spirit of the 1920s, with the belief that any problem could be solved by the application of good salesmanship and sound business practices. Although these "Regular Guys" were guilty of much of the hypocrisy, empty rhetoric, and lack of forethought of their fictional counterpart, George Babbitt, their optimism, contagious enthusiasm, and boundless energy—their "zip," to use Babbitt's word—transformed the region during the 1920s and played the key role in getting the movement to establish a national park in the Smokies off the ground.

During the 1920s, under the energetic influence of these individuals, both Asheville and Knoxville boomed. The population of both communities skyrocketed during the twenties. Asheville's numbers increased by 79 percent between 1920 and 1928, to over 50,000; while Knoxville grew from 77,818 in 1920 to 105,802 in 1930, a 36 percent rise. The skylines of both cities changed dramatically, as new construction projects sprouted as if overnight. Ashevillians built new high-rise city and county buildings, the George Vanderbilt Hotel, the fifteen-story Jackson Building, a new state-of-the-art high school, and a new domed First Baptist Church, and began the construction of the Beaucatcher Tunnel. Boosters in Knoxville built the eighteen-story Andrew Johnson Hotel; the fifteen-story General Building (later known as the Bank of Knoxville Building); new homes for the YWCA and YMCA; a beautiful new stone Church Street Methodist Church; and the Tennessee Theater, a two-thousand-seat Spanish-Moorish movie palace, one of the most elaborate and ornate in the South, complete with a Wurlitzer organ costing $50,000. Organizations intent on improving the quality of civic life abounded in both communities. Knoxvillians founded the East Tennessee Historical Society and organized a major campaign to renovate the historic Blount Mansion. Civic reformers transformed the city government, adopting the progressive council–city manager format. Ashevillians joined the Civic Music Association, founded a city-funded junior college, and sought to attract tourists through the city's new Rhododendron Festival.[2]

Nothing exemplified the spirit of boundless optimism and faith in the future more than the real estate booms that swept both cities during this period. In Knoxville, posh new developments sprang up at Looney's Bend, renamed Sequoyah Hills, and around the Cherokee Hills Country Club west of town and the Holston Hills Country Club east of the city. Asheville native Thomas Wolfe recorded his observations of the real-estate mania sweeping his hometown in the twenties: "It was fantastic! Everyone was a real estate man ... barbers, lawyers, clothiers. . . . And there seemed to be only one rule ... buy, always to buy ... and to sell again within any two days at any price. . . . When the supply of streets and houses was exhausted, new streets were . . . created in the surrounding wilderness; and even before these streets were paved or a house had been built upon them, the land was being sold, and then resold, by the acre, by the foot, for hundreds of thousands of dollars."[3]

The civic boosters of the region who emerged from this hothouse environment and came to dominate the park movement were by no means typical scenic preservationists. While they appreciated "God's good out-o'-doors," they saw the establishment of the park primarily as a means to further economic development and prosperity in their cities by attracting national publicity, tourists, and good roads.[4] Indeed, in the early days of the movement, many boosters had little first-hand knowledge of the Smokies, a fact often obvious from their exaggerated claims for the region. However, what they lacked in knowledge, they made up for in enthusiasm and energy. In a remarkably short time, boosters in both cities created formidable publicity machines that enabled them to persuade the people of the region, despite the active and powerful opposition of logging and wood-pulp industries and the utilitarians, that setting aside (or, as the opposition said, "segregating") a large part of the Smokies was a beneficial and valuable "use" of the land. At the same time, the boosters successfully convinced the National Park Service, influential preservation groups, and Congress that the Smokies deserved designation as a national park.

Two individuals who played an important early role in promoting the establishment of the Great Smoky Mountains National Park, Horace Kephart and Paul Fink, diverged somewhat from the booster norm. Kephart, the well-known author of *Our Southern Highlanders,* was a noted eccentric who had left his wife and children, as well as an excellent job as head of the Mercantile Library in Saint Louis, Missouri, to settle alone in a shack in the "back of beyond" of the Great Smoky Mountains near Bryson City, North Carolina. Kephart had an intimate knowledge of the Smokies and had covered a good deal of the area on foot doing research for his two major works, *Camping and Woodcraft* (1906) and *Our Southern Highlanders* (1913), and for the countless magazine and journal articles he had published. In 1910, Kephart was forced to move from his home on Hazel Creek when the Ritter Lumber Company purchased the land and began large-scale timber operations. He moved to a boarding house in Bryson City, where he witnessed the environmental destruction the lumber companies wreaked on much of the North Carolina side of the Smokies. Watching the devastation of his beloved mountains, Kephart became determined to try to preserve them in

Horace Kephart, one of the earliest and most influential park boosters. Photo by Kephart's friend and frequent backwoods companion, George Masa. Photo courtesy of Great Smoky Mountains National Park.

some way. "I owe my life to these mountains and I want them preserved that others may profit by them as I have."[5]

Paul Fink, from Jonesboro, Tennessee, was another avid outdoorsman. Having spent a considerable amount of time hiking and camping in the Smokies, particularly on the Tennessee side, he had developed a similar passionate love for the mountains and intense desire to protect them. Fink recounted his reaction, on a trip to explore the eastern end of the Smokies in 1919, to seeing logging operations after spending several days in the wilderness: "Here at Balsam we encountered the first evidence of logging operations since we had left Mount Collins. A great shock it was to us, to travel for days through a magnificent, truly virgin forest, where there was only the very faintest, scattered evidence man had ever been there before, and then step into the utter devastation the spruce logger leaves behind him."[6] Fink worshipped Kephart and tried to emulate his writing. Although he never achieved the degree of success that Kephart attained, Fink published numerous articles about his camping trips and about the human and natural history of the Southern Appalachian region.[7]

While their love of the outdoors and firsthand experience in the Smokies distinguished Kephart and Fink from many other park boosters, their Progressive ideology and desire to boost the economy of the region placed them squarely in the mainstream. Fink was a quintessential civic booster who loved his hometown of Jonesboro, the oldest town in Tennessee, as much as he loved the Smokies. He spent much of his life working to preserve the old buildings in his town and turn Jonesboro into a major tourist attraction. He saw the establishment of the park not only as a way to preserve the mountain scenery, but as a way to bring tourists and millions of dollars to his town and region. Kephart saw establishing a national park as the key to regional prosperity, as it would bring good roads to the area. Most area boosters shared this view. Kephart, however, anticipated this prospect with some ambivalence; surely it would change the region, and its pioneer character would be lost. Writing to his son in the early 1930s, when he believed that establishment of the park was assured, Kephart argued, "Within two years we will have good roads into the Smokies, and then—well, then I'll get out."[8]

Kephart and Fink began corresponding in 1919 and often discussed the possibility of preserving the Smokies as a national park or even as a national forest. To this endeavor Kephart brought contacts made through his publishing success and his writing skill, while Fink contributed energy, optimism, and perseverance. The pair began to explore ways to make a national park in the Smokies a reality and talked about their idea with anyone who would listen. In the early 1920s, though, few were listening.[9]

Even while they sought ways to save the Smokies from the lumberman's ax, both Kephart and Fink recognized the immense problems any such enterprise would face. Congress had placed a major hurdle in the path of any movement attempting to establish a national park in the East by declaring that it would provide no funds for the purchase of such lands. The states, or private individuals, would have to buy any national park lands in the East and then turn them over to the federal government for administration. Even if one could raise the money, however, or get the Forest Service to buy the land under the provisions of the Weeks Law, lumber companies showed little inclination to sell the scattered holdings of old-growth forest still in their possession. Kephart lamented this fact in a letter to Fink in 1920:

> I wish from my heart that I could encourage you in starting a propaganda to have the Government buy up the best forests here before they are destroyed; but there is no hope. The big timber companies that own those lands would not take $100 an acre for them and the Nat'l Forest Reservation Commission is allowed an average of less than $6 an acre for purchases. That will buy nothing but cut-over lands unfit for agriculture. . . . I hope our people will show a similar appreciation [to that of New Englanders developing the Appalachian Trail] of our far more extensive and attractive mountain playgrounds, some day; and that they will awake to the importance of protecting our fish and game. It makes my heart sick to see with what reckless selfishness these gifts of nature are being squandered.[10]

Not long after Kephart wrote these words, and particularly after the formation of the Southern Appalachian National Park (SANP) Committee, others in the region began to jump on the park bandwagon, developing that appreciation of the Smokies—or at least of its economic potential—that Kephart and Fink long had touted.

The park movement in Knoxville began almost immediately after the publication of Stephen Mather's annual report declaring his desire to see national parks in the East. In the summer of 1923, Ann Davis reportedly asked her husband, Willis P. Davis, on their return from a trip to the western parks, "Why can't we have a national park in the Great Smoky Mountains? They are just as beautiful as these mountains."[11]

No two individuals better exemplified the community spirit prevalent in Knoxville and Asheville that helped make the park a reality. W. P. Davis immediately took the establishment of a national park in the Smokies as his personal crusade and brought his considerable enthusiasm and energy to bear on the project. As general manager of the Knoxville Iron Company and a member of the boards of directors of both the Knoxville Automobile Club and the Knoxville Chamber of Commerce, Davis had the wealth and influence to be heard on the issue. Ann Davis proved almost as adept as her husband in promoting the park, through her involvement in Knoxville area women's groups, such as the League of Women Voters and the Knoxville Garden Club. In 1924, she surprised her husband and broadened her influence further by running for, and gaining election to, the House of Representatives of the Tennessee State Legislature. She became the first woman to represent Knox County there and was one of the first women elected to statewide office in the State of Tennessee.[12]

On 17 September 1923, W. P. Davis wrote to Secretary of Interior Hubert Work, urging him to look into the possibility of establishing a national park in the Great Smoky Mountains of Tennessee. Work responded that two important things had to be considered before a national park could be established in the area: "First, whether the area in fact is suitable from a scenic standpoint for national park purposes, and, secondly, if that is established affirmatively, how it can be acquired by the United States."[13]

Davis actively began seeking local support for the project, talking to anyone who would listen about his dream of a national park in the Smokies. On 22 October 1923, Davis took his idea to the directors of the Knoxville Automobile Club, which formed a special committee to pursue the project in conjunction with a like committee appointed by the Knoxville Board of Commerce. For the remainder of 1923, the committee called itself the Smoky Mountain Forest Reserve Association. In January 1924, however, the committee removed "forest reserve" from its name and became the Smoky Mountain Conservation Association.[14]

Knoxville park boosters made their motivations clear from the start. In discussing the formation of the special committee, the *Knoxville Sentinel* argued that the establishment of a national park in the area "will bring millions of extra dollars into the southland." These millions would come from the tourists who would flock to the region, particularly those tourists who were headed to Florida. The article also pointed out that tourists had spent $100 million in the previous year in the areas surrounding national parks. In an argument that demonstrated the ignorance of most inhabitants of the region concerning national park rules and regulations (and concerning actual conditions in the Smokies, long hunted beyond capacity), the paper argued that "no better place is offered for a national park than the Smoky Mountains, rich in scenery, pioneer history and hunting."[15]

The article continued by discussing another potential benefit: "With the establishment of a national park in the Appalachian region, roads would be built and maintained by the government, thus eliminating drawbacks offered motoring tourists."[16] During the 1920s, good roads became one of the primary political and civic issues in the region. Historian Francis B. Simkins called good roads the "third god in the trinity of Southern progress," one accorded the same enthusiasm as educational and industrial projects.[17] Many southerners saw good roads as a long-sought panacea that would stimulate regional economic development and finally put the South in the national economic mainstream. "Good Roads" boosters touted increased tourism as one of the chief benefits that their program would bring to the South. As the price of automobiles plummeted and automobile ownership in the South soared—the number of registered automobiles in the South increased from approximately 25,000 in 1915 to 146,000 in 1920—the demand for good roads soon followed.[18]

Good roads became a powerful political issue in both North Carolina and Tennessee in the 1920s. Under Highway Commissioner Frank Page, North Carolina developed a statewide system of hard-surfaced highways. Between 1921 and 1925, the state built 7,500 miles of highway, with all the main routes hard-surfaced, connecting all one hundred county seats. In 1920, Tennessee possessed only 500 miles of surfaced roads. Under the leadership of Gov. Austin Peay, this distance expanded to 5,000 miles by 1929.[19]

The prospect of good roads—in fact, any roads—held a particularly strong appeal for the virtually roadless regions of Western North Carolina and East Tennessee. However, the expense of road building in the mountains kept that activity to a minimum, even during the halcyon 1920s. "Good Roads" boosters knew that, if the federal government established a national park in the region, good roads—possibly even financed by Washington—would follow. With this goal in mind, they often led the way in local promotion of the park idea.

Indeed, involvement in the "Good Roads" movement in Western North Carolina and East Tennessee almost guaranteed that an individual would be involved in promoting national parks in the region. Joseph Hyde Pratt, who became known as one of the leading "Good Roads" proponents in the South during his tenure as North Carolina state geologist, from 1906 to 1917, led the early drive to bring a national park to Western North Carolina.[20] Both W. P. Davis and David Chapman served on the board of directors of the East Tennessee Automobile Club (ETAC). Other park boosters—including Claude Reeder and Cowan Rodgers, pioneer automobile dealers; and Russell Hanlon, secretary-manager of ETAC—also had strong "Good Roads" credentials. Good roads and national parks were bound together especially closely in East Tennessee. The ETAC and the Great Smoky Mountains Conservation Association shared office space and had the same board of directors. As Russell Hanlon recalled, "It was often difficult to determine which group was meeting."[21] It did not really matter, for the goals of both groups—area economic development, good roads, and increased tourism—proved to be the same.

While boosting the idea of a park and the economic benefits that it would bring to the region, Davis also began collecting information on the scenic importance of the Smoky Mountains. This was essential if the federal government was to be convinced that the area deserved inclusion in the national park system. In October 1923, Davis wrote to Wiley Brownlee, a locally prominent developer and manufacturer who lived in the Smokies near Gatlinburg, Tennessee, requesting a description of the mountains, with particular focus on aspects that would make them attractive to the National Park Service. Brownlee replied that it "would require the efforts of three or four poets to describe the beauties of these mountains." Brownlee touted the Smokies as "the largest body of highlands in the entire Appalachian range," noting that they contained "dense masses of luxurious flora," with "innumerable springs, brooks, creeks, and rivers; literally thousands of miles of speckled trout, rainbow, and bass." All of this lay "within a day's journey from all large cities east of the Mississippi River." Brownlee concluded: "If there is any section east of the Mississippi that can measure up to National Park standards, the Smokies are unquestionably it."[22]

Davis also worked to gain key support for the project from local politicians. By January, he had secured the backing of U.S. Rep. J. Will Taylor, the dominant Republican political figure in Tennessee, and Tennessee's U.S. Sen. John Shields. These connections paid off early, as Davis received an audience with Secretary Work and some unnamed members of the SANP Committee in early February 1924, over a month before the first official meeting of the committee.[23] Late in the spring, Senator Shields introduced a bill in the Senate, entitled "A Bill to Establish the Smoky Mountain National Park, and for Other Purposes" (67th Congress, S.B. 3012). The bill proposed to appropriate $10 million for the Department of Agriculture to purchase national park land in the Smokies. The wording of the bill reflects the continuing confusion between national forests administered by the Department of Agriculture and national parks administered by the Department of the

Interior. Although the bill never made it out of committee, it did give the Smokies valuable exposure as a potential national park site.

By early 1924, Davis's most important ally in promoting the national park project in East Tennessee, Col. David C. Chapman, a veteran of the Spanish-American War and World War I, became involved in the Smoky Mountains Conservation Association. Chapman, like Davis, was a prominent local businessman, president of the Chapman Drug Company, a local wholesale drug distributor. He also served on the boards of directors of the Knoxville Automobile Club and the Knoxville Chamber of Commerce.[24] Chapman quickly became the chief public spokesman for the Conservation Association, equaling Davis in his enthusiasm, energy, and salesmanship. From his days in the military, Chapman brought to the movement leadership ability, intensity, and a combative personality—valuable traits in the many instances when the movement to establish a park in the Smokies took on the character of a war.

Chapman saw the park as a means to an end, that of bringing to the region badly needed roads and resultant economic development. In his first recorded public statements concerning the national park issue, made at a Kiwanis Club meeting in January 1924, Chapman declared that, if a national park were established in the Smokies, "tourists by the thousands would pass through Knoxville to reach" this "veritable paradise of beauty." He went on to point out that four million people visited Colorado every year, yet 82 percent of the population of the nation lived closer to the Smokies. He felt that the latter mountains, "rising sheer out of the East Tennessee valleys[,] present a grander spectacle than the mountains of the west." Chapman lamented that the grand future he envisioned could not be realized unless the government built a suitable road into the region, connecting Tennessee with North Carolina.[25]

Once the SANP Committee had been established, the Smoky Mountain Conservation Association began an intensive study of the Smokies to generate the background information needed to create an attractive presentation. In May 1924, Davis, Chapman, Brownlee, and several other park boosters made a five-day inspection trip into the Smokies. Many of the boosters had their first close-up view of the region they wanted to see become a national park. The trip had three purposes: to see the proposed area at first hand, to promote road building into the area (officials of the Tennessee State Highway Department accompanied the group), and to establish rapport with park boosters in Bryson City, North Carolina. Horace Kephart led the Bryson

City delegation, which included S. E. Varner, chairman of the Swain County Commissioners, and Dr. Kelly E. Bennett, the mayor of Bryson City. The group concluded the trip with a banquet at Bryson City, at which Davis, Chapman, and Kephart captivated the group with visions of the economic benefits that would descend upon their respective areas with the coming of a national park and good roads. This trip initiated important relationships among boosters in Knoxville and Bryson City, one of the most important being that between David Chapman and Horace Kephart.[26]

This early cooperation between Bryson City and Knoxville boosters culminated in an editorial in the *New York Times* in late July 1924, supporting the establishment of a national park in the Smokies. The editorial heavily quoted W. P. Davis and Kephart and was characterized by the sort of hype and exaggeration typical of the promotion of the proposed park. The article spoke of the variety of trees "that have never been touched by the woodsman's ax," the clear streams teeming with fish, the accessibility of the site by automobile, and the fact that "only a few herdsmen, hunters, lumbermen and surveyors have penetrated the recesses of this wilderness." The article concluded by arguing that Congress needed to act quickly in order to save the region from spoliation, and that, "for all the delights of wilderness under the sun and stars, the region of the Great Smokies alone in the East has the resources required for a national playground."[27]

Other North Carolinians also began to organize to attract the attention of the SANP Committee, although most supported locations other than the Smokies. In late 1923, U.S. Rep. Zebulon Weaver of Western North Carolina introduced a bill to turn the Pisgah National Forest, near Asheville, into a national park.[28] The regional booster group, Western North Carolina, Inc., also began to look for ways to promote national park interest in the area. However, the strongest and best organized effort came from the Grandfather Mountain and Linville Gorge area. Nelson McRae, president of the Linville Improvement Company, owners of Grandfather Mountain and much of the surrounding area, led the way. This site received a key endorsement at a 4 July 1924, meeting of North Carolina civic organizations in Blowing Rock. The organizations endorsing the Grandfather Mountain–Linville Gorge area included the Chambers of Commerce of Asheville and Charlotte, the two largest metropolitan areas in Western North Carolina, and of Western North Carolina, Inc.[29]

The National Park Service earlier had considered the Grandfather Mountain area as a potential national park site. In 1917, the appropriation for the Department of the Interior carried a rider allowing its secretary to accept the donation of Grandfather Mountain as a national park. However, when Stephen Mather looked into the matter, he realized that the Linville Improvement Company intended to give Interior only the summit of the mountain and retain all the surrounding property. Mather turned down the offer, arguing that "the purpose of the National Park Service is not to inflate private land values."[30]

The SANP Committee decided to begin on-site investigations of possible locations for national parks in the region in late July 1924. A special fund, made up of donations from Park Service Director Stephen Mather, committee member William Gregg, and John D. Rockefeller Jr., covered the committee's travel expenses.[31] The committee put together a rather loose itinerary for a late July or early August trip to visit possible sites in Georgia, North Carolina, and Tennessee. Booster groups began feverish preparations for the committee's visit.

The president of Western Carolina, Inc., Joseph Hyde Pratt, organized the North Carolina portion of the trip. Pratt submitted a list of twenty possible sites in Western North Carolina that the committee might visit. The *Asheville Citizen* reported that "the visit of the national committee is expected to be one of the greatest boosts ever given to this section to bring to the attention of the world the scenic and recreational advantages of Western North Carolina."[32]

On 26 July 1924, the committee began a whirlwind inspection tour of the region. The trip quickly took on a circus atmosphere, as boosters attempted to convince the committee of the suitability of their particular sites. The group, accompanied by Secretary of the Interior Work, stopped first in Gainesville, Georgia, where a delegation of over sixty men, including Gov. Clifford M. Walker, U.S. Sen. W. J. Harris, and U.S. Rep. Thomas M. Bell, met them. They spent two days in the North Georgia mountains and on 28 July passed into North Carolina to view the resort town of Highlands. The town had been founded by the father of committee member Harlan Kelsey, who had spent much of his early life there.[33]

Pratt and members of Western North Carolina, Inc., met the committee at Highlands, and for the next five days the committee inspected sites in the mountains of Western North Carolina, although Secretary Work returned to Washington due to illness. The group visited Whiteside Mountain near Brevard, went to Asheville for a stay at the famed Grove Park Inn, and inspected Mount Mitchell, Blowing Rock, Grandfather

Mountain, and Linville Gorge.[34] Although careful not to single out any particular site, members of the committee told the press that, on their tour, they had seen numerous sites suitable for national park purposes. These remarks set off a frenzy of anticipation among Western North Carolina boosters.[35]

Although professing neutrality, it became apparent that both Pratt and the *Asheville Citizen* supported the Grandfather Mountain–Linville Gorge site. *Citizen* reporter George McCoy mentioned in two separate stories that, while Pratt did not wish to sway the committee in any particular way, he supported the Linville area as the most suitable site. In a story summarizing the committee's visit to Western North Carolina, McCoy emphasized the Linville site, although he argued that the *Citizen* was "so little concerned as to the exact location, knowing that it inevitably must largely lie in Western North Carolina." Western North Carolinians also banked on Harlan Kelsey's close ties to the area. Linville supporters reminded Kelsey that his father had first opened that area to tourist development in 1888, when he began the construction of the Yonahlossee Road connecting Blowing Rock and Linville.[36]

In the midst of the North Carolina visit, the Knoxville boosters became terrified that the aggressive North Carolinians had influenced the

Winter in the Smokies. Photo by Jim Thompson, 1920s.

The Chimneys, one of the signature sights of the Smokies. Photo by Jim Thompson, 1920s.

Mount Le Conte. The fields in the foreground mark the location of present-day Gatlinburg. Photo by Jim Thompson, 1920s.

committee unduly. They decided to take matters into their own hands, visit the committee in Asheville, and present their case. Because they had been given only an approximate date for the committee's visit, the Knoxville boosters also feared that the committee might not visit Knoxville and the Smokies at all. The day before this trip, David Chapman publicly criticized rival sites in North Carolina and Georgia: "The principal sections of North Carolina and Georgia have been cut over, and the only other great scenic area that has not been culled that would anything like compare with the Smoky Mountains is that tract of virgin timber situated largely in Tennessee and Graham and Cherokee Counties of North Carolina."[37] This competition between groups from the two states often would cloud the establishment and development of the park.

On 29 July, Chapman, Davis, Paul Fink, Rep. J. Will Taylor, and several other members of the Smoky Mountains Conservation Association traveled to Asheville and met the committee at the Grove Park Inn. The group displayed an album of photographs of the Tennessee Smokies taken by Knoxville photographer Jim Thompson. The Knoxville group met with the committee for three hours and received assurances that the Smokies would be given full consideration and that at least part of the committee indeed would visit Knoxville and the Smokies on this trip.[38]

Harlan Kelsey and William Gregg honored this promise and on 4 August arrived in Knoxville to inspect the Smokies. For the next five days, Knoxville boosters took the committee members on a tour of major points of interest in the mountains. Led by members of the Smoky Mountains Hiking Club, a group of about twenty-five hiked to the top of Mount Le Conte and camped on 6 August. Kelsey and Gregg spent the next three days on trips by car, horseback, and logging train to Cades Cove, Gregory Bald, Elkmont, and Clingman's Dome, inspecting not only the scenery, but also the rapid encroachment and destructiveness of the logging operations.[39]

Gov. Austin Peay joined the group for the last two days of the trip. Swayed by both the scenic beauty of the Smokies and the threat to that beauty, he became one of the chief boosters of the park project. The Smoky Mountain Conservation Association actively had solicited the support of Governor Peay and had urged him to come to East Tennessee and meet with the committee in support of the Knoxville bid. Both W. P. Davis and David Chapman had written to Peay, requesting his presence for the visit. Chapman virtually implored Peay to come: "It [the Smokies] contains the greatest mountain mass in the eastern half of America, and the greatest

hardwood forests that now stand or have ever stood at the greatest elevation. It meets all the requirements for a national park and unless speedy
action is taken it will be destroyed, as the lumber companies are pushing
their plans to take out the timber since they fear it may be taken over by
the government. Its destruction would be a serious crime against our culture and civilization, and its preservation as a national park would bring
to Tennessee great wealth and great prestige. We are therefore extremely
desirous of your presence and your influence."[40]

Knowing that the Smokies or any site in the East could not compete with the western parks in terms of scenic grandeur, Knoxville boosters
hit on new justifications for including the Smokies in the national park system: its wealth of "primeval forests" and its overall biological diversity. The
boosters arranged for the committee to meet with a trio of botany professors doing research in the Smokies that summer—H. C. Longwell of
Princeton University; Arthur Kendall of Washington University in St. Louis,
Missouri; and William Trelease of the University of Illinois. The scientists
encouraged the committee to nominate the Smokies for national park status because of the area's botanical uniqueness.[41] In a subsequent article in *The
Outlook* magazine, Gregg reiterated these arguments: "It may be admitted
that they [the Southern Appalachian Mountains] are second to the West in
rugged grandeur, but they are first in beauty of woods, in thrilling fairyland
glens, and in the warmth of Mother Nature's welcome."[42]

On 18 August, Kelsey wrote to Representative Temple, giving his impres-
sions of the trip. Kelsey expressed his awe at the beauty of the Smokies, the
size of the area, and its suitability for inclusion in the national park system:
"After viewing the Smoky Mountains from Le Conte all the way thru to
Gregory Bald, which overlooks the Tennessee River [actually the Little Tennessee River], I am convinced that that section is the one big thing in the
Southern Appalachians for us to consider." Kelsey based his support for the
Smokies on traditional notions of monumentalism: "For grandeur I know
of no other view in the Southern Appalachians that quite equals Le Conte."[43]

The first inspection tour of the SANP Committee stirred booster activ-
ity all over the region. The Washington press reported that U.S. Sen. W. J.
Harris had convinced Secretary Work to send a group to survey a site in
North Georgia, which "he expected . . . to be selected." Delegations from
Alabama, West Virginia, Kentucky, and Virginia began to demand that the
committee visit sites in their states.[44] In North Carolina, U.S. Sen. Marion
Butler urged the North Carolina legislature, already meeting in special ses-

sion, to appoint a commission to advance the claims of the state with the SANP Committee and with the Department of the Interior. Butler head-lined a telegram to the legislature with the warning: "North Carolina Must Get Busy Or We May Not Get National Park, It Looks As Though Geor-gia Is About To Win."[45]

With the active support of mountain area legislators, particularly Sen. Mark Squires, Rep. Harry Nettles and Rep. Plato Ebbs, the North Caro-lina General Assembly, on 23 August 1924, approved the appointment of a "Commission on the Part of North Carolina for the Purpose of Pre-senting the Claims of North Carolina for a National Park." The joint resolution called for a committee of eleven—three chosen by the presi-dent of the senate and five by the speaker of the house, with three ex of-ficio members: the speaker of the house, the president of the University of North Carolina at Chapel Hill, and the president of North Carolina State College (NCSC) in Raleigh.

The commission, then, would include North Carolina Speaker John Dawson of Kinston and E. C. Brooks, the state college president. Although neither man came from the western part of the state, both were avid sup-porters of the park idea. Brooks, from his prior experience as state superin-tendent of public instruction, brought a good deal of experience dealing with northern philanthropists, particularly the Rockefeller Foundation's General Education Board.[46] The other members of the commission included Harry Chase of Chapel Hill, Mark Squires of Lenoir, Harry Nettles of Biltmore, Plato Ebbs of Asheville, D. M. Buck of Bald Mountain, A. M. Kistler of Morganton, Frank Linney of Boone, E. S. Parker Jr. of Greensboro, and J. H. Dillard of Murphy. The commissioners held strong sympathies for the Linville–Grandfather Mountain site, as three came from that immediate area, and Kistler, in particular, had financial ties to the Linville Improvement Company. The General Assembly appropriated $2,500 to cover the expenses of the commission.[47]

This special commission began meeting in October 1924. Although only four members attended the first meeting, those present believed that it was important to get started immediately. The group designated Squires, of Lenoir, North Carolina, as the chairman, while Brooks became secre-tary. In spearheading the national park movement in North Carolina, Squires quickly would assume a role similar to that of David Chapman. Squires was convinced that a national park would solve the region's eco-nomic problems; moreover, he had a commitment to good roads, political connections from long years in the state legislature, and the determination to see the project through. However, Squires would not achieve the status in North Carolina that Chapman garnered in Tennessee, due to his combativeness, lack of tact, and recurring illnesses that sidelined him at crucial stages of the process.[48]

The commission authorized H. M. Curran of NCSC and the State Department of Agriculture to begin collecting data on the suitability of possible sites in North Carolina. At the commission's second meeting, Curran brought a map that included a proposed area of approximately one thousand square miles—a compromise solution, designed to quiet competing factions, that tied together most of the potential areas in the western part of the state. The commission also appointed a special committee, composed of Brooks, Buck, Dawson, Kistler, and Squires, to go immediately to Washington to lobby federal authorities on behalf of the proposed North Carolina site.[49]

The establishment of this commission would serve to differentiate the North Carolina national park movement from the one in Tennessee. Because of the interest of the General Assembly and the regional balance of the commission, the park movement in North Carolina, although strongly centered in Asheville, would be more statewide in character. In Tennessee, due to the intense political competition among the three grand divisions of the state—East, Middle, and West—the movement always would remain rooted in East Tennessee and dominated by Knoxvillians.

In Tennessee, too, the visit of the two members of the SANP Committee stimulated a great deal of activity. As one of their first priorities, Knoxville boosters enlisted the ongoing support of Gov. Austin Peay. Peay's progressivism, his love of the outdoors, and the favorable impression he formed on his first visit to the region made this an easy task. In addition, several of his closest East Tennessee advisors informed him that support for a national park in East Tennessee would benefit him politically in the upcoming election. Knoxville lawyer Williston Cox advised Peay that, if he continued his support for the park effort, "the Republicans [in East Tennessee] will certainly sit up and take notice."[50] Peay's close friend, Knoxville automobile dealer Claude Reeder, also advised Peay to back the park.[51]

Almost immediately, Peay took an active interest in the park project, especially as the prospect of early acquisition of land in the Smokies became a real possibility. At the urging of Davis and Chapman, Peay began negotiations with Col. W. B. Townsend, president of the Little River Lumber Company, to secure a 78,131-acre tract in the Smokies. Davis had expressed interest in the property for several months and had written to Secretary Work in early 1924, advising him of the possible availability of the land. The Forest Service had almost bought the land a few years before, and it already had been surveyed and the titles approved. Peay decided to try to get the state to purchase the land for a state park and then turn the property over to the National Park Service, once Congress agreed to designate the area as a national park.[52]

On 13 September 1924, Peay secured an option on the property from Colonel Townsend. The option would lapse on 1 February 1925, if the General Assembly did not agree to purchase the land. This action raised the hopes of Knoxville park boosters, who conjectured that the state's acquisition of such a sizable piece of land in the Smokies would favorably impress the SANP Committee.[53] The initiative elicited a particularly enthusiastic reaction from Davis: "I think it will be one of the greatest moves you have ever made in your administration. And then, after we have secured that property for a State Park, later when it comes to the National Park proposition, it will be mighty fine if our state could offer this land to the National Government for part of the National Park. . . . the comparatively small amount of expense involved in securing this property, would be infinitesimal in the actual results obtained by the State of Tennessee through this purchase, for there is absolutely no way of estimating the amount of money that would be spent by tourists in the many years to come."[54]

Meanwhile, the inspection work of the SANP Committee continued. On 12 September, W. A. Welch and Glenn Smith visited White Sulphur Springs, West Virginia. They continued from there to the Blue Ridge Mountains of Virginia, where they spent three days inspecting the area around Skyland resort and Stony Man Mountain. Both the site and the enthusiastic reception given them by several hundred boosters impressed Welch and Smith, and they announced that they would return with the full committee. The Blue Ridge site's location, only a few hours away from Washington, D.C., and the support of the powerful Byrd political machine of Virginia gave this site a decided advantage. In the next two months, various committee members visited northern Alabama, the Blue Ridge of Virginia, and the Smokies; and several on the committee reinspected sites they had already visited.[55]

After completing these inspections, the committee met in early December to consider its recommendations. On 12 December, the committee made its report to Secretary Work. The report began favorably for the Smokies boosters: "We have found many areas which could well be chosen, but the committee was charged with the responsibility of selecting the best, all things considered. Of these several possible sites the Great Smoky Mountains easily stand first because of the height of the mountains, depth of the valleys, ruggedness of the area, and the unexampled variety of trees, shrubs, and plants. The region includes Mount Guyot, Mount Le Conte, Clingman's Dome, and Gregory Bald, and may be extended in several directions to include other splendid mountain regions adjacent thereto."[56] In the next paragraph, however, the report discussed problems associated with the Smokies. The rugged terrain and the altitude made road building and development difficult and expensive, and excessive rainfall in the area might put a damper on development and recreation.[57]

Both North Carolinians and Tennesseans were shocked when the committee recommended the Blue Ridge Mountains of Virginia as the "outstanding and logical place" for a national park. The committee listed as reasons for this selection the proximity to the nation's capital and forty million people, the scenic beauty, the historical interest of the area, and the possibility of building a skyline drive along the ridges through the park.[58]

The news stunned park boosters in Knoxville and North Carolina, as both groups had convinced themselves that their sites would be chosen. The *Knoxville Sentinel* reported that "astonishment and amazement are the two words that describe the feeling of the Smoky Mountain Conservation Association." David Chapman asserted that "hidden influences" must be at work, as no national park site ever had been selected "merely on account of proximity." Russell Hanlon of the East Tennessee Automobile Association lamented the loss of an estimated $10 million that a national park would have generated for the region.[59] The headlines of the *Asheville Citizen* reflected the relative lack of commitment to the Smokies site and more resignation than resentment at the committee's decision: "North Carolina Fails In Fight For Playground." An editorial urged North Carolinians to move on and increase their cooperation with the Forest Service to further develop land in Western North Carolina that already was under Forest Service management.[60]

Neither of the two groups proved willing to surrender, however, and both North Carolinians and Knoxvillians began to urge their representatives in Washington to advance their cause in Congress, particularly as

Representative Temple had introduced a resolution (68th Congress, H.R. 10738) to appoint a special commission to establish boundaries for a Shenandoah National Park. In North Carolina, U.S. Sen. Furnifold Simmons took the lead in advancing his state's cause. As the senior Democrat on the Senate Finance Committee and the recognized leader of the Democratic Party machine in his state, Simmons held immense power in both the U.S. Senate and North Carolina.[61]

Simmons organized a meeting of the North Carolina Park Commission in Washington for 19 January 1925. He called on North Carolinians to present a solid front to Congress and to unite behind one park site; Simmons supported the Linville–Grandfather Mountain site. He publicly opposed designating the Smokies a national park site, as such a move would prevent crucial water power development in that region. Most important, Simmons threatened to organize the congressional delegations from several southern states to defeat any bill that proposed establishing a national park only in Virginia.[62]

The Tennessee congressional delegation also reacted aggressively to promote the Smokies site. Sen. Kenneth McKellar actively advanced Tennessee's claims in the Senate. In the House of Representatives, J. Will Taylor and Carroll Reece received the assurances of the chairman of the Public Lands Committee, Nicholas Sinnot, that the Smokies would receive fair consideration.[63]

By early January, National Park Service officials, Secretary Work, and the members of the SANP Committee realized that the threats from disappointed boosters and their congressional delegations seriously jeopardized the project's future. Unless they reached some sort of compromise, there would be no new national park in the Southern Appalachian region. The addition of the Smokies to Representative Temple's resolution seemed the logical and natural solution to the problem. The fact that the committee had ranked it as the most scenic area in the region and its location in two states gave the Smokies a major advantage over other sites. Moreover, the bill now would have the support of the three powerful congressional delegations from Virginia, Tennessee, and North Carolina. On 11 January 1925, Secretary Work faced political reality and issued a press release calling for Congress to establish two national parks in the East: "It is my opinion that this commission instead of confining its work to the Blue Ridge site should also be authorized by Congress to investigate into the cost of establishing a second national park in the Great Smokies area."[64]

At this point, the Smokies site finally began to gain the support of Ashevillians and of some important North Carolina politicians. Horace Kephart actively campaigned for the Smokies site with U.S. Rep. Zebulon Weaver. Kephart attempted to counteract the contention of Senator Simmons and others that the establishment of a national park in the Smokies would damage water power development in the region: "There is no water-power site of any consequence in the territory under consideration in the Smoky Mountains. The contemplated boundary would take in none but small streams. . . . On the other hand, the perpetual preservation of the Smoky forests would be the best thing possible for the water-power interests, be-cause it would preserve the stream flow of the river feeders. If those forests are all cut off, there will be droughts alternating with disastrous floods and immense deposits of silt in the dam basins. Ask the water-power people themselves if this is not so."[65]

Kephart also urged Weaver to consider the economic value of tourism to the region, especially as Western North Carolina lumber interests be-gan to oppose the Smokies site, due to their extensive holdings in the area: "What made Asheville and the other flourishing towns of Western North Carolina? How much did the lumber trade do for them? Was it not the climate and the scenery that attracted wealthy outsiders, first as tourists, then as residents, then as investors? There is the great commercial asset of this country. It lasts forever and forever grows in value. Consider the rise of Asheville real estate, and its future; then turn and consider what our mountain land is worth when the timber is all cut off."[66]

By the middle of January, Weaver and Rep. Charles Abernethy rec-ognized both the wisdom of Kephart's words and the political reality that North Carolina never would receive enough congressional backing to gain a national park site entirely within the state's boundaries. Both began actively to support the Smokies site. Abernethy's patronage proved espe-cially crucial, as he served on the House Committee on the Public Lands, which was considering the legislation.[67]

As the Tennessee congressional delegation worked to insure inclusion of the Smokies in any plans for national park expansion in the South, Governor Peay and Knoxville boosters worked to strengthen their case by attempting to get the state legislature to accept the option on the Little River Lumber Company property. Peay and the boosters hoped that, by securing the option on this land, they could convince Congress that they deserved consideration. On 24 January 1925, Governor Peay, a delegation from the Tennessee General Assembly, and W. A. Welch of the SANP Committee came to Knoxville to inspect the Little River land. Several hundred Knoxvillians greeted them at the train station. During the course of this visit, Peay secured both an extension of the option from Colonel Townsend and the bold and unprecedented public assurance of the Knoxville Chamber of Commerce that the City of Knoxville would contribute one-third of the cost of purchasing the Little River land.[68]

The lobbying efforts of Tennessee and North Carolina politicians and the efforts of Governor Peay, Knoxville boosters, and Horace Kephart paid off when Representative Temple and Sen. Claude Swanson of Virginia agreed to submit new legislation in each house of Congress. On 27 January 1925, Swanson and Senator McKellar introduced a bill in the Senate (68th Congress, S.B. 4109), and Temple introduced a bill in the House (68th Congress, H.R. 11980), calling for the determination of boundaries for national parks in both the Blue Ridge Mountains of Virginia and the Great Smoky Mountains.[69] Senator Simmons attempted to salvage the claims of the Linville–Grandfather Mountain supporters by proposing his own bill to have a special congressional committee composed of three senators and three representatives investigate the Blue Ridge, Great Smokies, and Linville sites and make their recommendations to Congress. However, this bill died in committee and never made it to the floor of the Senate.[70]

On 21 February 1925, Congress took the first major step in establishing a national park in the Great Smoky Mountains, when it approved the Swanson–McKellar bill and President Coolidge signed it into law (68th Congress, 43 Stat. 958). The last-minute addition of Mammoth Cave as a site to be mapped secured the support of the Kentucky delegation and put the bill over the top. The bill called for the secretary of the interior to appoint a special commission to determine the boundaries for each proposed park; allowed the secretary to receive donations of land and secure land options, once the commission had determined the boundaries; and appropriated $20,000 for securing options and for the expenses of the commission.[71] Secretary Work appointed all the members of the SANP Committee as the new commission to determine the boundaries of the parks and receive donations of land and money to secure options.[72]

After Congress designated the Smokies as a potential national park, booster organizations in Western North Carolina and East Tennessee began the work of convincing the Southern Appalachian National Park (SANP) Commission and Congress that the people of the region were willing and able to purchase the land necessary to establish a national park in the Great Smoky Mountains. For Tennesseans, getting the state legislature to accept the option offered by the Little River Lumber Company was the first order of business. Despite the active support of Governor Peay, traditional regional jealousies between the three grand divisions of the state and active opposition by some powerful East Tennesseans placed formidable hurdles in the path of park boosters. In order to sway legislators—many of whom viewed the Little River land as "stump land"—the Knoxville Chamber of Commerce chartered a special train to bring the legislature to Knoxville to inspect the land.[73]

The train arrived in Knoxville on 14 March 1925, and Knoxville turned out to promote the Smokies. The University of Tennessee's marching band greeted the legislators at the station, and a weekend of tours and entertainment ensued. On Sunday, 15 March, Knoxville boosters took the legislators by car to Townsend and then up the Little River Gorge to Elkmont by train. The lawmakers were treated to a luncheon at the Appalachian Club, where David Chapman addressed the group. Chapman recounted the tremendous benefits that would accrue to the state if it had a national park and reaffirmed Knoxville's willingness to finance one-third of the purchase price. After the luncheon, the party rode the train back through the Little River Gorge to Townsend and continued its tour in cars over Rich Mountain and into Cades Cove. The group arrived in Knoxville by nightfall and boarded the train to return to Nashville.[74] The next day, the *Knoxville News* practically gushed about the legislature's visit: "There is no doubt that even the most prosaic of the lawmakers was mightily impressed with the beauty of the scenery thru Little River Gorge and up Rich Mountain and thru the pass, giving a panoramic view of billows of mountains and the valleys between."[75]

Despite the success of the legislature's visit, park boosters knew that several powerful groups and individuals still opposed the bill. David Chapman, Chamber of Commerce Secretary-Treasurer Carlos Campbell, Knoxville auto dealer and Peay crony Claude Reeder, and U.S. Rep. J. Will Taylor went to Nashville to lobby on behalf of the bill.

In the Tennessee House of Representatives, Ann Davis (only the third woman to win election to that body) sponsored the bill. Davis had shocked her husband in 1924 when she declared her intention to run for office, so as better to promote the park idea she first had proposed to him the previous year. W. P. Davis wrote to his wife frequently, giving her information to

use in trying to convince her fellow legislators to support the bill. Invari-
ably these letters came around to grossly exaggerated—but effective—
arguments concerning the economic benefits for Tennessee if the state
gained a national park:

> It is only a matter of a few years until the accumulated wealth
> should pay the entire debt of the state, and instead of having to
> be closed fisted and niggardly in our appropriations for the Uni-
> versity, for the schools and for every other purpose that will ben-
> efit the people of the State of Tennessee we will have millions
> more to spend for every purpose necessary for the prosperity,
> happiness and peace of our citizens, and it will be a crime if we
> do not now while we have this opportunity buy this property and
> furnish a nucleus to the government for the establishment of a
> National park, and every member of the Legislature who votes
> for the small appropriation needed to purchase the land called for
> will be blessed by prosperity forever, and he who has sufficient
> vision to see the need and meets it now will never regret it.[76]

In early April, the bill came before the Tennessee legislature. The state
senate approved the purchase bill on 1 April and also approved a bill establishing a state park and forestry commission to buy land and turn it
over to the federal government "if and when a national park in the Smokies
is created."[77] The bill did not fare as well in the House of Representatives,
where it failed on 8 April by a vote of 47–45. The *Knoxville Journal* attributed the bill's failure to the recent large appropriation made for the
University of Tennessee and the unwillingness of many Middle and West
Tennessee legislators to spend so much money on East Tennessee in one
legislative session.[78] Governor Peay immediately launched an offensive,
announcing that passage of this bill, next to the eight-month school bill,
would mean more to Tennessee than any other measure being considered
by the legislature. He also called to his office several legislators who had
voted against the bill and encouraged them to change their votes. The next
day, supporters reintroduced the bill into the House of Representatives,
along with a bill authorizing Knoxville to pay one-third of the purchase
price, and it passed 58–32.[79] On 10 April, Governor Peay signed the bill
into law (Chapter 57, Public Acts of 1925) and presented the pen to Ann
Davis in recognition of her significant role in the process.[80]

The bill contained two important provisos which would come back to
haunt park supporters in later years. The first allowed the Little River

Lumber Company to retain the timber rights to sixteen thousand acres in the middle prong of Little River for fifteen years, enabling them to continue to cut the old-growth timber in this area and prohibiting the state from condemning the land during this period. The second proviso authorized the Tennessee State Park and Forestry Commission to purchase the Little River land officially "only in the event that the United States of America shall by proper legislative Act of Congress, within two years from the passage of this act, have first designated said lands to be included as a National Park area, to be maintained as such by the United States of America."[81] Indeed, it seems obvious that many legislators cast their votes for the Little River Purchase Bill in the strong belief that the park never would become a reality and that the state hence never would have to come up with the money. Moreover, a third problem soon became evident, as the commitment that the City of Knoxville would pay one-third of the purchase price had been made not by any elective body in Knoxville, but by the Knoxville Chamber of Commerce.[82]

Despite these problems, the success of the bill produced a great deal of optimism among park boosters in both states. At the urging of the SANP Commission, boosters in Knoxville and Asheville followed the example of the people of the Blue Ridge of Virginia and began organizing to promote, raise funds, and buy additional lands for the proposed national park. William Gregg, Glenn Smith, and William Welch of the commission played especially active roles in supporting local efforts, visiting the region, giving speeches, writing newspaper articles, and even opening discussions with lumber companies in the Smokies.[83]

On 5 June 1925, Knoxville kicked off its promotion campaign with a luncheon hosted by the presidents of Knoxville's five national banks. Mayor Ben Morton presided, and U.S. Sen. L. D. Tyson spoke on behalf of the park project, proclaiming, "We are not going to fail."[84] The group decided to incorporate the Great Smoky Mountains Conservation Association (GSMCA) and raise $50,000 to promote the Smokies and purchase additional land that might become available. Knoxville boosters raised $8,300 at this meeting, with $1,000 of it donated by William Gregg.[85]

Asheville boosters displayed less enthusiasm than their Knoxville counterparts. The North Carolina Park Commission (NCPC) held a meeting in Asheville on 18 June to discuss the possibility of cooperating with Tennessee in efforts to gain a national park in the Great Smoky Mountains. David Chapman and other members of the GSMCA attended the meeting, along with William Gregg and William Welch. However, several members of the NCPC and a number of prominent Western North Carolina national park enthusiasts remained committed to the Linville–Grandfather Mountain site. Local timber interests, who wanted to see the Smokies turned into a national forest so that they could continue to have access to the land, threw their support behind the Linville group.

The meeting began on a bad note for Smokies boosters, as Linville–Grandfather Mountain supporters expressed their intention to continue to press the SANP Commission to choose their site; they refused to support the Smokies site. Gregg responded to this challenge by asserting that their lack of support would damage everyone's chances of gaining congressional approval. He reminded them, "We must all sacrifice something for the general good. Some of you must also sacrifice your own preferences if North Carolina is to grasp her opportunity."[86] Finally, Plato Ebbs, a state senator, NCPC member, and officer in the Asheville Chamber of Commerce, made a motion that the NCPC cooperate with Tennessee to support the Smokies site. The commission voted in favor of Ebbs's motion. Smokies supporters had won a significant victory.[87]

Despite the commitment of the NCPC to back the Smokies project, public support in Western North Carolina remained lukewarm, and opposition from timber companies and Forest Service employees began to mount. The Champion Fibre Company, the largest landowner in the Smokies, stood at the forefront of the resistance. Champion actively lobbied the SANP Commission to forget the Smokies and allow the Forest Service to administer the land. Champion stood to gain tremendously from such an arrangement, which would enable the firm to sell its lands to the federal government at a profit, gain tax relief, and still have access to the timber and pulpwood necessary for its operations at low prices. Champion Fibre Company Chief Forester W. J. Damtoft wrote to Harlan Kelsey, arguing that "to create a National Park out of an area merely because of its beauty is to depart from past policy of having Parks only where there are unique topographic features or unusual natural phenomena." Moreover, he said, any area fit for national park status "should acclaim itself and should not have to be hunted."[88] Both Damtoft and Champion President Reuben Robertson emphasized the economic importance of the timber in the Smokies to their particular operation and to the overall economy of Western North Carolina.[89]

In July, the Western North Carolina Lumber and Timber Association passed a resolution declaring that "the National Park System is not adapted to the needs of Western North Carolina." The resolution went on to condemn "the agitation to establish one in the Smoky Mountains." The association justified its position based on its opposition "to the segregation of enormous areas of forest lands and lands suitable for growing forests into dead hands, where it cannot be used, no matter how vital its use may be to the industries of this State, and to the material needs of this nation."[90]

Continuing conflict between utilitarians and scenic preservationists manifested itself, as Forest Service employees also worked to stir up opposition to the Smokies project throughout Western North Carolina, despite declarations by both the secretary of agriculture and the director of the Forest Service that the Forest Service had withdrawn its interest in the Smokies. Verne Rhoades, forest supervisor of the Pisgah National Forest (and a graduate of the local Biltmore Forest School, the first school of forestry in America), led the utilitarian opposition. Harlan Kelsey visited the region and reported to fellow members of the SANP Commission that forest rangers in Western North Carolina had told area residents that "they would have their homes seized at a very low figure and would be excluded from the area and might just as well give up hope if the National Park took in that area."[91] Reuben Robertson revealed to Kelsey that local Forest Service employees had confided in him that they had withdrawn from the area "only temporarily" and would take over the area when the national park project failed.[92] Smokies boosters also accused Forest Service employees of distributing unsigned literature warning Western North Carolinians of the disaster to come if the park became a reality.[93]

A relative lack of public interest, however, proved the most serious problem in North Carolina. Gregg reported in July, "In spite of our 'victory' at Asheville and the vote of the North Carolina Commission endorsing the Great Smoky National Park proposition, the interest is rather lukewarm."[94] The reticence of Western North Carolina's largest and most influential newspaper, the *Asheville Citizen,* was particularly damaging. Gregg expressed his disappointment that the *Citizen* had printed unsigned letters expressing the concerns of the timber interests and had made favorable editorial comments about these concerns.[95]

Glenn Smith reported a mixed message after meeting in the Smokies with Mark Squires and A. M. Kistler of the NCPC. Both supported the Linville–Grandfather Mountain site but, after seeing the Smokies at first hand, reportedly had become "sold" on the site. However, Squires, the

NCPC chairman, told Smith that he did not believe the people of North Carolina would "put up a cent by popular subscription or in donating any land for national park purposes."[96] Smith lamented to SANP Commission Chairman H. W. Temple, "I am afraid that there is a good deal of politics mixed in connection with the establishment of the national park in North Carolina."[97]

The SANP Commission responded aggressively to Western North Carolina opposition and apathy. At its 18 July meeting, the commission drafted two public announcements to try to stimulate more interest in the park project in Western North Carolina. In its first announcement, the commission warned the people of North Carolina that, due to opposition and apathy in the area, "the Commission may find it necessary to modify its boundaries as originally contemplated and consider the advisability of the creation of a national park which will lie largely in the State of Tennessee."[98] The commission also drafted a follow-up statement more specifically pointing the finger at Champion and the other large Western North Carolina timber companies and stressing the urgency of the situation:

> The original Tennessee area is large and scenic; about one-half of the North Carolina project originally designated seems available, but the holdings of two or three of the largest timber corporations are difficult to acquire as virgin areas; if they are not secured until after the timber is cut off they will not be fit for a national park for recreational use. The companies referred to are at the present time in active operations on some of the higher elevations and are removing the spruce and balsam in their entirety. The spruce and balsam areas which have been cut over do not reforest themselves, and immediately become covered with an almost impenetrable thicket of blackberry and other undesirable growths peculiarly susceptible to forest fires.[99]

The commission's threat bore almost immediate fruit. The *Asheville Citizen* and its copublisher Charles Webb dropped their position of relative neutrality and aggressively advocated for the park. Webb soon became the most important ally of the park movement in Asheville, almost single-handedly bringing the enthusiasm of Asheville boosters up to the level of their Knoxville counterparts. He also demonstrated a willingness to take on the timber companies and the utilitarians. On 27 July, Webb ran an editorial entitled "What Are We Doing For The Park?" In it he warned the people of Western North Carolina that they were being left behind by Virginia and Tennessee. He then issued a call for action: "Isn't it about time that the people of Western North Carolina should come together in their ideas and ambitions for conserving the Smoky Mountain area, and make definite plans for carrying their ambitions into reality?"[100] On 11 August, the board of directors of the Asheville Chamber of Commerce publicly endorsed the park project for the first time, and board members personally pledged to purchase two hundred acres in the park area.[101]

Webb and the *Citizen* continued their promotional onslaught throughout August and September. The 16 August front page contained a cartoon entitled "No Time For Lethargy," showing a man designated "Western North Carolina" sleeping, while Tennessee boosters struggled to pull in a big fish labeled "National Park." The Tennesseans shouted at the sleeping North Carolinian, "Hey, there! Wake up and give us a hand!"[102] On the editorial page, Webb gave his strongest endorsement yet for the park and pointed out its potential benefits to Western North Carolinians: "It would mean the real making of Western North Carolina as the 'playground of Eastern America,' and innumerable tourists would come among us to spend their money and many of them to make their homes among us. Its benefits to the present generation and the people of the future are simply inestimable."[103] Webb challenged the people of Western North Carolina not to allow a "few individuals" motivated by "personal interests" to deprive the region of this golden opportunity. In the conclusion of the editorial, Webb pledged that the *Citizen* would purchase 100 acres of Smokies land for the park.[104]

Webb became such an avid supporter of the park that he personally wrote to Secretary of Agriculture William M. Jardine, informing him of the activities of Forest Service personnel in opposition to the park. Webb wrote that he understood that the Forest Service had withdrawn from the area, yet Forest Service employees in Western North Carolina had issued "organized, systematic propaganda . . . making the most outrageous misrepresentations, terrifying and alarming the populace." Webb asserted that he knew the employees had done this without the secretary's knowledge or consent, but he felt the need to call it to his attention so that he could take proper action.[105]

The support of the *Citizen* and the Asheville Chamber of Commerce led to the chartering of a new organization to start a statewide promotion and fundraising campaign on behalf of the park. Asheville boosters established Great Smoky Mountains, Inc., on 2 September 1925, to cooperate with the

Knoxville-based GSMCA and the SANP Commission. The group elected
Asheville Chamber of Commerce President Roger Miller as executive secretary and Horace Kephart as field secretary. It also established a $13,000
fund to pay for necessary publicity and travel expenses.[106] The next day, the
Citizen reported that "North Carolina people are beginning to more fully
appreciate the proposal of a National Park."[107]

Throughout the summer and early fall, the Great Smoky Mountains
National Park project secured additional key endorsements and valuable
publicity which helped the project gain momentum. Knoxville boosters took
advantage of the gathering of the nation's press at nearby Dayton, Tennessee, for the Scopes trial in July 1925. Park supporters traveled to Dayton to
try to persuade both members of the national press and major figures involved
in the trial itself to visit the Smokies. On 24 July, boosters counted it a major coup when Clarence Darrow and John Scopes visited Elkmont as guests
of David Chapman. After a horseback ride to the top of Gregory Bald,
Darrow gave a ringing endorsement of the Smokies to the gathered press:
"I have been in most of the national parks of this country and I have seen
many mountains, but never have I seen any view to surpass this. By all means
this should be conserved as a national park."[108]

Smokies boosters also began to take advantage of the talents and reputation of Horace Kephart. The *Asheville Times,* the *Knoxville News,* and
the local Bryson City, North Carolina, newspaper all published articles
by Kephart on the importance of preserving the virgin timber of the
Smokies and the economic benefits of national parks. William Gregg
encouraged him to have the articles published in every paper in North
Carolina and even agreed to finance any expenses involved, up to $500.[109]

In August 1925, the Smokies project received a crucial endorsement and
a valuable convert. Arno Cammerer, assistant director of the National Park
Service and Stephen Mather's point man on national parks in the East, visited the Tennessee side of the Smokies. With David Chapman, Paul Fink,
and members of the Smoky Mountains Hiking Club, Cammerer climbed
Mount Le Conte, where he witnessed a spectacular sunset and sunrise; toured
Cades Cove; and climbed Gregory Bald. After this three-day visit, Cammerer
wrote to Park Service Director Stephen Mather, telling him about his trip
and giving his impressions. Cammerer emphasized the major point of his
visit: determining whether the Smokies would "measure up to national park
standards" for scenery and recreation potential. Cammerer included photographs to illustrate his point to Mather: "Most of the area is absolute virgin

wilderness and presents particularly unique flora."[110] Cammerer concluded his report on a strong note, arguing that the proposed national park area presented "scenery of such supreme character, nationally instead of locally considered, that it will measure from every standpoint up to the best in our national park system." Cammerer also demonstrated his prescience when he predicted to Mather that, in a short time, the number of visitors to the Smokies "would far exceed in number . . . those in any other national park in the country."[111] This report gave the Smokies project credibility where it counted. From this point on, the National Park Service and especially Cammerer provided critical support and encouragement.

During this trip, Cammerer also developed close personal relationships with many park boosters on the Tennessee side of the Smokies. These proved both a blessing and a curse for the park movement. Cammerer corresponded with a number of Knoxville boosters and sprinkled his letters with fond references to songs and experiences from his camping trips into the Smokies. He and David Chapman became particularly strong friends, evidently enjoying many of the same pleasures. They often alluded to trips to the "Cosby district," a section of the Smokies notorious for its moonshiners. Later, during an era of national Prohibition, these visits would prove problematical for the movement, as opponents used allegations of drinking, womanizing, and consorting with moonshiners to call into question the character and judgment of the two men. These relationships also caused a good deal of jealousy on the North Carolina side of the Smokies and led to accusations—still common today—that the National Park Service favored the Tennessee side.

Another key endorsement came in September, when Robert Sterling Yard, president of the National Parks Association, visited the Smokies for nine days. Yard had criticized the inclusion of cut-over lands in the Smokies and Shenandoah projects, and had argued that the push to establish these parks had to do more with politics than with scenic values. Yard's influence in the scenic preservation movement made his support crucial to the national credibility of the Smokies project. In the *National Parks Bulletin* of November 1925, he published his impressions of the Smokies. Readers had to look no further than the title and subtitle of the article to get Yard's view: "A National Park in the Great Smoky Mountains: Reporting a Region of Lofty Mountains and Ridges, Deep Canyons, Many Waters, and Original Forest, Which Will Uphold in Full Measure the Standards of the National Parks System, in Which It Will Ably Represent the Characteristics of the

Appalachian Mountain System." The article continued, describing the imposing mountains, variety of flora, waterfalls and streams, and even the quaint and interesting mountain folk.[112]

In a period of less than two years, regional park boosters had confounded their enemies and surprised even themselves. They had transformed the movement for a national park in the Smokies from idle wishes in the minds of Horace Kephart, Paul Fink, and Ann Davis into two vibrant and effective organizations—the Great Smoky Mountains Conservation Association and Great Smoky Mountains, Inc.—that had galvanized support in their respective communities. The groups in both North Carolina and Tennessee had effective and energetic leadership in David Chapman and W. P. Davis in Knoxville and Mark Squires, Horace Kephart, and Plato Ebbs in Western North Carolina. Both communities also had the firm and enthusiastic support of local newspapers, as Edward Meeman and the *Knoxville News* (soon to become the *Knoxville News-Sentinel*) and Charles Webb and the *Asheville Citizen* provided positive coverage and publicity. Politicians and individuals with statewide constituencies had jumped on the bandwagon as well. Gov. Austin Peay, U.S. Rep. J. Will Taylor, and U.S. Sen. Kenneth McKellar aided the cause in Tennessee; while U.S Rep. Zebulon Weaver, U.S. Rep. Charles Abernethy, and E. C. Brooks, president of North Carolina State College, lent their support and influence in North Carolina. The support of scenic preservation leaders, including the members of the Southern Appalachian National Park Committee, National Park Service Assistant Director Arno Cammerer, and National Parks Association President Robert Sterling Yard, gave the movement credibility on the national level.

While celebrating these successes, park boosters realized that the battle had just begun. All they really had were a couple of enthusiastic but underfunded organizations, a promise to buy 76,000 acres of mostly cutover land in Tennessee, tentative national park recognition from Congress if they could demonstrate their ability to purchase the needed land, and a new dream: that, in one of the poorest parts of the country, they could come up with the millions of dollars necessary to buy that land. Meanwhile, in both states, opponents of the park showed no inclination to give up their fight; indeed, they had demonstrated their willingness to resist the park movement at every turn. Park boosters soon realized that they needed to combine their enthusiasm, vigor, and (to use Babbitt's word) "zip" with perseverance and patience for the long, slow process ahead.

4.

A "Mighty Undignified" Campaign

Ten million dollars! That figure stood foremost in the minds of park boosters as the amount of money that 427,000 acres in the Great Smoky Mountains reportedly would cost. That huge sum was an immense challenge for one of the poorest regions of the country, a barrier seemingly as impenetrable as a rhododendron hell in the Smokies. In order to make the Great Smoky Mountains National Park a reality, boosters launched a fundraising campaign that reached a level of hype that would have embarrassed even George Babbitt. When opponents claimed that a national park in the Great Smoky Mountains was a "fairy dream on a goat hill," a "playground for idlers," a "vision out of the air," and even a ticket straight to hell, boosters countered that it would be "an inexhaustible gold mine," a "Mecca for tourists," the "best investment ever offered to the people of East Tennessee," the "Goose with the Golden Eggs," and a "modern combination of Aladdin's Wonderful Lamp, the touch of Midas, the Magic Urn, and the weaving of straw into gold by Rumpelstiltskin." Indeed, campaign workers pulled out all stops in order to tap into every possible money source in the region and beyond. The campaign led them from the piggy banks of school children and church collection plates to the bulging wallets of millionaires. Boosters sought funds in the halls of elementary schools, at high schools and colleges, in local businesses and industries, in churches and civic organizations, at country clubs, in the legislative assemblies of Tennessee and North Carolina, and even on the banks of the Hudson River, where they approached wealthy philanthropists.

To make matters more difficult, Congress had made it clear on a number of occasions that it would not purchase land for national park purposes. This placed the burden of raising such a sizable amount on the two states and on local communities. Optimistic and self-assured though they were, park boosters knew that raising that much money would be extremely difficult. Park opponents felt that park boosters had little chance of achieving their goal but still fought hard at every turn to insure that they did not.

The scramble for funding began on 24 September 1925, when members of the GSMCA and Great Smoky Mountains, Inc. (GSMI), met in Knoxville. There they established an interstate committee to coordinate fundraising efforts. Plans were made to launch the North Carolina campaign in late November and the Tennessee campaign on 7 December. David Chapman was named chairman and Plato Ebbs secretary.[1] On 2 October, the group met again, this time in Asheville, and began negotiations with the New York firm of Tamblyn & Brown, who specialized in managing such endeavors for nonprofit organizations.[2] On 26 October, GSMCA and GSMI signed a contract with Tamblyn & Brown, officially launching the fundraising drive.[3]

An investigation by a Tamblyn & Brown staff member, Charles Trimmer, immediately pointed out a major problem for fundraisers: a lack of interest and a general unwillingness to contribute to the project by individuals outside the park region, particularly in Tennessee. Trimmer talked to prominent citizens in Nashville and Memphis and received little encouragement to extend the fundraising campaign beyond the eastern end of the state. Luke Lea, editor of the *Nashville Tennessean* and arguably the most powerful and influential man in the state, told Trimmer flatly, "Nashville people are not interested in this project. They never have been interested in it and they never will be interested in it, regardless of any kind of publicity campaign you might put on."[4]

In Memphis, Trimmer met with U.S. Sen. Kenneth McKellar, who expressed his support for the project but echoed Lea's contention that boosters would have great difficulty raising funds outside the Knoxville area. Fundraising in West Tennessee would prove especially difficult, McKellar argued, as East Tennesseans had blocked an expenditure of federal funds for a Memphis viaduct. McKellar felt that private funding never would bring in sufficient funds and that only large amounts of federal and state funding would make the park a reality.[5] E. H. Crump, Memphis political boss, told Trimmer that West Tennesseans felt much more kinship with Arkansans and Mississippians than with East Tennesseans. When Trimmer asked Crump if a dignified campaign in Memphis might raise support for the project,

Crump replied, "My dear sir, any campaign that could stir up interest for that project would have to be mighty undignified."[6]

Despite these limiting factors, GSMCA, GSMI, and Tamblyn & Brown agreed to set a goal to raise $1 million for the campaign by 1 March 1926.[7] State and area goals reflected the differing attitudes toward the park in the two states. Each state had a goal of $500,000, but Knoxville would raise three-

David Chapman led the fight for the park in Tennessee. Photo courtesy of Great Smoky Mountains National Park.

Mark Squires led the fight for the park in North Carolina. Photo courtesy of Great Smoky Mountains National Park.

fifths of Tennessee's quota (including an $85,000 credit for Knoxville's proposed contribution toward the purchase of the Little River land), and the rest of East Tennessee would raise $200,000. Reflecting the broader statewide appeal of the project in North Carolina, that state's goals were set at $250,000 for Asheville; $150,000 for the rest of Western North Carolina; and $100,000 for the rest of the state.[8]

After setting these goals, park boosters and the professionals from

Tamblyn & Brown began a period of intensive organization preparatory to the start of the campaign in late November and early December. Each group put together lists of potential donors and ranked them according to their giving potential. Other groups began soliciting local civic groups to secure their endorsements and support. Finally, organizers established a separate fundraising committee in every participating county, each with its own local goal, and smaller district committees within each county responsible for contacting fifteen to twenty potential donors.[9] Campaign organizers also set up women's committees to publicize the park and solicit funds from local women's groups.[10]

In further preparation for the campaign, boosters and Tamblyn & Brown staff worked on every conceivable angle to promote the park and the campaign. Committees began to prepare booklets and leaflets to send to potential donors and local newspapers and to distribute at fundraising gatherings. The GSMCA published a thirty-two-page booklet entitled "Great Smoky Mountains." The booklet emphasized the worthiness of the Smokies as a national park site and the economic benefits that would come to East Tennessee when the park became a reality; it also tried to answer the criticisms of lumbermen and hunters. The boosters estimated that a national park in the Smokies would attract five hundred thousand tourists and bring at least $50 million into the region annually. Photographs, most taken by Knoxville photographer Jim Thompson, documented the region's spectacular scenery.[11]

North Carolina's version of this publication, written by Horace Kephart and entitled "A National Park in the Great Smoky Mountains," hit the same themes, although Kephart placed major emphasis on the good roads the project would bring to the region. The North Carolina booklet also contained a number of photographs, these taken by George Masa, a Japanese immigrant and Asheville photographer. Masa was Kephart's friend and camping companion.[12] Thompson's and Masa's photographs played an important publicity role throughout the campaign to establish a national park in the Smokies. These photographs brought the beauty of the Smokies home to people of the region. Although most lived within one hundred miles of the proposed park, many had never seen the view off Andrews Bald or the Chimney Tops; the sunrise off Myrtle Point; the rushing streams of Deep Creek and the Oconoluftee, Little Pigeon, and Little rivers; the huge poplars of Greenbriar; or the pastoral setting of Cades Cove.

Campaign organizers put together a variety of other materials for use by campaign workers in their fundraising efforts. They produced guidelines for speakers, giving them a brief history of the park movement, an explanation of the differences between a national park and a national forest, an explanation of the urgency of getting a bill before the current Congress, and future plans for a nationwide fundraising effort.[13] Knoxville organizers also came up with a list of suggested slogans for people to use as they solicited funds. These appeals focused on a park's economic benefits to the region and appealed to civic pride:

- A dollar invested now in the Great Smoky Mountains National Park Fund will bring a tenfold return by 1927.
- Knoxville started the movement to establish a National Park in the Great Smokies, and Knoxville never started Anything it couldn't finish.
- If you believe that it pays to attract tourists to Knoxville and Eastern Tennessee, help create a National Park in the Great Smokies.
- California is richer by a million dollars every day because of its tourists. Tennessee will enjoy the same prosperity when the Great Smoky Mountains National Park is open.[14]

Someone even wrote several songs promoting the park and the fundraising campaign:

> We want a Park, a National Park
> As Western people have,
> One with big trees, flowers to the knees
> As only Smokies have,
> With mountains blue and scenic view
> And all so wonderful and new—
> We want a Park, a National Park
> As Western people have.
> (Sung to the tune of "I Want A Girl")
>
> The Sun shines bright
> On the Smoky Mountains Park
> In summer the tourists are gay.
> By'n'by good roads will bring millions to our Park
> And then all will prosper every day.
> So work real hard, my lady,
> And work men too, I say,
> For the outlook's bright
> For the Smoky Mountains Park:
> The Smoky Mountains Park's not far away.
> (Sung to the tune of "Old Kentucky Home")[15]

Campaign organizers designated the month of November as a period of intensive publicity for the Smokies and the fundraising campaign. The Chambers of Commerce in both Asheville and Knoxville organized motorcades to publicize their cities and the Smokies project. The Ashevillians toured the entire state, going all the way to Wilmington on the coast, while the Knoxville group focused its efforts in East Tennessee. The Asheville group, containing twenty-four cars, went to Charlotte, Wilmington, Raleigh (where Gov. Angus McLean held a reception for the group), Durham, Greensboro, Winston-Salem, and High Point, and concluded in Marion. Roger Miller and other leaders of the North Carolina fundraising campaign rode in a limousine and distributed literature and set up displays of photos and maps at every stop. Various speakers, including William Welch of the Southern Appalachian National Park Commission, Mark Squires, and North Carolina State College President E. C. Brooks, addressed the hosts in each city, emphasizing the benefits that would come to the entire state with the park.[16] In a letter to Representative Temple, Welch commented on the marked change in attitude that had occurred in North Carolina: "They are no longer skeptical and cold as they were on my last visit there—on the contrary, they are very enthusiastic and are arousing tremendous enthusiasm among all of the people."[17]

The Knoxville group toured much smaller towns in East Tennessee, such as Cleveland, Madisonville, Sweetwater, Lenoir City, Loudon, Maryville, and Athens. They also distributed literature and told listeners of the benefits—new roads, floods of tourists, and advertisement of the region—that would come with the establishment of the park.[18]

Boosters employed a variety of other means to publicize the park and the fundraising campaign. Favorable editorials filled local newspapers, especially the *Asheville Citizen* and the *Knoxville Journal*, regaling readers with accounts of the fabulous scenery of the Smokies and the economic potential of a national park. On 1 November, the *Knoxville Journal* carried a guest column on the front page written by nationally known magazine writer, Rollin Lynde Hartt, who had taken a trip through the Smokies in a limousine and recorded his impressions of the experience: "No where have I beheld anything so lovely and at the same time so majestic as these incomparable Great Smokies. Their veil of dreamy blue mists, their royal robes of primeval forest, their gracious contours, and their romantic mystery and splendor combine to set them off as altogether the most enchanting scenery imaginable." Hartt continued with the sort of hyperbole that characterized much of the popular writing of the twenties and much of the promotion of the park. He argued that establishing a national park in the Smokies not only would make the "thrilling sport of mountaineering by limousine" available to everyone, but also would bring tremendous business opportunities through an "enormous increase in tourist traffic" and prolific advertising for both states. Some tourists might even be tempted to stay and make their homes in the region. The ultimate prize, according to Hartt, would come when the protection of the Smokies assured the success "of the hydroelectric projects which will develop an American Ruhr in this region."[19] Few, if any, noted the irony of establishing a national park so that the surrounding area could become like one of the most polluted regions of the world.

The *Asheville Citizen* emphasized the benefits of advertising the park: "Western North Carolina is going to grow according to the volume and the excellence of the advertising given her. . . . And now Western North Carolina is given a chance to secure the continuous service of the finest advertising agency on earth: the United States Government. By assuring establishment of the Great Smoky Mountains National Park, she can put Uncle Sam to work on the job of acquainting all nations with her beauty, grandeur, riches and opportunities."[20]

The *Citizen's* estimates of the amount of revenue a national park would generate for Western North Carolina rose higher and higher as the start of the fundraising campaign approached. In a 13 September editorial, the *Citizen* estimated that the park would bring $40 million annually to the region.[21] By late November, on the eve of the kickoff dinner for the North Carolina fundraising campaign, that figure had grown to $100 million.[22]

Both booster groups held mass meetings to promote the campaign, particularly among area businessmen. On 7 November, in a meeting with fifty leading businessmen from East Tennessee towns, Knoxville Mayor Ben Morton called the establishment of a national park in the Smokies a "sound investment." Even if the park never was established, the advertising that the region received would make up for any money spent on the process. William Welch elaborated on the same theme, arguing, "If you people take the money you spend annually in advertising and bought this park for a national playground, you would get an unequaled return on your investment."[23]

The kickoff dinner for the North Carolina campaign brought over two hundred people to the George Vanderbilt Hotel in Asheville. William

Gregg made the keynote address and carefully explained the differences between the National Park Service and the Forest Service. In a direct challenge to local timber interests, Gregg argued that "the Forest Service could not 'just as well' handle the Great Smoky area."[24] The speech of Jim Stikeleather, district highway commissioner, highlighted the evening. Stikeleather pointed out that three events had heralded the great epochs of Asheville and Western North Carolina's growth and progress: George Vanderbilt's decision to build an estate in the area, the coming of developer E. W. Grove to the region, and the building of the Battery Park Hotel. Stikeleather argued that the establishment of the Great Smoky Mountains National Park would usher in a period of prosperity greater than those produced by all of the previous three combined.[25]

The 8 December Knoxville kickoff dinner at the Civic Building attracted two hundred and fifty people. Cowan Rodgers argued, "This is Knoxville and East Tennessee's greatest opportunity to let the world know who we are, what we are and what we have to offer." If the park became a reality, Rodgers continued, "millions will annually come through our gates and scatter the golden shekels in our midst." David Chapman stirred the crowd when he pronounced, "This is our time; this is our tide; it is impossible for us to fail."[26]

As the promotional phase saturated the region with park propaganda and the campaign organization was in place and ready to go, opponents of the project launched a major counterattack. On 25, 27, and 29 November, the Champion Fibre Company placed full-page ads in the *Asheville Citizen*, headed "The Champion Fibre Company And The Proposed Smoky Mountain National Park." Champion argued that the establishment of a national park in the Smokies would withdraw "for all time and regardless of changed economic conditions one of the very large natural resources of Western North Carolina from all industrial use."[27]

The company reminded area residents that Champion employed two thousand Western North Carolinians and had four hundred stockholders in the region. The establishment of a national park in the Smokies would threaten the livelihoods of these individuals. Champion pointed out that the region could not depend on tourism alone to bring prosperity. Rather, it needed a balanced economy that would include industrial activity. Turning the Smokies over to the Forest Service would benefit both tourism and industry, providing the recreational activities that would attract tourists, while allowing for scientific forest management and continued industrial use. The ad also contended that loggers had already cut over 75 percent of the Smokies and that the region thus no longer met the standards for national parks. Additionally, the Forest Service could purchase the land under federal law, relieving North Carolinians of the burden of financing the purchase of land for a national park. The ad concluded with a call for reflection: "Under all these conditions we feel that the people of Western North Carolina would do well to pause and consider whether a sufficiently careful analysis of all factors involved in this proposition has been made, before they take action which may commit them for generations to come."[28]

A similar ad appeared in the 6 December edition of the *Knoxville Journal*. Moreover, an article published in *Manufacturers Record* on 12 December 1925 was entitled "An Industrial Argument for the Smoky Mountain Forest Area." It quoted extensively from the Champion ad.[29]

On 6 December, two other lumber companies—the Whitmer-Parsons Pulp and Lumber Company of Swain County and the Suncrest Lumber Company of Haywood County—published a full-page ad in the *Citizen*. This ad echoed many of Champion's arguments but made some additional points. Park boosters had drastically underestimated the cost of purchasing the land for the park, the ad claimed. While boosters asserted that they could buy the land for $10 million or less, Whitmer-Parsons and Suncrest argued that "$15,000,000 would not buy the properties." The ad concluded with a plea for consideration of the effect of a national park in the Smokies on Western North Carolina timber company employees and their families: "We furnish employment to over two thousand persons, who with their families would aggregate six thousand persons. If the Park goes through as proposed, the raw product [timber] that these two plants depend upon, will be segregated and operations will be crippled at one plant and destroyed at the other. Is it not an overwhelming responsibility to take the income away from six thousand persons and invoke visions out of the air to provide for them?"[30]

The campaign by the timber companies distressed park boosters and dramatically increased the difficulty of meeting fundraising campaign goals, particularly in Western North Carolina. The *Knoxville Journal* reported that "the fundraising campaign in that region promises to be complicated by the organized opposition of certain lumbering interests, and by a battle royal between those interests and the hotel owners, the newspapers and the business interests of the cities of Western North Carolina, which are lined up firmly on the side of the national park."[31]

However, Western North Carolina park boosters had come too far to back

down. Led by Charles Webb and the *Asheville Citizen*, boosters responded
aggressively to the timber company challenge, in order to save both the
fundraising campaign and the Smokies project itself. The *Citizen* led the
charge with dramatic pictures, editorials, and cartoons. The 29 November
edition of the paper contained "before and after" photos of logging operations in the Smokies. The "before" photo, entitled "The Murmuring Pines
and the Hemlocks," represented the "virgin growth untouched by axe and
unmarred by the destructive march of the devouring hosts of the lumber
industry." The "after" photo, entitled "Bleak Skeletons, Monuments to Lumbering," depicted the "naked skeletons of former sylvan monarchs, sacrificed
to feed industry that eats without thought for the moment."[32] The same
edition of the *Citizen* contained an editorial that challenged the Champion
ad point by point.[33] On 3 December, *Citizen* editor Charles Webb alleged
that, while the timber interests fought to retain access to the Smokies, five
hundred thousand cords of pulp wood lay rotting on the ground in Swain
County for lack of a market. He continued by calling the timber companies'
push for a national forest a "smoke screen set up to allow the uninterrupted
cutting of timber in the beauty spots of this section."[34]

   Citizen cartoonist Billy Borne joined the fray with front-page cartoons
on 8 and 9 December. The 8 December cartoon, entitled "The Goose
With the Golden Eggs," showed "Opposition" preparing to chop off the
head of a goose labeled "Proposed Smoky Mountains National Park" with
an ax marked "Selfish Interests." The golden eggs of "Tourists," "Prosperity," "Millions of Dollars Annually," and "Progress" lay scattered on the
ground.[35] The 9 December cartoon featured a "Lumberman" preparing
to cut down a large fruit tree, with the fruit labeled "Tourists," "Progress,"
"Millions of Dollars," "Unexcelled Scenery," and "Motorists."[36]

   The *Knoxville Journal* also weighed in with an argument designed to
provoke the ire of East Tennesseans against the timber interests. A 10
December headline read: "Smoky Deforestation May Ruin Power Sites."
The article quoted State Geologist Hugh D. Miser as warning, "East
Tennessee's magnificent prospects as a great industrial center, to follow
the development in time of its more than a 1,000,000 watts of potential
hydroelectric power, is but a dream if the national park campaign fails."[37]

   Despite the fight with the timber companies, fundraising proceeded as
planned. Organizers were relieved when the first town to launch its campaign, Bryson City, North Carolina, the hometown of Horace Kephart, exceeded its quota on the first night by pledging over $25,000, with more than

Cartoons created by Billy Borne were displayed prominently on the front page of the *Asheville Citizen* to promote the fundraising drive for the park and to counter opposition by timber companies. Used courtesy of *Asheville Citizen-Times*.

COME ON, LET'S GO!
By BILLY BORNE

THE GOOSE WITH THE GOLDEN EGGS
By BILLY BORNE

two hundred citizens contributing.[38] Asheville launched its campaign on 1 December and by 19 December, the end of the first phase, had received commitments for over $160,000, including $133.84 from Asheville's public school children.[39] Knoxville began its campaign on 7 December, raising over $91,000 in thirty-six hours and over $215,000 by 20 December, with $12,000 given by Knoxville's banks.[40]

As park boosters canvassed Knoxville and Asheville, the *Asheville Citizen,* the *Knoxville News,* and *Knoxville Journal* kept the campaign in the public eye. The papers touted the benefits a national park would bring to their respective areas: "unprecedented growth, development, progress, and prosperity"; increasing the membership of every church in the community; and even pleasing the average mother, who appreciates "the out of door playground for her children."[41] Reporters used hard evidence from statistics on national park visitation, given by Stephen Mather in his annual report, and even rhapsodized that a national park in the region would "operate as splendidly and as incredibly as a modern combination of Aladdin's Wonderful Lamp, the touch of Midas, the Magic Urn, and the weaving of straw into gold by Rumpelstiltskin."[42]

After the holiday season, boosters renewed and expanded the campaign into the towns and communities surrounding Asheville and Knoxville. Campaign organizers received mixed results in surrounding communities. A few followed Bryson City's lead and quickly subscribed their quotas. However, the process moved much more slowly in most towns, with overall apathy constituting the primary problem.[43]

In Haywood County, North Carolina, the home of Champion Fibre Company and Suncrest Lumber Company, apathy seemed the least of the boosters' troubles. On 27 January, boosters held a rally in Waynesville to kick off the Haywood County campaign to raise its quota of $30,000. The meeting did not go according to plan, however, as Champion and Suncrest employees packed the hall and took over the meeting, turning it into an anti-park rally. W. J. Damtoft, Champion's chief forester, addressed the group and recounted the economic damage in lost jobs and lack of opportunity that the establishment of a national park would bring to Haywood County.[44]

"Bat" Smathers, a lawyer for Suncrest, turned the rally into something akin to a revival meeting, when he argued that the "forces of evil" inspired all of this talk about recreation and pleasure seeking. He gave his own unique interpretation of the scriptural example of Adam and Eve, who, he asserted, were corrupted by being allowed to live a life of ease in the Garden of Eden. He concluded his talk by pounding the podium and shouting: "This mad age of pleasure and recreation is carrying us to hell as fast as possible!"[45]

This setback failed to deter park boosters, however, and they planned another meeting for Haywood County on 4 February. This meeting went much better for campaign organizers, and citizens of Haywood County "threw down defiance to the organized opposition to the movement" by pledging $10,000.[46] Indicative of the power of the arguments used by park boosters, Haywood County campaign organizers held a barbecue and victory rally at the Haywood County Courthouse one month later, to celebrate reaching their $30,000 campaign goal.[47]

In the early part of 1926, park boosters began to expand the publicity campaign beyond East Tennessee and Western North Carolina. The East Tennessee Chamber of Commerce organized a train tour to Florida, complete with the Knoxville High School Band, to promote both tourism in East Tennessee and the park project. On 31 January, 170 boosters left Knoxville for the seven-day promotional tour. As a mascot, the boosters took along an eagle captured in the Smokies, planning to release it in Miami. A member of the Knoxville High band even wrote a theme song for the tour:

> We're from Knoxville, Tennessee
> That's where all good folks ought to be.
> Although our present is cloudy, and our skies are dark,
> We're here to boost our Smoky Mountain National Park.[48]

David Chapman and other park boosters joined the trip, handing out literature and speaking about the proposed park at every stop.[49]

North Carolina boosters also cast a wider net. On 13 February boosters held a mass meeting in Raleigh, attended by many prominent North Carolinians, including Governor McLean. Josephus Daniels, a Raleigh newspaper publisher, former ambassador, and quintessential southern Progressive, gave the park project a strong endorsement, calling it a necessity for the state.[50] In late March, the Asheville Chamber of Commerce organized its own promotional tour to boost tourism and the park. The "Land of the Sky Goodwill Tour" took boosters on a special train to Atlanta, Birmingham, New Orleans, Houston, Dallas, and Oklahoma City.[51]

Despite these activities and promotions, however, both states fell well short of their goals. Boosters extended the original 1 March deadline for the end of the fundraising campaign to 1 April.[52] Members of the Southern Appalachian National Park (SANP) Commission, fearing that the campaign would not reach its goal before Congress adjourned, urged campaign organizers to redouble their efforts.[53] Harlan Kelsey warned the people of East Tennessee and Western North Carolina that "failure to put this thing through in the present congress means the death knell of the park program. . . . If we fail now, we are through."[54]

In East Tennessee, David Chapman sounded the alarm. Headlines in the *Knoxville Journal* for 21 March read: "Chapman Declares Park Campaign Is Nearing Failure." In the accompanying article, Chapman complained that, while Knoxville carried the fundraising load, apathy in the rest of East Tennessee threatened to derail the project.[55] An editorial in the *Knoxville Journal* challenged Knoxvillians to redouble their efforts: "Knoxville cannot afford to become a laggard and a civic slacker in the march of progress."[56]

The Knoxville community responded with a frenzy of activity to try to reach the Tennessee goal by 1 April. Mayor Ben Morton termed the situation a "grave emergency" and called for a meeting of the presidents of every civic club, bank, Sunday school class, labor union, factory, fraternal organization, or missionary society at the Lyric Theater on 11 March.[57] More than three hundred Knoxvillians showed up for the meeting. The Knoxville High School Band played, and Mayor Morton, David Chapman, and W. P. Davis urged the crowd to canvass their membership to help meet the fundraising goal. Boosters asked local ministers to observe Sunday, 14 March, as "Smoky Mountains Sunday" and to urge their congregations to support the drive. Community Chest leaders agreed to postpone their annual fundraising drive until after 1 April. Russell Hanlon organized another motorcade to canvass surrounding towns, and Mayor Morton declared Tuesday, 16 March, as Great Smoky Mountain National Park Day: "I call upon all citizens, so far as circumstances will permit, to lay aside their usual business and professional work on that day to devote it to the especial and particular business of procuring this national park."[58] The Alex McMillan Realty Company published a full-page ad in the 12 March *Journal,* pledging $10,000 to the park fund if nine other firms in East Tennessee would do the same. The ad concluded with the challenge: "The Smoky Mountain National Park is the best investment ever offered to the people of East Tennessee. WE MUST NOT FAIL!!"[59] On Great Smoky Mountain National Park Day, canvassers received over $43,000 in pledges; and in one week they raised $72,000.[60]

Money began pouring in from every direction. The bell boys at the

Farragut Hotel lined up in military formation and each donated a dollar. Knoxville's African-American community contributed $170.50.[61] Students at nearby Carson-Newman College donated $610, and students at Knoxville High School pledged $2,490.[62] Boosters encouraged elementary school children, Boy Scouts, and Girl Scouts, to rob their piggy banks and contribute all they could. The *Journal* recounted the touching story of one elementary-age boy who desperately wanted to contribute one dollar, so that he could receive one of the founders' certificates given to everyone who donated a dollar or more. Unfortunately, he had only ninety cents. The boy's hopes were fulfilled, however, when his younger brother gave him a dime so that he could proudly collect the certificate.[63]

As 1 April approached, fundraising activities became even more frenzied. On 26 March, the *Journal* published on its front page membership forms for the "Unsolicited Club," to be used by those who had not been approached to give. An individual could join by making a five-dollar pledge and sending in a dollar.[64] On 28 March, the Alex McMillan company made its $10,000 pledge unconditional. The next day, the Knoxville Clearing House, the organization that represented all Knoxville's major banks, raised its pledge from $12,000 to $25,000. On 30 March, amid a recall campaign, the Knoxville City Council voted unanimously to honor the earlier informal commitment made by the Knoxville Chamber of Commerce, agreeing to issue bonds worth $150,000 to pay for one-third of the Little River Lumber Company's property.[65] Finally, on 3 April, the *Journal* announced that Tennessee had reached its quota.[66]

Park boosters in Asheville worked to meet the 1 April deadline as well. Although fundraising in surrounding towns proved more effective in Western North Carolina than in East Tennessee (Bryson City alone raised $47,500, almost double its quota), North Carolina passed the deadline still well short of its goal. On 5 April, however, the Asheville Chamber of Commerce held a last-minute meeting and raised the final $35,000 in only twenty minutes, putting North Carolina over the top.[67]

The four-month fundraising effort had accomplished much more than meeting campaign goals. The drive also had attracted national media attention to the Smokies. The 30 December 1925 edition of the nationally circulated magazine, *The Outlook*, contained an article by William Gregg, "Two New National Parks?" which asked for national support for both the Smokies and the Shenandoah projects.[68] Another national magazine, *World's Work*, published "The Last of the Eastern Wilderness," an article by Horace Kephart on the Smokies. The article, heavily illustrated with Jim Thompson photographs, concluded with a challenge to the nation: "Here today is the last stand of primeval American forest at its best. If saved—and if saved at all it must be done at once—it will be a joy and a wonder to our people for all time. The nation is summoned by a solemn duty to preserve it."[69] The *New York Times* also published several favorable articles and editorials on the proposed park.[70]

Most important, however, the campaign had energized communities in both North Carolina and Tennessee in support of the park effort and had thwarted the very serious challenge mounted by Western North Carolina timber and pulp companies. Although the arguments used by boosters might not have pleased purists, the promotion and fundraising campaign had created thousands of passionate converts to the Smokies project and, to some extent at least, to the cause of scenic preservation. Despite the successful fundraising drive and the enthusiasm for the park that had developed in the region, however, boosters knew that $1 million in pledges meant little if Congress did not approve a park bill or if the states and wealthy individuals would not provide the remainder required to purchase the land.

As soon as the success of fundraising campaigns in North Carolina, Tennessee, and Virginia became apparent—Virginia national park boosters had raised $1.2 million to purchase land for Shenandoah National Park—the SANP Commission issued a report to Secretary of Interior Work, recommending both Shenandoah and the Great Smoky Mountains as national park sites. Fearing that the legislative session would end before Congress could pass favorable legislation, Work rushed a report on the two potential parks to both houses of Congress on 13 April 1926.[71] The next day, Representative Temple introduced into the House a bill (69th Congress, H.R. 11287), which was referred to the House Committee on the Public Lands.[72] On 23 April, Sen. Claude Swanson of Virginia introduced an identical bill into the Senate (69th Congress, S.B. 4073) on behalf of himself and Sen. Carter Glass of Virginia, Sen. Furnifold Simmons and Sen. Lee Overman of North Carolina, and Sen. Kenneth McKellar and Sen. L. D. Tyson of Tennessee. This bill was referred to the Senate Committee on Public Lands and Surveys.[73]

The bill itself called for the establishment of national parks in the Blue Ridge area of Virginia and in the Great Smoky Mountains when the states had purchased a minimum amount of suitable land. For the Smokies to come under the administration and protection of the National Park Service, Tennessee and North Carolina would have to purchase and turn over to the federal government 300,000 acres within a 704,000-acre area designated by the secretary of the interior. The bill contained two important provisos, however. First, the federal government could buy none of the land. Second, the National Park Service could not undertake general development of either park until "a major portion of the remainder of such area shall have been accepted" by the secretary of the interior. For the Smokies, this meant that the Park Service would provide only basic fire protection and law enforcement until the states had turned over 502,000 acres.[74]

The bill immediately drew protests from park boosters. Many misunderstood and thought that they had to acquire all of the 704,000 acres, which included several areas with large settlements, especially in Tennessee. This would make it extremely expensive to purchase the requisite land. According to David Chapman, the error "stirred up a hornet's nest here and a lot of resentment" among homeowners in the area.[75] Others pointed out that the minimum requirement of 300,000 acres also would prove an impediment to establishment of the park. The fundraising campaign had set up a schedule whereby subscribers did not have to make their final payments until after the government established the park. If boosters could not collect on these pledges, they could not hope to purchase such a large amount of land.[76]

Before the bill came to the respective committees for consideration, park supporters won an important victory which strengthened their cause in Congress. At its convention in late April, the North Carolina Democratic Party considered the possibility of inserting a plank in the party platform in support of the park. The *Asheville Citizen* immediately understood the significance of this action: "Should a plank endorsing the Great Smoky Mountain Park be inserted in the State Democratic party's platform, it would mean the absolute assurance of the park for Western North Carolina, since the Democratic party's endorsement in North Carolina means the execution of the plan immediately following the general election."[77] On 29 April, State Sen. Plato Ebbs used his leverage to secure the party's support. The simple wording of the endorsement belied its significance: "The efforts of the state should be further exerted toward making the Smoky Mountains National Park an accomplishment."[78]

The park bill came before the House Committee on Public Lands for consideration on 11 May 1926. The proceedings began with a statement by Representative Temple, who explained the investigative work and recommendations of the SANP Commission. He also told of the local financial support for the projects reflected in successful fundraising drives in Virginia, Tennessee, and North Carolina. He stated that the adoption of a pro-park plank in the North Carolina Democratic party's platform forecast "an appropriation of a considerable amount from the State treasury." Temple emphasized that the addition of these two new national parks would cost the federal government nothing until the states turned the land over "in fee simple" to the secretary of the interior. At the conclusion of Temple's report, Representative Abernethy from North Carolina, a member of the Committee on the Public Lands, introduced an amendment to the bill that would reduce the minimum acreage in the Smokies for Park Service administration from 300,000 acres to 150,000.[79]

Several others followed up on Temple's remarks. Rep. Zebulon Weaver emphasized the urgency of protecting the Smokies because of its importance as a watershed for an area of great potential water power development, the small population in the proposed park area, and the close proximity of the park to centers of population. William Welch told of plans to launch a national fundraising campaign to raise additional funds for both Shenandoah and Smokies parks, averring, "I have practically been assured now as much money from people at large as has already been contributed by those two States."

David Chapman argued that most of the people living in the designated park area, especially the area most likely to be included in the park, worked at temporary jobs in lumber camps. Chapman also spoke on behalf of Representative Abernethy's amendment, telling the committee of the difficulties involved in procuring 300,000 acres as a minimum area. Mark Squires spoke next and assured the committee that the State of North Carolina would make a sizable appropriation for securing park land. The session concluded with comments from Shenandoah proponents and a summation by Arno Cammerer, giving the Park Service's stamp of approval to the project. The committee then went into executive session, where it amended the bill to reduce the minimum acreage in the Smokies and voted the bill out for consideration by the full House.[80]

The Senate Committee on Public Lands and Surveys held hearings on the same day. The process moved more slowly, as members debated whether they should include a provision in the bill to make sure that the land donated for the parks should be contiguous and compact. Several senators from western states had witnessed significant problems with parks that had extensive inholdings of private property. Sen. George Williams of Missouri protested park supporters' efforts to push the bill through too quickly: "While I am in sympathy and in hearty accord with this movement, I shall not be stampeded or rushed until we have a thorough understanding here in the record of what this thing really is."[81]

The Senate committee meeting turned into a much more free-wheeling affair than the more formal House hearing, with give and take among members of the committee and park supporters, such as Senator Swanson from Virginia, Senators Overman and Simmons from North Carolina, Stephen Mather, and William Gregg. Committee members wanted assurances that these parks actually had a chance of becoming viable and comparable to the western parks, and that the federal government would not have to pay any money for land in these parks. Finally, the committee delayed action until the next day.[82]

When it resumed, the hearing began with Senator McKellar's introduction of the amendment added to the House bill on the previous day. After a good deal of discussion, the committee approved the amendment, so that the bills in both houses would have identical wording in order to avoid any delay in putting the bill through a conference committee. The only significant opposition in the Senate committee came when Sen. Robert Stanfield, the chairman, read a telegram sent by the Champion Fibre Company. The company emphasized the hardship that a national park in the Smokies would place on the company if it lost its primary source of timber, which "can not be replaced." The telegram continued, "We do not oppose the park idea in principle, but feel that a location could and should have been selected which would not have involved such serious industrial interference nor such tremendous costs of acquisition."[83] Surprisingly, Champion's telegram elicited no comment from the senators; and the committee wound up the proceedings, went into executive session, and voted the amended bill out to the Senate floor.[84]

The amended bill sailed through both houses on 14 May, and President Coolidge signed it (69th Congress, 44 Stat. 616) into law on 22 May. The *Asheville Citizen* hailed the event: "We are dazed with victory. . . . We have acquired a gold mine—an inexhaustible gold mine in the park. . . . Why the very passage of the measure has given us a wealth of the best publicity."[85]

Several factors combined to help move the park bill through Congress so rapidly. First, the establishment of the park had strong bipartisan support. J. Will Taylor served as a member of the Republican National Committee and was the referee of patronage in Tennessee.[86] H. W. Temple also commanded a good deal of respect in Republican circles. Democrats Sen. Claude Swanson and Sen. Furnifold Simmons held high positions in the Senate due to their seniority, and Kenneth McKellar served on the Senate Appropriations Committee. The yoking of the Great Smoky Mountains project with Shenandoah also helped the bill get through. This gave the bill the backing of three congressional delegations and greatly improved the odds of passage. Indeed, the six senators from the three states had a combined tenure of eighty years in the Senate.[87]

Unquestionably, the fundraising and political activities within the individual states also helped the bill. The $1.2 million in pledges raised by Shenandoah boosters in Virginia, the more than $1 million raised by Smokies boosters, the national publicity generated by these drives, the option on the Little River land gained by the Tennessee legislature, and the adoption of a pro-park plank by the North Carolina Democratic Party—all these helped convince members of Congress of the dedication of all three states to seeing these parks become reality. Perhaps most important, however, the passage of this bill cost Congress nothing. Any money that Congress would have to spend on these parks would come well down the road, when (or if) the states collected the necessary money and the secretary of the interior accepted the land for national park purposes.

Both states celebrated the joint victories in meeting their fundraising goals and in getting the park bill through Congress. Tennessee boosters held a victory banquet on 28 May at the Whittle Springs Hotel, with over two hundred people attending. Gov. Austin Peay delivered the keynote address: "The Park is going to be Tennessee's greatest advertising asset. No one can estimate what it will be worth to Tennessee in wealth or population."[88] Knoxville boosters presented David Chapman with a loving cup, designating him the "Hero of the Hour." In accepting the trophy, Chapman asserted that they had completed the greatest part of the work and that the establishment of the park was mainly a matter of routine.[89]

North Carolina boosters held their banquet on 21 July at the Battery Park Hotel in Asheville. Arthur W. Page, son of Walter Hines Page and editor of the national magazine, *World's Work*, gave a strongly aesthetic and emotional argument concerning the human need for national parks: "It [the park] is a part of saving our souls. It is one of the pieces of equipment in the fine art of living. It is a part of the intellectual overhead of civilization. This overhead I believe to be the most essential part of our civilization." The highlight of the festivities came when Mark Squires presented to the City of Asheville the pen used by President Coolidge to sign the park bill into law.[90]

In August 1926, headlines in the *Knoxville Journal* expressed the optimism of park boosters in both states: "Chapman Declares Park Assured." The accompanying article quoted David Chapman as challenging any doubters: "A Great Smoky Mountain national park of at least 235 square miles, within the states of Tennessee and North Carolina, is assured beyond any doubt, notwithstanding reports to the contrary." Chapman continued by arguing that the money already raised would prove sufficient to buy the required minimum area of 150,000 acres.[91]

However, as opponents of the park movement once again went on the offensive, Chapman's words proved more fantasy than fact. On 6 September 1926, Jim Wright—an attorney for the Little River Lumber Company, a landholder in the park area, and a staunch supporter of making the Smokies a national forest rather than a national park—organized a meeting of road builders and property owners in the Smokies at the Appalachian Club in Elkmont, Tennessee. Over two hundred people attended the meeting, including C. N. Bass, Tennessee state highway commissioner; Jim Stikeleather, a former park supporter and a member of the North Carolina Highway Commission; East Tennessee Division Engineer Frank Webster; Roscoe Marvel, Western North Carolina developer and owner of the Kenilworth Inn in Asheville; the Little River Lumber Company's President W. A. Townsend; and "mountaineers from every hill and cove in the Smokies."[92]

Wright organized the meeting to encourage the building of roads into the Smokies area. He told the crowd, "It is my ambition to put a road into every cove and valley, and up every mountain. And as long as I can get the money for the work I intend to do it."[93] Wright also promoted the idea of running several major highways over the Smokies connecting North Carolina and Tennessee. One speaker from North Carolina asserted that he had built a road into a virtually worthless piece of mountain property and had increased its value to one thousand dollars an acre.[94]

Park boosters reacted in horror at the prospect of such a road-building program. They feared that roads built into the region would boost the value of mountain property so much that the states could not afford to buy the land, thus killing, or at least seriously delaying, the park project. The *Knoxville News* spelled this out on the front page of its 7 September edition: "And If Roads Are Built In The Park Area Before The Land Is Bought For Park Purposes, The Value Of The Land Will Be Enhanced

And The Public Of Knoxville And Tennessee And North Carolina And Other States Will Have To Dig Deeper Into Their Pockets." The *News* pointed out that spending money on land for the park would prove the wisest course: "For we know that if we get the park, the federal government will build the roads—and fine ones!"[95]

Wright's plan threw a serious roadblock in the way of park boosters. His talk also provided a glimpse into the future, for Wright would become the Tennessee park movement's chief antagonist. Wright had attended the first Knoxville booster gathering organized by W. P. Davis back in 1923 but had dropped out of the group when it became apparent that Davis's interest lay in promoting a national park and not a national forest. Observers have attributed Wright's long fight against the park to a variety of factors. Wright himself often referred to his love of the mountain people and his fear that a national park would displace them. He also spoke of the waste of money if land was purchased for a national park when the federal government would buy the land if it became a national forest. However, Wright also had a major financial interest in seeing the Little River Lumber Company land become national forest land instead of national park land. Wright earlier had negotiated an option with the Forest Service to purchase the Little River land and stood to gain a sizable commission if the sale went through. However, the withdrawal of the Forest Service from the region eliminated this prospect. In addition, Wright held a good bit of property in the Elkmont area, and he hoped to boost its value through the road-building campaign. David Chapman even attributed Wright's opposition to the park movement to a rivalry that had developed between the two when they pledged the same fraternity at the University of Tennessee. Whatever Wright's motivation, the vehemence and persistence of his opposition, his skills as a lawyer, and his powerful political connections made him a constant thorn in the side of park boosters and an ever-present threat to the success of the endeavor.[96]

An even more immediate threat to the park movement, however, was W. A. Townsend's announcement at Wright's Elkmont meeting that he was not bound by the option on the Little River Lumber Company land that had been secured by the Tennessee Legislature the previous year. Townsend declared that the option had expired before the state accepted it; although he had given a verbal commitment, he argued, "There is not a pen scratch on paper anywhere." Townsend also expressed his frustration at dealing with park supporters: "What has become of the national park? Where are the leaders of this park movement? If there are any, why aren't they doing something?"[97]

Jim Wright had picked an ideal time to launch this attack on the park. David Chapman had left on an extended vacation in Europe in August to recover from the previous year of exhausting promotion and fundraising and did not plan to return until October.[98] Governor Peay had just completed the toughest battle of his political career, defeating Hill McAlister in the August Democratic primary by some 8,000 votes. Peay's victory, however, was good news for park supporters, as the narrow triumph resulted from a vote of 29,731 to 13,831 in East Tennessee.[99]

Peay's support for the park movement had paid major political dividends, as he won 68 percent of the East Tennessee vote in the 1926 Democratic Party primary. In 1922, he had finished a weak third there, in a four-man field, with 27 percent of the vote. Peay now owed a major political debt to East Tennesseans, who had saved him from defeat by a McAlister candidacy backed by the powerful E. H. Crump machine of Memphis and *Nashville Banner* publisher E. B. Stahlman's Nashville machine.[100]

When Peay learned of the Elkmont meeting and the statements of Colonel Townsend, he immediately set out to pay on that debt. Peay dashed off a letter to Townsend the day after the meeting: "I am greatly disturbed by reports seen in the press purporting to be some remarks of yours at a recent road meeting. My dear Colonel, the whole country is looking at Tennessee now. The park is practically assured. For you to refuse your option would be disastrous. You are a part of that scheme. It means so much to the fine standing and regard for you by all of our people in future years. Don't let yourself, I beg, turn away from the culmination of this project."[101] Peay's letter had the desired effect, and on 10 September the *Knoxville Journal* reported that Townsend had declared himself an "advocate and friend" of the park. He was ready to begin negotiations to complete the purchase of the Little River land.[102]

Despite assurances to Arno Cammerer that negotiations should go off with "no hitch" and that the state would complete the purchase in thirty days, Townsend did not transfer the deed until 22 March 1927.[103] Peay met with Townsend on 21 September, and the colonel agreed to keep the price the same as in the previous contract. They met again after the November general election and finalized terms of the agreement after Townsend had resubmitted the matter to his board of directors. After they renegotiated the deal, it took several months to search the title, as over three hundred individuals previously had owned parts of the land. Peay finally signed a warrant to release the state's share of the purchase price, and the Knoxville City Council gave final approval to the release of its share in late February 1927.[104]

Just when it seemed that the purchase finally would go through, after two and a half years of negotiations, opponents, led by Jim Wright, filed a taxpayer suit contesting the legality of the purchase under the terms of the Tennessee Legislature's act to accept the Little River option on 10 April 1925 (Chapter 57 of the Acts of 1925). The claimants maintained that the bill allowed the state to purchase the land only for national park purposes. Since the Little River Lumber Company had retained timber rights on part of its land, the state could not convey the title in fee simple as the National Park Service required; therefore the land could not be used for national park purposes for fifteen more years. The Davidson County, Tennessee, chancery court immediately placed an injunction on the purchase. The state finally got the injunction lifted on 22 March, and the $273,557.59 purchase price—$182,371.73 from the State of Tennessee and $91,185.86 from the City of Knoxville—was transferred to Colonel Townsend. At last the 76,507-acre tract belonged to the state.[105] Park opponents appealed to the state supreme court, and almost two years and two new legislative actions later (Chapter 54, Acts of 1927; and Chapter 1, Acts of 1929), the suit finally was dismissed.[106]

David Chapman hailed the purchase of the Little River land as clearing the way for "an early realization of the project," despite the cloud of litigation, criticism from some circles concerning the retention of timber rights by Little River, the purchase of cut-over land, and accusations that the state had paid too high a price. Chapman defended the transaction on all counts, arguing that, even when the Little River Lumber Company concluded its cutting, ten thousand acres of virgin timber would remain on the tract. In addition, the purchase price of $3.57 an acre fell far below the average price of $4.96 an acre paid by the Forest Service for similar lands in the Southern Appalachians between 1912 and 1925. As for cut-over lands, Chapman, ever the promoter, asserted that people should consider most of the Little River land "second growth lands" which rivaled "in beauty and majesty the virgin areas."[107]

Even as Tennessee finally concluded the Little River purchase, North Carolinians moved ahead in securing significant legislative support for the park project. During the later months of 1926, Mark Squires, Plato Ebbs, and E. C. Brooks began preparing legislation to introduce in the General Assembly's upcoming session. The bill called for a $2 million bond issue to provide money to purchase land for the park. Brooks also urged that the North Carolina Park Commission launch a publicity campaign, giving greater attention to the potential economic benefits that a national park would bring to the state.[108] On 27 January 1927, the bill received a crucial endorsement from U.S. Sen. Furnifold Simmons, the undisputed leader of the North Carolina Democratic Party, who pledged his "whole hearted support" for the park movement and encouraged the legislature to pass the bond bill.[109]

Despite Simmons's support, however, park boosters still lacked the crucial endorsement of Gov. Angus McLean, who remained, at best, lukewarm in his support of the project. NCPC Chairman Mark Squires, who had developed an intense dislike for McLean, did not improve matters when he publicly criticized the governor's inaction.[110] The Western North Carolina timber industry pressured McLean to oppose the bond issue. A. M. Kistler echoed the timber interests' line when he wrote to McLean telling him about copper deposits that miners had discovered in the park area and advising him, "I cannot help but feel that economically it is wrong to establish a park at that particular point, from a State standpoint solely."[111] Champion Fibre Company's President Reuben Robertson wrote to the governor, telling him that the federal government might not accept the Little River lands and that the "same uncertainty would probably rise with reference to lands purchased in North Carolina." Robertson urged the governor to remain neutral on the issue, as this matter was "manifestly a proposition which the Legislature should consider on its own responsibility."[112]

Park boosters went on the offensive to try to push McLean off the fence. *Asheville Citizen* editor Charles Webb wrote, "The time has come when you must take some position in the matter. Your friends here in Western North Carolina are certainly expecting it. We have stood by you in every way possible and it will be a sore disappointment to all of us if you do not help us now. The fact is, the success of this measure now depends absolutely upon your taking a positive position in favor of it."[113]

Supporters set up a joint session of the state legislature on 3 February and brought in Rep. Henry Temple, Arno Cammerer, and William Welch to speak to the group. Temple talked of the peace and security in the Smokies that he had found nowhere else. He also told the legislators that the closeness to population centers would make the Smokies a "Mecca for tourists" and that the state would soon recoup any expenditure from the collection of gasoline taxes. Cammerer pointed to the recent boom in national park visitation and emphasized that, while western parks attracted millions with only a summer season, the Smokies would be open almost all year. He argued that while the federal government had asked the state to come up with $2 million to purchase land, when the Park Service took possession of the land, the agency would develop it and build roads. Welch told of the scientific importance of the Smokies, the importance of preserving them as a living laboratory, and the eagerness of wealthy philanthropists to contribute to the project.[114]

On 3 February, Plato Ebbs of Asheville introduced the bond bill into the Senate, and Harry Nettles of Buncombe County and Mark Squires (formerly a state senator but now a representative) submitted the bill to the house. Legislative leaders scheduled discussion of the bill for a joint session of both appropriations committees on 8 February. Boosters called on all park supporters to attend this session. Park boosters appealed to forty different organizations in Asheville and Western North Carolina to "be on hand to extol its [the bill's] merits." The Chamber of Commerce organized a special train to take supporters to Raleigh, and the *Asheville Citizen* considered this a "crisis time," terming it a "case of now or never with the Great Smoky Mountains National Park. The fate of this project so tremendously potent of good for North Carolina will be decided by the Legislature within a few days. If the decision is favorable to the measure appropriating $2,000,000 to buy park lands the park will become a reality; if it is unfavorable the park will never be more than a faded dream."[115]

Governor McLean met with park boosters on the morning before the committee meeting. The group implored him to come out in favor of the proposition. Asheville attorney J. D. Murphy, unable to attend the meeting, wired the governor, begging him to "Please rise to the occasion."[116] Charles Webb, in Florida at the time, also sent a telegram, putting the proposition in no uncertain terms: "Your personal friends in Western North Carolina who supported you in your primary campaign and have loyally stood by you since you have been governor feel that you should now stand by them. Your failure to actively support [the] park matter will mean its defeat and no power on earth can keep them from blaming you for it."[117] Despite this pressure, McLean maintained his silence.

Even without McLean's support, park boosters gained a partial victory at the joint appropriations committee meeting. The meeting lasted over three and a half hours, with speeches by both park boosters and opponents. Lawyers of the Champion Fibre Company, led by Haywood Parker, provided the only public opposition to the bill. The *Citizen* did report, however, that twenty to twenty-five timber company lobbyists, including former State Highway Commissioner Joseph Hyde Pratt, who once had been a park booster, had worked the halls and lobbies actively in the days before the meeting. At the conclusion of the meeting, House Appropriations Committee members disappointed park boosters by deferring action on the bill until they could study it further. However, a 14–7 favorable vote by the senate committee encouraged them.[118]

The next two weeks proved a roller-coaster ride for park proponents, as the fortunes of the park bill waxed and waned. On 12 February, Governor McLean went to Washington to meet with Governor Peay, Secretary Work, and officials of the National Park Service. McLean told reporters that he only sought information on the park issue and expressed his concern that the legislature might appropriate money to buy land for a park that might never come into existence. He wanted assurances that, if North Carolina appropriated money, Tennessee would match it and the federal government would accept the land already acquired by Tennessee. He also wanted information from Secretary Work and from the Park Service about the amount of virgin forest the land must contain and how much of the total area each state had to purchase.[119] Despite receiving the written assurance of Secretary Work that he would direct the National Park Service to make a study of the area "as soon as weather conditions will permit" to answer McLean's questions, the governor told reporters that he would make no endorsement of the bill and would leave it for the legislature to decide, "especially as it involves an appropriation which only the General Assembly can make."[120]

Park boosters became increasingly discouraged with McLean's recalcitrance and the continued delays in the lower house; they feared that a seemingly endless stream of damaging amendments would jeopardize approval in the senate. Finally, on 15 February, park proponents amended the bill so that funds would become available only after adequate funds had been assured to purchase enough land "for general development for National Park purposes." By the secretary of the interior's definition, this condition meant that approximately $10 million would be needed to buy the required 427,000 acres. The amendment charged the NCPC, the governor, and the Council of State with certifying the availability of the money before the state would issue its bonds. The bill's supporters added provisions allowing the park commission to gain injunctions against timber companies to prevent them from cutting timber on proposed park lands and allowing the NCPC to begin condemnation suits immediately.[121]

The amended bill quickly gained Governor McLean's approval, which assured its passage. Indeed, many opponents, and probably the governor himself, gave their support because they believed that the new conditions never would be met. Even if the Tennessee Legislature matched North Carolina's funding, park supporters would have only half the money required. Like the park bill in the U.S. Congress, this bill was a cheap vote for most legislators—one sure to be popular with many constituents but one which deferred the commitment of funds into a future unlikely ever to arrive. The bill passed the senate on 16 February with only one dissenting vote and passed the house on 22 February; Governor McLean signed it on 25 February.[122]

In addition to the $2 million bond issue, the bill gave the eleven-member NCPC the power to buy land for park purposes. The commission also received the crucial power of eminent domain, which allowed it to "condemn for park purposes land and other property."[123] In March, the commission held a meeting in which it dissolved Great Smoky Mountains, Inc., and transferred all of the organization's records and funds to the commission.[124]

The passage of the North Carolina bond bill put the onus on the Tennessee Legislature to follow suit, especially as the issuance of North Carolina bonds depended upon the procurement of sufficient monies to complete the park. Intense fighting in the legislature between Peay supporters and Crump and Stahlman's anti-administration forces heightened the pressure. Park boosters feared that the anti-administration group would fight any park bill, simply because the governor supported it. To make matters worse, Governor Peay suffered a mild heart attack in February, right after his return from the Washington conference with Secretary Work and Governor McLean. He left the state for several weeks to recuperate in Florida.[125] As the legislative session neared its end, park supporters rushed to introduce a bill. Lawmakers would not meet again for two years—years in which the entire park movement could die.[126]

During Peay's convalescence, Knoxville park boosters worked with lawyers to draw up a bill similar to the recent North Carolina park bill. The group decided to ask for a $1.5 million bond issue, as the NCPC had agreed to give Tennessee a $500,000 credit for the purchase of the Little River land.[127]

The bill immediately received some crucial endorsements. A Knoxville delegation met with Peay on 30 March, and the governor publicly gave his support.[128] U.S. Sen. Kenneth McKellar telegraphed his endorsement on 2 April. Although McKellar consistently had supported park legislation in Congress, some questioned whether he would support the bill, inasmuch as he had close political connections to the anti-administration group, particularly E. H. Crump. When others close to the anti-administration group voiced their support, park boosters began to hope that the park bill would survive the bitter political infighting.[129]

However, some members of the anti-administration faction saw this as an opportunity to strike a blow against the governor. The *Nashville Banner,* E. B. Stahlman's paper, called the Little River purchase a political payoff for East Tennessee's supporting Peay in the last election. Indeed, Peay had benefited tremendously from East Tennessee support in both the tight primary race and the November general election, when he became the first Democratic gubernatorial candidate since the Civil War to win the popular vote of East Tennesseans over a Republican candidate. Others tried to fan dissension by accusing park supporters of trading votes with the anti-administration group to insure passage of the park bill. One state senator called the park a "fairy dream [on a] goat hill [in a] far corner" of the state. A member of the house declared, "I do not believe the State's financial condition is such to make a gift to the Federal Government for a playground for idlers at the expense of the tax payers of the State."[130]

To combat opposition to the park bill, Knoxville boosters relied on two familiar tactics: bringing out the heavy artillery for a joint session of the legislature and inviting the legislature to visit the Smokies. Legislative leaders called the joint session on the eve of the trip to the Smokies. Representative Temple, William Welch, and Arno Cammerer replayed the speeches that they had delivered to the North Carolina General Assembly. The high point of the proceedings came when Josephus Daniels urged the Tennessee Legislature to "preserve for all time a place remote from the city life, where men may refresh their souls and commune with their Maker. Let us look to the hills from whence cometh our help."[131]

On the morning of 16 April, the University of Tennessee band greeted the special train bringing eighty to ninety legislators to the Smokies. Boosters attempted to keep the trip as nonpartisan as possible. Governor Peay did not make the trip, due to his health and fears of antagonizing anti-administration legislators. Knoxville boosters took the group in a "gigantic motor cavalcade" to the top of Rich Mountain for lunch overlooking Cades Cove, where, according to the *Knoxville Journal,* "the adjectives expended exceeded those encompassed in Webster's unabridged." The group then received a motorcycle escort to the Mountain View Hotel in Gatlinburg.[132]

That night, park supporters hosted a banquet at the hotel, with several boosters speaking on behalf of the so-called "Match North Carolina Bill." U.S. Rep. J. Will Taylor reminded the legislators: "You have heard of what North Carolina has done in this matter. Remember, if you will, that we are the child of that great state, and is it meet that the child should falter? Any that do are mighty poor children, and if we can't do as well as the Old North state or improve on her actions, we are mighty poor children." Mark Squires hit the same note when he challenged the group: "Shall it go unheeded that we [North Carolina] threw the torch?" In a surprise move, W. P. Haynes, leader of the anti-administration forces, was called upon to speak. Haynes did not give his endorsement but did give boosters hope for a fair hearing when he commented, "This proposition does not smack of politics, and for that reason it shall be considered solely on its merits."[133]

The next day, a few of the hardier legislators hiked to the top of Mount Le Conte, but most took an auto trip to Elkmont. Much to the chagrin of park boosters, someone—allegedly Jim Wright—had posted signs along the way reading: "Inside Park Area: Will Our Homes Be Condemned?"[134] W. P. Davis made an attempt at "damage control" when the group arrived at Elkmont. He told the legislators, "In no case will a resident of the area be forced out of his home. To the contrary, all residents will be urged to remain, and will in most cases be employed by the park."[135]

Despite Davis's efforts, however, once the legislature returned to Nashville, the issue of what would happen to the people living in the park area became a major topic of discussion. Jim Wright and fellow attorney John Jennings, also a property owner in the Elkmont area, used the image of the state's forcibly removing poor mountaineers from their homes as an effective weapon in lobbying against the park bill. The *Knoxville Journal* quoted Rufus Hommel, an orchard owner at Elkmont, as telling a group of legislators that the people of the mountains did not want the park, because it meant "running them out of their homes and the return of the vacated areas to a howling wilderness."[136]

On 19 April 1927, park boosters amended the bill to exempt from the power of eminent domain the most populated areas within the 704,000-acre area designated by the secretary of the interior, especially those areas where the property owners were wealthier and better connected politically. The areas immune from condemnation proceedings included Wears Valley, the Cherokee Orchards, Gatlinburg, Sevierville, and—indicative of the political influence of Jim Wright and his friends—the summer cottages at Elkmont and the Indian Gap area, both in the heart of the park. The amendment included a provision for a Tennessee Great Smoky Mountains Park Commission, comprised of the three-member Tennessee Park and Forestry Commission and four persons appointed by the governor.[137]

The amendments quieted much of the opposition, but the park bill still had several hurdles to clear before becoming law. Park boosters were encouraged when the bill passed the senate on 21 April by a 23–8 margin. The next day, however, the bill became involved in a major controversy in the house, when someone placed on every member's desk a copy of the 1924 bill introduced into the U.S. Senate by John Shields, Tennessee's former senator. The bill had called for the purchase of land by the federal government under the Weeks Law to create a national park in the Smokies under the administration of the Department of Agriculture. An anonymous note—again attributed to Jim Wright—accompanied the copies of the bill, encouraging the representatives to delay their action and push Congress to pass the Shields bill, so that the land could be acquired by the Forest Service at no expense to the state. The note also called for the governor to sell the Little River land to the Department of Agriculture to recoup the state's and Knoxville's bond investment. Unfortunately for the opposition, park boosters got in touch with Shields, who immediately telegraphed the speaker of the house: "I now favor the bill before you, believing it to be the only hope for a national park in the Great Smoky Mountains."[138]

On the eve of the vote in the lower house, a new problem faced the park boosters. Governor Peay vetoed the general appropriations bill that his opponents had pushed through the legislature. Peay vetoed the bill and even threatened to issue an injunction stopping payment on the bill if the legislature overrode his veto, because it gave a $750 bonus to each state legislator. The *Knoxville Journal* reported, "Smoky Mountain National Park legislation is riding the top of a volcano tonight and its eruption may prove disastrous in the extreme."[139]

Although the crisis delayed the vote on the park bill by one day, as the legislature voted to override Peay's veto, it did not have an adverse effect on the final outcome. The bill passed the house on 26 April by a healthy margin of 60–33, and Governor Peay signed it into law the next day (Chapter 54, Acts of 1927).

Once again park boosters celebrated. The front page of the *Knoxville Journal* contained a cartoon showing a sun labeled "Success" rising over the mountains, with a long line of cars headed for the mountains. A front-page editorial in the same issue maintained that "it would be no hectic dream or stretch of fancy to predict that[,] in less than ten years from the time a national park is open to the world[,] Knoxville will have a population of 200,000." A local real estate company even placed an ad in the paper reading: "If You Had A Dollar's Worth Of Knoxville Real Estate Yesterday, It's Worth $1.50 Today."[140]

Despite the celebrations, boosters in both states knew they had a long way to go to secure the necessary funds. Although park boosters now had commitments of almost $5 million, most of the money would not become available until the states had enough money on hand to complete the project. While the State of Tennessee held title to 76,000 acres of potential park land, a taxpayers' suit under appeal to the state supreme court loomed. Most important, boosters knew that, despite recent victories, serious, determined, and well-financed opposition to the park would continue in both states.

Park supporters suffered a damaging loss in October 1927, when Austin Peay died of a cerebral hemorrhage. Peay's replacement, Speaker of the Senate Henry Horton, lacked Peay's commitment to the park project, as well as his administrative abilities.[141] In assessing Horton's abilities, E. H. Crump asserted: "If one of the learned mathematical professors were to condescend to throw away much time in discussing temporary Governor Horton, he would no doubt brand him the square root of zero."[142]

Park boosters now began to look outside the boundaries of their states to secure the additional $5 million needed to buy the land for the park. From the very beginning of the movement, the National Park Service and boosters had attempted to interest wealthy Americans in making large donations to the project. Stephen Mather personally tried to use his influence and salesmanship to line up wealthy contributors. In February 1925, he wrote to George Eastman of the Eastman-Kodak Company, urging him to consider securing the large property holdings of the Champion Fibre Company, because "I know your love for the primitive forests."[143] Mather also tried to interest his fellow alumni of the University of California (UC) at Berkeley in buying the area around Mount Le Conte from Champion as a memorial to Joseph Le Conte, former UC professor of geology. Both these endeavors produced no money, and Annie Florence Brown of the UC Alumni Association responded that most of the alumni would "consider the amount rather impossible for us at so great a distance from the desired object."[144]

Park boosters also tried to interest corporations and wealthy individuals in the project. W. P. Davis attempted to get the Aluminum Corporation of America (ALCOA) to donate some of its large holdings in the Smokies to the park, as a way of protecting its water supply. Davis assured ALCOA's President Arthur Davis that "a National Park surrounding your dams and locks would be the greatest protection you could possibly have, and that protection you would always have."[145] Russell Hanlon, secretary of the Knoxville Automobile Club, sent W. P. Davis a newspaper clipping concerning New York millionaire Leopold Schepp, who publicly requested help in dispersing his fortune. Hanlon suggested that a committee go to New York and approach Schepp, as "the Great Smoky Mountain National Park would be a wonderful place for him to put some of his surplus money, as it would thus provide a recreational area for all of Eastern America, and would be a lasting monument to his memory."[146] Davis encouraged Mark Squires to approach the Duke family for a substantial contribution. He argued that perhaps the family would like to make a donation in honor of recently departed family patriarch and tobacco baron James B. Duke: "It would be an appealing thing to say to the Duke family, that if they made a very substantial contribution, say a million or more dollars for the park fund, Indian Gap would be called 'Duke Pass.'"[147]

One of the grander schemes of the park boosters involved the attempt to interest Henry Ford in the project. In October 1926, when Ford visited Lincoln Memorial University, a delegation from Knoxville drove a fleet of Lincoln cars to the campus at Harrogate, Tennessee. The group persuaded Ford to visit the proposed park area the next day, but Ford seemed to be more interested in local character Wiley Oakley than in the mountains.[148]

The SANP Commission had given primary responsibility for securing large pledges on the national level to William Welch. As general manager of the Palisades Interstate Park, Welch knew many wealthy northeastern philanthropists, especially those with an interest in preservation projects. In the midst of the fundraising campaigns in North Carolina, Tennessee, and Virginia, boosters formed the Appalachian National Parks Association, Inc., to facilitate fundraising for the proposed Great Smoky Mountains and Shenandoah national parks. The group chose Welch as chairman and gave him the responsibility of raising funds for both parks among the eastern elite.[149]

Welch continually assured park boosters, Park Service officials, and members of Congress that he had lined up a number of large contributions. Indeed, in September 1927, he told Arno Cammerer that he had twenty people interested in the project and expected to receive pledges of about $2 million.[150]

However, in January 1928, Welch dropped a bombshell that brought the project to its lowest point since 1924. In a letter to Secretary of the Interior Hubert Work, he resigned as a member of the SANP Commission and announced, "I have not collected any money or secured any definite pledges."[151] Cammerer wrote to David Chapman, expressing his consternation: "At present we are all a bit stunned and confused, such a complete failure on the part of one man is incomprehensible."[152] To Chapman and other park boosters, it appeared that more than three years of hard work and sacrifice had come to naught. The park bonds voted by both states were worthless without the total amount in hand, and the funds collected locally would not even cover the legal fees necessary for purchasing the land. Indeed, it seemed that the dream of a national park in the Smokies might be only what the critics had contended, a "vision out of the air."

Fortunately for the park project, Arno Cammerer launched his own fundraising campaign to rescue the enterprise. Even before the Welch debacle, Cammerer had worked to secure contributions from wealthy individuals. He operated, however, strictly outside his official capacity as assistant director of the National Park Service. As he wrote to David Chapman, "My position is a peculiar one. I am not acting in these contacts officially, as you know. . . . I am not to be seen on the surface, because the Department's attitude necessarily is that they have no official connection until the park is handed them on a silver platter, so to speak."[153] As Cammerer worked behind the scenes in late 1927 and early 1928, the North Carolina and Tennessee park commissions secretly paid his travel and entertainment expenses.[154]

Beginning in May 1927, Cammerer kept up a running conversation with John D. Rockefeller Jr. and his representatives, encouraging the oil baron to make a sizable contribution to the park effort. Cammerer met personally with Rockefeller on 4 August 1927 and "filled his briefcase with all the photographs of the Big Smokies I had collected."[155] Rockefeller expressed interest in the project, and at this point the courtship began in earnest. Cammerer kept up a steady stream of correspondence with Rockefeller, emphasizing the urgency of securing land in the Great Smokies before the timber companies cut over all the old-growth forest. Cammerer told Rockefeller that "sixty-odd acres of primeval forest land included in the proposed park boundaries are being cut each day, in the lumberman's anxiety to get all the timber possible off the land before it is acquired for park purposes."[156]

On 26 September 1927, Cammerer's efforts paid dividends, as Rockefeller pledged $1 million to the project and promised to provide an additional $500,000 if others pledged $3 million before 1 January 1928. Rockefeller urged secrecy ("so as not to run up the price of these lands") and speed ("so as not to delay for one unnecessary day the continuing destruction of primeval forest land which the park embraces").[157]

On 14 November, Cammerer obtained a pledge for $50,000 from Henry Ford's son Edsel, who promised that he would give more if the Park Service had not secured the full amount by the middle of 1928.[158]

After the Welch announcement, Cammerer began to work feverishly to save the subscriptions already pledged. He took a leave of absence from the Park Service and went to New York City, promising Chapman, "I'll do my damndest, and angels can't do more."[159] Cammerer's efforts produced more than even angels could have expected. On 23 January 1928, Rockefeller wrote to Cammerer and offered to withdraw his $1 million pledge but match the gifts of both states, dollar for dollar, totaling either $4.5 million or $5 million, to purchase the necessary acreage for the park. Rockefeller proposed to make this gift in honor of his mother, through the Laura Spelman Rockefeller Memorial. He asked only that the Park Service place a tablet in the park honoring her and containing the words: "This Park is given, one-half by the peoples and commonwealths of the States of North Carolina and Tennessee, one-half in memory of Laura Spelman Rockefeller."[160]

For John D. Rockefeller Jr., involvement in the Smokies project was both natural and logical. He had an intense, even a religious, love of nature and eventually gave more to conservation projects, particularly national parks, than any other individual in history. He donated tens of millions of dollars to Acadia, Grand Teton, Sequoia, Shenandoah, Yellowstone, and Yosemite national parks, to Mesa Verde National Monument, to the Palisades Interstate Park, and to the Save-the-Redwoods League.[161] In addition, several of Rockefeller's largest conservation projects involved saving old-growth forests from destruction. Rockefeller gave $2 million to save the California coastal redwoods and $1.65 million to save the sugar pines of Yosemite.[162] Thus, the need to save the last great area of old-growth forest in the eastern United States from the timber companies made the Smokies a particularly attractive project.

Moreover, the southern location of the Smokies made the project one that would attract Rockefeller notice. By 1921, Rockefeller already had given over $130 million to the General Education Board to finance the construction of new primary and secondary schools in the South, to subsidize southern teachers' colleges, to promote scientific farming methods in the region, and to improve the quality of education for southern African-

Americans. He spent additional millions through the Rockefeller Sanitary Commission for the Eradication of Hookworm Disease to ameliorate sanitation and health care in the South.[163] The economic benefits that a national park purportedly would bring to the region undoubtedly constituted a major selling point for Rockefeller's involvement in the project.

Cammerer immediately began preparations to receive the gift. He wrote to David Chapman and Mark Squires on 28 January, telling them that an individual had offered the gift but not revealing the name of the donor. He also explained the conditions of the gift. It would be made as a memorial "to an individual, now deceased, who possessed a lovely Christian character." A memorial tablet was to be placed in the park, and the nature of the inscription was described. Cammerer asked them to inquire in official channels if their states would accept such a gift.[164] With an enthusiastic response from these two, Cammerer proceeded to organize a three-member board of trustees (consisting of himself as chairman, Chapman, and Squires) to receive and disperse the donated funds.[165]

Throughout the month of February, both sides worked out the details of the bequest; and on 6 March, Kenneth Chorley, Rockefeller's "point man" on conservation and preservation projects, traveled to the region to tie up loose ends and be on hand for the public announcement of Rockefeller's gift. Cammerer accompanied Chorley on this trip. Chorley first met in Knoxville with Gov. Henry Horton, the state treasurer, and members of the Tennessee Great Smoky Mountains Park Commission, to insure that the state would make bond funds available for the project, to check estimates of the cost of land, and to examine evidence of the availability of locally raised funds.[166]

Finding the Tennessee situation acceptable, Chorley and Cammerer traveled on to Raleigh to meet with Gov. Angus McLean and the North Carolina Park Commission. McLean obviously was shocked that funding for the park had been secured at all, much less so quickly. Mark Squires met the pair upon arrival and informed them that the governor was obstructing issuance of the state's park bonds. Squires told the men that the governor "had been playing with the lumber interests and was now embarrassed by the influence exerted by them."[167] On the next day, Chorley and Cammerer met with the governor, who apologized for the delay but stressed that he had to make sure the state had complied with all the provisions of the bond act and that the project had a reasonable chance of success. McLean firmly asserted that his slowness of action did not in any

Tennesseans went to Washington, D.C., on March 6, 1928, to finalize the $5 million Rockefeller donation. Front row: Former Gov. Ben Hooper; Willis P. Davis, Knoxville; E. E. Conner, Tennessee Park Commission (TPC); David Chapman, TPC chair; Gov. Henry Horton; John Noland; Knoxville Mayor James A. Fowler. Back row: Kenneth Chorley, Rockefeller representative; Arno Cammerer; Wiley Brownlee; J. M. Clark, TPC; Marguerite Preston, TPC staff; Ben Morton, former Mayor of Knoxville; Frank Maloney; Cary Spence; Russell Hanlon; and Cowan Rodgers. Photo courtesy of Great Smoky Mountains National Park.

way demonstrate a lack of interest or disapproval of the project. Chorley later recollected that "this statement was repeated so many times that one could not help but question its sincerity."[168]

At this point the Rockefeller bequest paid the first of many major dividends. The sheer weight of the gift, the power and influence of the Rockefellers, and now the full-fledged support of the National Park Service virtually forced Governor McLean to order issuance of the bonds. McLean had tried to delay the process further by calling for a meeting of all of the principal participants in Washington in a "week or two," before he released the bonds. Cammerer replied that he saw no need for such a meeting and that "every day's delay meant further cutting of virgin timber."[169]

Chorley clinched the matter and backed McLean into a corner when he asserted that the trustees of the Laura Spelman Rockefeller Memorial were satisfied that the project would succeed and that "the only thing remaining to be done to make the Memorial's pledge fully operative was the issuance of the North Carolina State Bonds."[170] Faced with the fact that he and he alone obstructed the entire project, McLean turned to his attorney general and gave his assent to release the bonds. Given the fact that the public announcement of the Rockefeller bequest had occurred two days previously, McLean had little choice.[171]

The public disclosure of the Rockefeller gift set off celebrations in both states. As Chorley reported, "Knoxville went wild with excitement. It could be compared with nothing but Armistice Day."[172] Knoxville newspapers published extra editions, factories blew their whistles, and churches rang their bells. The *Asheville Citizen* reported, "Universal joy reigns in Asheville and all sections of Western North Carolina . . . the mountain metropolis was suddenly surcharged with an atmosphere of confidence in itself and its future the like of which has never been felt here before."[173] The *Charlotte Observer* burst into psalm over the gift: "Praise be to the Laura Spelman Rockefeller Fund, the Smoky Mountains National Park is saved!"[174]

Crowds mobbed Chorley everywhere he went, as people asked him to convey their appreciation to Mr. Rockefeller. This reception moved Chorley to write in his report on the trip: "Measurement of the relative value of gifts of money is perhaps hopeless and useless, but I cannot help but have the feeling that this gift and the way it was made is one of the best things the Memorial has ever done. It has placed Mr. Rockefeller Senior and Mr. Rockefeller Junior and the Memorial in an extremely high position in a section of the country where apparently very little was known of their work, and probably less of an understanding of the high accomplishments they have in mind, to say nothing of the joy and happiness that the establishment of this Park will bring into the lives of so many people."[175]

Making this dramatic gift, however, did not end Rockefeller involvement in the project. Although Rockefeller himself did not take a particularly active role in the park, his associates, and particularly Chorley, kept close tabs on the project to insure the success of the endeavor. As two historians of Rockefeller philanthropy, John Ensor Harr and Peter Johnson, have observed, with Rockefeller, "giving was not easy or frivolous, but painstaking in the extreme, . . . he insisted on full value and careful accountability in every financial transaction."[176]

With the Rockefeller donation in hand, park boosters believed that they finally had achieved their goal and that establishment of the park would be only a formality. Indeed, park boosters had defied the odds; they had gained pledges of over $1 million from the people of the region, had secured $4 million in funding from their respective state legislatures, and, in the greatest surprise of the campaign, had received $5 million in matching funds from the Laura Spelman Rockefeller Memorial Fund. As E. H. Crump had predicted, the campaign had become "mighty undignified," as boosters battled both timber companies and politicians who tried to undermine the movement, dragged their feet, and voted yes on park legislation only when they believed the project would never succeed.

Aside from the obvious victory involved in raising the needed money, the fundraising campaign produced other important benefits. It galvanized the support of the people of Western North Carolina and East Tennessee. Even if they had given only a few pennies, residents of the region saw the Great Smoky Mountains National Park as *their* park, a place in which they had invested their money, time, and energy. For no other park in the national park system, aside from the sister park Shenandoah, would this sense of ownership be stronger. As a result of the successful statewide campaigns for legislative funding, the park gained additional support outside the immediate region. Among politicians in both states, opposition to the park—at least public opposition—became a liability. Throughout the campaign, the park also gained a great deal of national publicity, with favorable articles appearing in practically every magazine of mass circulation in the nation, especially after the Rockefeller bequest seemed to assure the park's establishment. Finally, the park gained the ongoing support of the Rockefeller Foundation, with its resources, connections, and influence, all of which proved instrumental in completing the park project.

Even as they celebrated their amazing accomplishment, though, boosters soon discovered that even greater challenges and tougher battles lay ahead. A few short months would see the onset of the Great Depression, causing the park project immense difficulties. Moreover, boosters soon discovered that, while they had money to buy land, they did not have willing sellers. Indeed, the people who owned much of the land designated for the park were the same people who already had fought the project for years. They demonstrated no inclination to cooperate in the transfer of their land to new owners.

5.

A Battle to the Finish:
Buying the Land

The injury report described the following: missing front tooth, black eye, cut lip, and two broken ribs. It was perhaps an appropriate report for the offensive line of the University of Tennessee football team in the age before face masks and rib pads, but an unexpected one coming from a meeting of the Tennessee Great Smoky Mountains Park Commission. All the injuries described were incurred by one individual, David Chapman, at a meeting (that is, brawl) on 9 January 1933. The recent appointment of five political cronies of Gov. Henry Horton (including his Knox County campaign manager, George Dempster) and Chapman's removal as chairman of the commission, although he remained on the commission, set the stage for the fireworks. At the meeting, Chapman circulated a statement arguing that, in the four months that the new commission had been on the job, it had spent $11,000 and had acquired only one-fourth of an acre of land for the park. In response, Dempster, the new chairman, called Chapman a "goddamned liar." Although older and much smaller, Colonel Chapman's combative spirit propelled him across the room, where he landed the first blow, knocking Dempster out of his chair. A brawl ensued, and later allegations charged piling on, kicking, and the possible use of a cane, all by Dempster's allies. Whatever happened, all reports agree that Chapman received the brunt of the damage to both body and reputation.[1]

No event in the final stages of the park movement better symbolizes the struggle required to establish the Great Smoky Mountains National Park than the Tennessee Great Smoky Mountains Park Commission brawl. While optimism had soared upon announcement of the Rockefeller bequest, and while park boosters believed that the toughest battles already had been fought in winning federal recognition and raising the necessary funds, they soon came to realize that the war had only begun. The process of buying the 427,000 acres necessary for the park would take twelve years and require two financial bailouts by the federal government. The major battle involved attempts to purchase the land owned by four major timber companies: Champion Fibre, Suncrest Lumber Company, Ravensford Lumber Company, and the Morton Butler Lumber Company.[2] The holdings of these companies not only contained a significant portion of the land that the park commissions needed to purchase in order to satisfy the terms of federal park legislation—over 180,000 acres—but the lands held by these companies comprised the most scenic and ecologically important land within the proposed park boundaries, including virtually all of the remaining old-growth forest in the Smokies.

Unfortunately for park boosters, these companies proved less than eager to sell their land, at least not without receiving compensation that they perceived as fair or, in most cases, generous. Failing this compensation, the timber companies proved determined to fight to the last level of appeal. The park commissions, like David Chapman in his fight with George Dempster, came to the battle with decided disadvantages. The timber companies came to the fight with deep war chests which enabled them to hire the best attorneys, employ the most skilled investigators, and, in at least one well-documented case, bribe individuals to keep condemnation cases tied up in the courts for years. The timber companies also had an advantage with rural juries in East Tennessee and Western North Carolina, as jurors often perceived the timber companies as important local benefactors whose payrolls and property taxes contributed crucial economic resources to the area. The proposed park, in contrast, offered few immediate, tangible benefits and would remove thousands of acres of land from local tax rolls. The battle in the courts and the difficulty of collecting pledge money during the Great Depression quickly depleted the resources available to the park commissions.

Planning acquisition of land needed for the park had begun well before the necessary money was raised. Both states had created the apparatus to carry out the work of surveying, appraising, condemning if necessary, and purchasing land for the park, even before the Rockefeller donation was secured. In March 1927, the North Carolina General Assembly had empowered its state

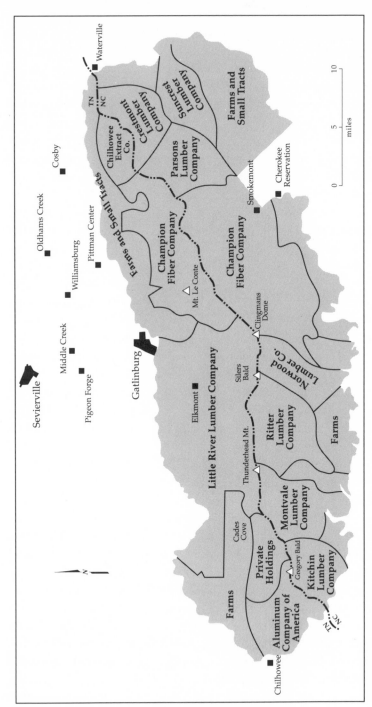

Ownership of land in the Smokies in the late 1920s.

park commission to purchase land in the name of the state. Ironically, the NCPC hired Verne Rhoades, the former forest supervisor of the Pisgah National Forest and an early leader of opposition to the park project, as executive secretary to head the land-purchasing process. Rhoades soon demonstrated his value to the park movement, however, with his unquestioned knowledge of local land and timber values and his loyalty to the park cause.[3]

Tennessee, in April 1927, had converted its three-member State Park and Forestry Commission into the seven-member Tennessee Great Smoky Mountains Park Commission (TGSMPC). After much debate over the composition of the commission—David Chapman argued that the commission should be dominated by Knoxvillians, as they had "done practically all of the work"—Governor Peay appointed the three members of the old commission; the former mayor of Knoxville, Ben Morton; and an individual from each of the counties that touched the park, including former Governor Ben Hooper from Cocke County.[4] The governor named Chapman to chair the commission. Although he did not have the professional knowledge that Verne Rhoades possessed, Chapman personally took charge of land buying on the Tennessee side. Peay defended his appointments by arguing that the commission needed individuals familiar with land values in each county.[5]

With money in hand after the Rockefeller bequest, the two park commissions began to lay the groundwork for purchasing land. Both commissions hired crews to survey the area designated by the National Park Service. They also hired timber experts to "cruise" the tracts and estimate the value of timber on the property. This undertaking became especially complex, because the timber estimators had to take into account the cost of getting the timber out of the forest. In addition, timber estimators for the timber companies and those for the park commissions often came up with widely disparate figures for the same tract of land. Problems often arose when timber company cruisers based their estimates on timber prices in the early twenties, when prices had peaked. Park commission cruisers, on the other hand, used the currently depressed prices for timber and pulpwood. The park commissions consulted a number of experts and even traveled to Wisconsin and Pennsylvania to get the best possible information on timber prices. Appraisers then had to bring all this information together and arrive at an estimate of the value of the property.[6]

The park commissions gathered teams of lawyers to do the extensive legal work required. Searching titles and determining ownership of over 6,600 separate tracts proved particularly difficult, as many tracts—even land owned by timber companies—had disputed titles or incomplete records. Lawyers spent hundreds of frustrating hours searching titles, even on tiny tracts on steep land that had been given away by the Wonderland Park development near Elkmont, in a promotional scheme to attract buyers. The lawyers also had to prepare condemnation cases, which required gathering mountains of data and expert testimony for suits against the large timber and pulp companies. Indeed, condemnation hearings consumed a tremendous amount of the park commissions' time and money.[7]

Before serious negotiations with the larger companies could begin, the park commissions had to get the companies to cease timber operations in the park area. Arno Cammerer had assured John D. Rockefeller Jr. that his gift not only would insure the success of the project, but would stop timber cutting in the area immediately. The Rockefeller people continually bombarded both park commissions and the National Park Service with queries as to why all timbering activities in the Smokies had not ceased. Although most of the timber companies stopped operations in the park area soon after the announcement of the bequest, two companies continued to cut their timber. In July 1928, Cammerer reported to Kenneth Chorley that only one company, the Suncrest Lumber Company, continued to operate on the North Carolina side; and only the Little River Lumber Company, which had retained timber rights to almost 16,000 acres of the 76,000 acres it had sold to the State of Tennessee in 1927, continued to operate in Tennessee.[8] Despite the cessation of most timber cutting in the park area, however, Rockefeller officials still expressed concern over the activities of Suncrest and Little River.

In particular, the Suncrest Lumber Company became a thorn in the flesh for both the Rockefeller people and the NCPC. In April 1928, Mark Squires met with A. J. Stevens, president of Suncrest Lumber Company, to try to get him to cease operations on proposed park land. Stevens refused and appealed to Kenneth Chorley and Arno Cammerer to give the company more time to fulfill existing contracts; otherwise, it might be "thrown into bankruptcy."[9] Although Squires vowed to "put an end to his activities" and instituted condemnation proceedings, Suncrest responded by challenging the constitutionality of the North Carolina Park Act, thereby preventing the NCPC from obtaining an injunction to stop Suncrest from cutting timber in the park area.[10]

The Suncrest challenge delayed the selling of North Carolina park bonds once again and allowed Governor McLean to continue to drag his heels on actually transferring $2 million to the NCPC. As long as questions lingered over the constitutionality of the North Carolina Park Act, investors would refuse to buy the bonds. Indeed, Francis Christy, an attorney who investigated the continuing timber cutting in the Smokies for the Rockefeller Foundation, advised Mr. Rockefeller not to buy the North Carolina bonds to help the project along, because "it is possible that the Supreme Court of the United States might hold the North Carolina act to be unconstitutional, in which case the bonds will be void."[11]

The federal courts finally resolved the issue in January 1929. On 14 January, a three-judge panel of the U.S. Circuit Court of Appeals ruled in favor of the park commission. However, Suncrest appealed to the Supreme Court and asked the court for a restraining order to prevent the park commission from interfering in its lumbering activities. On 17 January, Chief Justice William Howard Taft denied Suncrest's motion. When this news became public, a state district court judge issued a restraining order against Suncrest and ended the threat to the timber.[12] The *Asheville Citizen* hailed the event, commenting, "For the magnificent virgin timber which is to be embraced in the park to have been slaughtered for commercial purposes would have been a crime against the future."[13]

Despite considerable pressure from the Rockefeller Foundation, Tennessee had no such success in stopping the Little River Lumber Company's activities in the park area. When the TGSMPC tried to get a bill through the legislature that would allow the commission to condemn Little River's timber rights, the firm retaliated. John D. Rockefeller Jr. began receiving letters that accused the commission of wasting money and cheating small landowners. All the letters also encouraged Rockefeller to withdraw his money from the park commission.[14]

In January 1929, the Rockefeller Foundation asked attorney Francis Christy to visit Knoxville and investigate these charges. When Christy arrived, several individuals whom *Knoxville News-Sentinel* editor Edward Meeman characterized as "lumber company stooges" contacted Christy and regaled him with stories of waste, fraud, and overall injustice by the TGSMPC. One individual even tried to get Christy to drink whiskey with him and share dinner with him and two "luscious maidens," in an obvious effort to put Christy in a compromising position that would embarrass both the park commission and the Rockefeller Foundation. Reminiscing later about these events, Christy recalled that, upon returning to his hotel room after a visit with Meeman, he half-expected "to find the Tennessee equivalent of Mata Hari under the bed." Christy reported to the Rockefeller Foundation that the charges had no basis in fact, and Rockefeller maintained his support, having "no intention of being pushed around by the lumber companies."[15]

Having failed to get the Rockefeller Foundation to withdraw its funds, Little River and Jim Wright used their political clout to get the state legislature to launch an investigation of the TGSMPC. A special investigating committee held five days of hearings in Knoxville in early March 1929. Rambling testimony by Jim Wright dominated the hearings. Wright condemned both the faulty legislation that had created the park commission and the activities of the park commission itself. He attacked the park commission, and David Chapman in particular, for dealing with uneducated and defenseless mountain folk in a fraudulent and coercive manner. Wright later published his testimony at his own expense in a seventy-one-page hardcover book.[16] Chapman's and Arno Cammerer's visits to moonshiners in the "Cosby district" came back to haunt them when former governor and former park commission member Ben Hooper charged Chapman, Cammerer, and other members of the commission with drinking and carousing with women while on official business. The chairman of the investigating committee, W. B. Latham, gave Wright and Hooper unlimited time but allowed David Chapman and Arno Cammerer only a few minutes to defend themselves and the TGSMPC.[17]

Although the majority of the investigating committee found no wrongdoing on the part of the commission, Latham introduced legislation to enlarge the commission by four, to make the governor the chairman in lieu of Chapman, and to restrict the park commission's power of condemnation (House Bill No. 1202). Wright and Hooper lobbied the legislature in support of the bill. W. B. Townsend, president of the Little River Lumber Company, mailed letters to all members of the legislature, to Knoxville businessmen, and to the Knoxville newspapers, reminding them that the company had monthly payrolls of $25,000 to $30,000 (most of which eventually wound up in the pockets of Knoxville merchants), and this money would disappear if the TGSMPC forced the company to shut down its lumbering operations.[18]

However, park supporters launched a strong counterattack. Cammerer warned the legislators that, if the bill went through, he would not certify the release of Rockefeller funds to purchase park lands in Tennessee.[19] The

Rockefeller Foundation also worked secretly behind the scenes, putting pressure on some key legislators to keep the bill from coming to a vote.[20] In addition, park supporters held a two-and-a-half-hour mass meeting in Knoxville to voice their support for Chapman and the park commission. At the meeting, three Cocke County farmers dressed in overalls testified to Chapman's and the park commission's fairness.[21] On 13 April, the legislature adjourned without voting on the bill.[22]

Wearied by the fight and ready to move on to more profitable enterprises, the park commission gave up its attempt to gain condemnation power over the Little River timber. The company's political clout, and the fact that the commission's own timber cruisers discovered that the company had "little timber of consequence left," led Chapman and the commission to back off.[23] Even so, the commission pursued a successful lawsuit requiring the Little River Lumber Company to live up to its contract and quit destroying timber under ten inches in diameter with their use of skidders.[24] Despite this particular success for the commission, the Little River Lumber Company continued cutting timber in the park area until 1939.[25]

Amid these early challenges, the two park commissions purchased enough land from small landowners so that, by February 1930, they could turn 150,000 acres over to the Department of the Interior. This met the minimum requirement to begin Park Service administration and protection of the area but fell far short of the 427,000 acres required for development as a full-fledged national park. On 6 February, Gov. Henry Horton, Gov. O. Max Gardner, all the members of the Tennessee Great Smoky Mountains Park Commission (TGSMPC) and the North Carolina Parks Commission (NCPC), Rep. Henry Temple, Glenn Smith of the Southern Appalachian National Park Commission, and Horace Kephart traveled to Washington to present the deeds to Secretary of the Interior Ray Lyman Wilbur.[26] As he offered the deeds to the North Carolina land, Governor Gardner hailed this action as "the first concrete step toward the actual consummation of this project."[27] The turning over of these deeds and the beginning of administration by the National Park Service marked a significant step for the park movement, but no lands had been purchased as yet from the large timber companies which controlled the vast majority of land in the Smokies (other than Little River, on whose former lands logging operations continued).

The Champion Fibre Company held the largest and most important of these properties—indeed, the very "heart of the park." It owned more than ninety-two thousand acres in Tennessee and North Carolina, including such scenic areas as Mount Le Conte, Mount Guyot, Mount Collins, Mount Kephart, Clingman's Dome, the Chimney Tops, Andrews Bald, Rainbow Falls, and Alum Cave. In addition, the property contained what Park Service officials reported as the "largest body of primitive hardwood timber and the heaviest stand of red spruce yet remaining in eastern America."[28]

Both park commissions knew that purchasing the Champion lands would be a difficult and complicated proposition. Champion's President Reuben Robertson and Chief Forester W. J. Damtoft had organized much of the early opposition to the park movement. At the same time, they had begun laying the groundwork for a generous settlement if the time came when they were forced to sell. As early as 1925, Robertson had pointed out to North Carolina officials that, in addition to land and timber, any appraisal of the property had to include railroad lines, logging camps, and sawmills. He also argued that any estimate of the property's value should include compensation for the adverse financial impact on the Champion Mill at Canton, North Carolina, due to the mill's dependence "on the peculiar products of Smoky Mountain lands for their continued and successful operation."[29] Robertson particularly emphasized the value and irreplaceable nature of the red spruce on its holdings.[30] In an expression of its willingness to work with the park commissions and its "desire to expedite a settlement in any way that we can," Champion in July 1929 made an initial offer to sell its holdings in North Carolina and Tennessee for $9,063,099.75. Acceptance of this offer would have required the park commissions to spend almost all their money on less than one-fourth of the needed land. In addition, the other timber companies would have demanded similar settlements, making the completion of land purchases a financial impossibility.[31]

To combat Champion's claims and counter the offer, Verne Rhoades launched an extensive investigation into spruce prices and into operations similar to Champion's in other parts of the country. He used his connections within the National Park Service to obtain, through the Department of Commerce and the Treasury Department, records of Champion's import activities. He also gained access to Forest Service and National Forest Reservation Commission records in order to determine more accurately the value of spruce and of land similar to Champion's that had sold recently.[32] In September 1929, Rhoades and S. F. Chapman, a land buyer with the NCPC, traveled to Wisconsin and Pennsylvania to study the operations of the Rhinelander and Hammerhill paper companies, and even inquired into the cost of importing Russian spruce.[33] After months of investigation, Rhoades concluded that Champion had faked the purchase of a load of Canadian spruce at an extremely high price in order to demonstrate the inordinate cost of importing spruce pulpwood.[34] With Rhoades's data in hand, the park commissions proceeded to make a verbal counteroffer to Champion of $3,250,000. Robertson sneered at the offer, which "was not even reduced to writing," and declared that the park commissions "should no longer expect us to withhold cutting operations on the land within the park area."[35]

In response to Champion's threat, the TGSMPC instituted condemnation proceedings in Sevier County Circuit Court on 1 January 1930.[36] Champion pulled out all stops in order to obtain a favorable appraisal from the court. They retained New York attorney John W. Davis, a trustee of the Rockefeller Foundation, as special counsel for this case.[37] They earlier had hired Charles Evans Hughes but lost his services when President Hoover appointed him chief justice of the Supreme Court.[38] The company also spread flyers around Sevier County entitled "The Champion Fibre Company a Good Taxpayer" and signed "Tax Payer." The flyer pointed out that Champion had paid $26,688.75 in taxes to Sevier County in the previous three years, an amount that the county would lose if Champion sold its lands to the TGSMPC. The flyer continued by arguing that "the propaganda that the people will be repaid by tourist travel is empty twaddle." It concluded, "Some Park officials are treating property holders in Sevier in a manner that suggests tyranny instead of allowing the Great State of Tennessee to continue as the Protector of its citizens and their property. Tennessee is a Grand Old Commonwealth, when let alone, when its powers are exercised by reasonable and patriotic men."[39]

The case finally came before a five-man jury of view in November 1930. Champion selected two jurors, the TGSMPC chose two, and the four jurors together selected a fifth member. The jury spent more than two months going over the property and listening to expert testimony presented by both sides. Champion valued its property and the incidental damages that would accrue from its loss at over $6 million. The park commission estimated the value of the property at less than $500,000. They argued that Champion had purchased the property for $643,000 at a time when prices peaked due to the high demand for timber during World War I. In addition, commission lawyers pointed out that Sevier County assessed the property at only $323,000 for tax purposes.[40]

In the midst of the jury's investigation, Robertson met with Chapman, Mark Squires, and other members of both commissions to try to negotiate a settlement. In apparent confidence that the jury would find in favor of the TGSMPC, David Chapman dramatically reduced the park commissions' earlier offer of $3,250,000 to $1,500,000. Robertson asked, "For the Tennessee portion?" When Chapman replied that this offer was for all of Champion's property in the Smokies, Robertson retorted, "Ridiculous—that is really childish—I wouldn't think of submitting that to my directors."[41]

On 15 January 1931, the jury issued a majority report awarding Champion $2,325,000 for its land in Tennessee plus $225,000 for incidental damages to its plant in Canton. David Chapman asserted that, if the courts upheld this decision, it would mean the death of the park; and that, at the rate awarded to Champion (approximately $65 an acre), it would take $27 million to buy the necessary land. Chapman also argued that the TGSMPC had paid, on the average, only $15 an acre for land already purchased and that the price awarded to Champion amounted to "50 percent of the entire assessed value of all lands in Sevier County." Champion's attorney, J. H. Frantz, barely concealed his glee at the verdict and taunted Chapman and others who criticized the award: "We had hoped for a little more, but since the report was made by five high-class men of Sevier County who spent three months going over the property and studying evidence, we feel that it would not be good taste to criticize them."[42]

Park supporters immediately accused Champion of exercising undue influence on the jury. Arno Cammerer wrote to Horace Albright, now Park Service director, that the jury had lacked supervision, with no judge present for the presentation of testimony; that Champion representatives had taken members of the jury to "places for entertainment purposes"; and that members of the jury "could read the papers and be accessible to anyone who wanted to approach them."[43] Four years later, park supporters discovered how badly Champion wanted a favorable settlement in the case, when the federal government indicted Sevier County attorney Clyde Bogart for tax evasion. Part of the income that Bogart failed to report included a $15,000 check from the Champion Fibre Company, dated during the time the TGSMPC had hired Bogart as a local legal expert to aid in jury selection and other matters related to the Sevier County case.[44]

The Sevier County verdict placed the TGSMPC and all park supporters in a deep quandary. They could take a "non-suit" and start over with a new jury of five, appeal to a higher court with a judge and a jury of twelve, or look for some alternative.[45] Pressure to make a quick decision became intense, when Champion announced its intention to resume timber operations on its property "as soon as may be practicable." Champion President Reuben Robertson accused the State of Tennessee of taking "undue advantage of its position as a sovereign" and argued that the value of the Champion lands—"the heart of the Park, the real Park lands"—could not be compared to the value of the "fringe lands" and the cut-over lands already purchased. Robertson defended his intention to resume timber operations by arguing that the park commissions did not have enough money to buy the necessary land and "that the establishment of the Park by you [David Chapman] is a hopeless proposition." Robertson put even more pressure on the park commissions by releasing this information to the press and having John Davis forward a copy to the Rockefeller Foundation.[46]

Despite David Chapman's contention that the situation would "develop into a sort of endurance contest" and that park forces eventually would win, officials of the National Park Service and the Rockefeller Foundation began pushing for some sort of negotiated settlement.[47] John Davis and Reuben Robertson met with Park Service Director Horace Albright in February and urged him to act as an arbitrator between Champion and the two park commissions.[48] Albright asked both commissions to appoint representatives with power to act on the matter. These representatives were to meet with him and the Champion people in Washington on 27 April.[49]

Negotiations began on the appointed day, with David Chapman leading the Tennessee delegation and E. C. Brooks serving as chief spokesman for the NCPC, due to the illness of Mark Squires. Reuben Robertson represented Champion's interest, and Horace Albright and Arno Cammerer mediated the negotiations. After three days of intense discussions, which on several occasions seemed to reach an impasse, the parties agreed on a purchase price of $3 million for the entire 92,814 acres in both Tennessee and North Carolina. Ironically, the selling price fell $250,000 short of the offer made by the park commissions two years earlier, which Champion had rejected, and it exceeded the Sevier County jury's award for Champion's Tennessee property by only $400,000. Albright attributed the agreement to Champion's desire to avoid additional expensive litigation; the stipulation that the firm would receive the money within ten days; and the desire of the North Carolina and Tennessee park commissions to move the project along and bring some hope to their regions, hard hit by local bank failures.[50] Robertson especially complimented

Albright and Cammerer on the "wonderfully patient, tactful, and fair-minded manner in which they conducted the negotiations."[51]

Celebrations ensued in both Asheville and Knoxville, as park boosters once again assured supporters that "the park is formally and irrevocably established."[52] An editorial in the *Asheville Citizen* hailed the event as a great day for Asheville and its future: "The tide has now turned for Asheville and for Western North Carolina. The outlook for this city and section is steadily brightening. The winter of our discontent is over. The clouds that loured over us are lifting. We can say at last in all sincerity that there is no city whose prospects for the future are richer with hope than those which now stretch out before the people of Asheville."[53]

An editorial in the *Knoxville News-Sentinel* expressed similar sentiments when it asserted that, with the announcement of the Champion settlement, "bright sunshine broke thru the clouds of depression which have hung over Knoxville and East Tennessee."[54] The Knoxville High School Band and a crowd of over five hundred greeted Chapman and Ben Morton when they returned from Washington.[55] On 1 May, the *News-Sentinel* printed a poem hailing Chapman as a "fearless champion":

> To bring to man, what God to Man had given . . .
> Reached is the goal, for which so long he has striven,
> Finished the course, which he so bravely chose. —
> Le Conte smiles gently from his throne of rocks:
> "Salute your Colonel Chapman, Father Knox!"

An editorial also called for an unnamed peak in the Smokies to be named for Chapman.[56]

Although Robertson repeatedly contended that Champion had accepted a price "which stops far short of compensation," his motives for selling the land were hardly altruistic. They were grounded in sound business considerations. The company gained a great deal from this transaction at a crucial time in its corporate history. As the Great Depression deepened, Champion was strapped for cash and confronted with stiff competition from Scandinavian pulp companies. The large infusion of capital at this time enabled Champion to launch a major expansion of the Canton plant. The company ordered over $100,000 worth of new machinery to begin manufacturing chlorine and caustic soda, to rework the plant so that it could utilize cheaper pine fiber instead of spruce or hemlock, and to add paper-making machinery. Champion purchased the necessary equipment at an exceptionally low price, due to the Depression. The company also used part of the money to expand its operations into Texas, where it purchased piney woods and built a new paper mill. Indicating the benefits that accrued to Champion with this purchase, the Canton plant operated at full employment throughout the Depression.[57] The settlement also helped Champion's public relations. The *Citizen* lauded the company: "There could not be a finer example of the subordination of personal interests to the general interests."[58]

On the heels of that settlement, the NCPC reached a similar agreement with Suncrest Lumber Company for its 33,000 acres. The two sides' valuations of the property differed widely, with the park commission valuing the Suncrest property at $400,000 and Suncrest valuing it at $3,800,000. In 1931, three court-appointed commissioners appraised the property at $522,255.33, but Suncrest appealed the decision.[59] In September 1932, a special jury valued the property at $600,000, and Suncrest and the NCPC agreed on this as the purchase price. However, the park commission had to settle for half interest in the property, as it had only $300,000 on hand.[60] It finally paid off the remaining $300,000 in May 1934.[61]

Despite the euphoria inspired by the Champion purchase, the turning over of 138,000 additional acres to the Park Service in November 1931, and the purchase of the Suncrest property, the movement toward establishing a national park ground to a halt over the next year, due to financial difficulties. The Great Depression and resultant bank failures in Asheville and Knoxville seriously diminished the financial resources available to the two park commissions. Once again these commissions had to seek new sources of funding to keep the project alive.

One problem resulted from the inability of many of the Park Fund subscribers to pay off their pledges. Verne Rhoades assessed the situation in Asheville for Arno Cammerer in 1931: "I can say frankly that so many people are out of work and out of funds, with their business on the ragged edge, that I believe it to be absolutely impossible to collect very much from private sources, even when subscriptions were made in the best of faith. The people simply do not have the money, and hundreds and hundreds of taxpayers have lost their property since the bank failure in November, 1930."[62]

David Chapman echoed Rhoades in describing the problems in Knoxville: "Conditions have been growing worse here for many, many months and each month seeing some of our subscribers wholly unable to pay, who, always heretofore have been good."[63] Under pressure from the Park Service and the Rockefeller Foundation to come up with more money, both park commissions filed suits to attempt to collect the pledges. However, the expense and negative public reaction made it a short-lived attempt.[64] Indeed, of almost $1 million pledged, the park commissions collected only a little over $420,000.[65]

Bank failures in both states, too, tied up funds for the purchase of park lands. In Tennessee, the Great Smoky Mountains Conservation Association (GSMCA) had $48,000 in the failed East Tennessee Bank.[66] The NCPC had over $132,000 tied up in failed banks. Although all these funds were insured, it took several years of litigation against the insurance companies—another unexpected expense for the park commissions—to gain reimbursement.[67] Arno Cammerer expressed his consternation over the situation in a letter to Kenneth Chorley: "I am fast losing all the black hair on my head helping out these various park commissions in the east."[68]

For Cammerer and the two park commissions, the situation grew dramatically worse in 1932 and 1933. During this period, the appointments of members of both park commissions expired. Despite the time and effort donated, their relative success under difficult circumstances, and several audits that had revealed no misappropriation of funds, the commissions were the targets of political turmoil in both states. In Tennessee, the park commission became entangled in the crumbling of Luke Lea's political machine, the end of Henry Horton's administration, and the takeover of state politics by the E. H. Crump machine in 1932.[69] In North Carolina, the park commission found itself replaced by individuals loyal to the Shelby machine, which had gained control of the state Democratic party in 1930, with the defeat of Sen. Furnifold Simmons.[70]

The appointments of the members of the TGSMPC expired in August 1932. Despite pressure from Arno Cammerer and a delegation of Knoxvillians who visited Governor Horton and urged him not to change the composition of the commission, the governor appointed five of his cronies to the commission. It was to be headed by his Knox County campaign manager, George Dempster. Horton retained only two members of the old commission, David Chapman and John Clark. A variety of accusations flew around the appointments. Some argued that Horton's appointment reflected Luke Lea's desire to gain control of park commission funds, so as to bolster his failing banking empire. Others argued that Jim Wright and other landowners in the Elkmont area had engineered the change to get higher prices for their property.[71]

The situation became even worse when the new commission failed to elect Chapman as chairman. The commission elected Knoxville's former mayor, James Trent, as temporary chairman; in November, George Dempster was selected as permanent chair.[72] Over the next six months, the activities of the new park commission became chaotic at best, with the new majority firing several longtime employees, including W. R. Mize, Sevier County land buyer; Frederick Ault, secretary-treasurer; and Marguerite Preston, office manager. Supporters of Chapman and members of the new commission regularly exchanged barbs in the newspapers, with each side accusing the other of various malfeasances.[73]

The culmination of events came on 9 January 1933, with the legendary brawl between Chapman and the commission's new chairman, George Dempster.[74] As a result of the fight and public embarrassment over the conduct of the new commission, newly-elected Gov. Hill McAlister received a great deal of pressure to do something about the commission. At the governor's behest, Knox County McAlister supporters Thurman Ailor and Harold Wimberly investigated the sentiments of East Tennesseans concerning the Horton-appointed commission. Wimberly urged McAlister to abolish the commission altogether.[75] Ailor agreed, asserting that, even though many people in the area still supported David Chapman, many Knoxvillians believed "that to a large extent he has lost his grip on public confidence." Ailor continued that the situation provided an ideal opportunity to put the park project wholly in the hands of McAlister's supporters; "in order to get rid of the others, he [David Chapman] can also be very handily dispensed with."[76]

Despite letters of support for Chapman from Horace Albright and declarations of public support from East Tennesseans, McAlister did not name Chapman as a member of the newly created State Park and Forestry Commission, which took over the duties of the Tennessee Great Smoky Mountains Park Commission through legislative action on 7 April 1933.[77] The members of the State Park and Forestry Commission—George Berry, Charles Cullom, and Frank Rice—all had the recommendation of Sen. Kenneth McKellar and others associated with the Crump political machine.[78] To serve as executive secretary, with chief responsibility for day-to-day operations of the new commission, McAlister named a twenty-eight-year-old Knoxville attorney, Harold Wimberly, who had been McAlister's Knox County campaign manager. None of these four individuals had any previous involvement with the park movement.[79]

The decision came as quite a blow to Chapman, who had stood in the forefront of the East Tennessee park movement for almost ten years. The decision to oust Chapman seems particularly ironic given the public acclaim Chapman had received on the heels of the Champion purchase. Indeed, Knoxvillians had successfully petitioned the Tennessee Nomenclature Commission to name a peak in the Smokies near Mount Guyot for Chapman.[80]

Despite McAlister's action, Chapman remained intimately involved in the completion of the park. In 1934, McAlister named Chapman as an "honorary member" of the State Park and Forestry Commission, and both Wimberly and officials of the National Park Service frequently sought his advice.[81] In addition, Chapman retained his leadership of the Great Smoky Mountain Conservation Association, which held over $40,000 earmarked for the purchase of park lands.[82]

The NCPC suffered a similar, if not quite so dramatic, fate in July 1933, when Gov. J. C. B. Ehringhaus replaced North Carolina's eleven-member commission with a new five-member commission.[83] The old park commission had been attacked in the state legislature for paying excessive attorney fees and general mismanagement of funds. To some degree, the commission had set itself up for such accusations by hiring its own chairman, Mark Squires, as "special counsel." Squires received $21,400 for his services between October 1928 and June 1933.[84] Although audits and investigations never revealed any malfeasance of any kind by the commission, individuals connected with the Shelby political machine—now in control of the North Carolina Democratic party—used the employment of Squires as an excuse to replace the old commission members who had been appointed when the Furnifold Simmons machine ran the state.[85]

As in the Tennessee case, membership on the newly appointed North Carolina Park Commission (NCPC) had much more to do with political loyalties than with park involvement. An editorial in the *Asheville Citizen* lamented the fact that only one of the new commission members resided in the park area and only two had donated to the park fundraising campaign. The editorial continued in wonderment: "It seems strange, nevertheless, that with so many men in North Carolina who have worked for the Great Smoky Mountains National Park for years, with so many men who have given liberally of their time and money to bring the park into being, the Governor should have passed over them in making these appointments."[86]

The replacement of the NCPC seemed especially pointless as the old commission already had purchased most of the land on the North Carolina side of the park, and the new commission had little left to do. Mark Squires tried to put the situation in perspective as he became a "private citizen" once more: "Appointed as we were, to please a thought deemed fanaticism and folly, we have brought the movement to a position [where] our successors will have nothing to do. The hard work has been accomplished, the obstacles overcome and those now our detractors have done nothing to speed us on our way."[87] E. C. Brooks consoled Squires, "I recall that Moses was permitted to stand on a high elevation and see the Promised Land, but another was permitted to lead the people. But as I have studied history somewhat, I am led to believe that Moses still has more credit than Joshua."[88]

In July 1933, efforts to secure the Great Smoky Mountains National Park largely shifted from Knoxville and Asheville to Washington, D.C.; and from the Tennessee and North Carolina park commissions to the federal government. Even as the fulfillment of their dream came closer to reality, the David Chapmans and Mark Squireses, who had brought the movement so far, had to let go of the reins. In order to see the project through to its successful completion, they had to turn control over to Arno Cammerer, Secretary of the Interior Harold Ickes, Sen. Kenneth McKellar, and President Franklin D. Roosevelt.

This shift held important implications not only for the future of the Great Smoky Mountains National Park, but also for the future of environmental protection in the United States. Under Roosevelt's New Deal administration, the federal government for the first time assumed the responsibility not only for setting aside lands for national parks already in the federal domain or accepting lands purchased by the states, but also for actively purchasing such lands.

Franklin Roosevelt's involvement with the Smokies came out of his interest in conservation and his concern for economic and employment opportunities in the South, which he deemed "the nation's number one economic problem." Completion of land purchases and the development of the park offered excellent opportunities to create thousands of jobs through the newly established Civilian Conservation Corps.[89]

Roosevelt's Secretary of the Interior Harold Ickes had a strong interest in the park project, too, and brought the Smokies situation to FDR's attention. Ickes encouraged Roosevelt to issue an executive order allocating $1,550,000, the amount North Carolina and Tennessee officials estimated to be necessary to complete land purchases for the park. Ickes argued that this action "would greatly enhance the effectiveness of and enlarge the opportunity for employment of men under the provisions of the Emergency Conservation Act of 31 March 1933, and would in addition contribute in a large and desirable way toward the fruition of the public objectives and program for the establishment of this national park."[90]

President Roosevelt initially issued an executive order on 28 July 1933 (No. 6237), but, because of the wording of the Act of Congress of 22 May 1926 (44 Stat. 616), which forbade the federal government from purchasing land for the park, he had to rescind the order. He revised it so that land purchased with these monies would not be considered as donations by the states but would be added to the park later, through Congressional enactment. The president issued the revised order on 28 December 1933 (No. 6542).[91]

Although Roosevelt had used a subterfuge to get around the wording of the original park bill, he had set an extremely important precedent: the federal government was purchasing land directly for a national park. This action would transform the national park system, making possible its rapid expansion in the East. It would also make the process of park establishment much more political, as Robert Sterling Yard had warned earlier; pet park projects now became an integral part of pork-barrel politics in Washington.

In addition to $1,550,000 from the federal government, Arno Cammerer received permission from the Rockefeller Foundation to release, unmatched, the final $500,000 of the $5 million Laura Spelman Rockefeller Fund.[92] Rockefeller agreed to do so, on the condition that Congress reduce the minimum acreage necessary to establish the park officially, so that the $5 million still would have provided half the land necessary to establish the park.[93] To satisfy the Rockefellers, Congress passed the appropriate legislation, providing that an area of four hundred thousand acres "within the minimum boundaries of the park shall be established as a completed park for administration, protection and maintenance."[94] Ironically, 15 June 1934, the date of the passage of this bill—which received no mention in newspapers in either Knoxville or Asheville—has become recognized as the official birthdate of the park.[95]

The intervention of the federal government in the park project accomplished several important things. First, it brought funds desperately needed to move the project toward completion. Second, it took the completion of the park out of the hands of state commissions and placed it in the hands of federal officials. From 1934 until the dedication of the park in 1940, a project that had been dominated by local action increas-ingly would come under federal control.

Even as the federal government began its intervention, however, the NCPC completed its final major land purchase: 33,000 acres belonging to the Ravensford Lumber Company. The purchase of this property fol-lowed an all-too-familiar pattern. The NCPC appraised the property at between $500,000 and $600,000, while Ravensford set its value at between $4 and $5 million. In August 1933, after a fifteen-day hearing, three court-appointed commissioners established the value of the property at $975,000.[96] The state appealed the case to Superior Court, which, to the appellants' consternation, set the price at $1,107,190. This price included $50,000 for railroad property that never had been discussed previously.[97] After several months of wrangling, in which Ravensford demanded an additional $63,000 (for taxes, insurance, and maintenance paid out after the NCPC forced the company to cease operations in 1929), the parties finally settled on the $1,107,190 price in April 1934. Together the two sides had spent an estimated $100,000 or more in legal fees.[98] On 1 May, Assistant Park Service Director George Moskey took almost $1.5 mil-lion to Asheville to make the final payment to the Suncrest Lumber Company and to pay the entire Ravensford judgment. At this point, North Carolina had purchased all of the property needed for the park in that state, and Arno Cammerer predicted that the formal opening of the park would take place by the summer of 1935.[99]

The focus of park supporters now moved to Tennessee and the last major land purchase, the property of the Morton Butler Lumber Com-pany. Negotiations with the Morton Butler family had been going on since at least 1926, when Stephen Mather urged Morton Butler not to sell or develop his land in Blount County. As usual, however, the Tennessee Park Commission's valuation of the 26,000 acres of old-growth forest differed widely from that of the Morton Butler Company. In addition to compen-sation for timber on the property, the Butlers also wanted a cash settle-ment for the potential value of water power development on Abram's Creek, which ran through the property.[100]

Negotiations dragged on for years, with neither side willing to give ground on its estimation of the value of the property. In 1928, Morton Butler died, but his sons and their lawyers kept up negotiations. By 1932, the National Park Service became so frustrated with the pace of negotia-tions that it briefly considered leaving the property outside the park boundary. However, this idea soon fell by the wayside, inasmuch as the Morton Butler property overlooked Cades Cove, an area designated by the Park Service as a principal development site. Both Arno Cammerer and Park Superintendent Ross Eakin argued against its elimination from the park, as either timber or tourist development overlooking Cades Cove would ruin this prime area.[101]

In 1935, the issue finally went to court. As the Park Service had taken over land purchasing for the park at this juncture, the decision was made to begin proceedings in federal court. James Cooper, a former Tennessee assistant attorney general who had handled a number of condemnation hearings for the Tennessee Park Commission but who now worked for the Justice Department, presented the government's case. Government witnesses, including David Chapman, set the value of the Morton Butler land at $400,000. Witnesses for Morton Butler set the land's value at $1.5 million, although Blount County valued it at only $149,416 for tax purposes in 1934.[102] After proceedings that lasted over a month, the five-man jury set the property's value at $800,000. Cooper argued that the decision was way out of line with current land and timber values and recommended against purchase at that price, even if the Park Service had to leave the property out of the park.[103]

The government appealed the case, despite Cooper's fears that the outcome might cost the government even more money, as had happened in several North Carolina cases. Prior to the start of the case, he wrote to Gov. Hill McAlister, "All I can do is to do my best to prepare it for trial and try it as best I can, and trust to the integrity of the citizenship of the country to protect the Government, which in ordinary times is a forlorn hope."[104] Cooper put on quite a show for the jury of twelve, lining up dollar bills along the rail of the jury box and explaining the "enormity" of Morton Butler's claim of $1.4 million, an amount that, if lined up end to end, would stretch for 125 miles, from Maryville to 17 miles beyond Chattanooga. To Cooper's pleasant surprise, the jury reduced the previous award by over $300,000, setting the price of the property at $483,500.[105]

Despite final success in purchasing the Morton Butler tract, the park movement once again saw a shortage of funds bring the process to a grinding halt. The two park commissions had estimated in 1933 that it would take a little over $2 million to complete land purchases. However, higher-than-estimated jury awards, especially in North Carolina, and large attorney fees left almost $750,000 worth of land unpurchased in Tennessee.[106] The Park

Service was pressured to decrease the minimum amount of land needed before development work would begin, so that the park could be officially opened. Arno Cammerer resisted these efforts because he believed that, if development began, Tennessee would lose all incentive to complete the necessary land purchases, leaving large privately owned areas within the park. Experience in other parks had taught Cammerer that, if inholdings went unpurchased, owners would dramatically increase their asking price for these properties once development began, making it increasingly difficult to buy them. In addition, he feared that these inholdings would "be used for all sorts of purposes adverse to our park administration."[107] The major problem remained, however, since neither Tennessee nor the Park Service possessed the funds necessary to purchase these lands.

At this point, Tennessee realized one of the benefits of having Sen. Kenneth McKellar, the state's senior senator, on the House Appropriations Committee. McKellar added amendments to a bill for the purchase of lands in the Tahoe National Forest, authorizing the appropriation of $743,265.29 to complete the acquisition of land for the Smoky Mountain National Park (75th Congress, S.B. 2583). The bill passed the Senate in August 1937, passed the House in February 1938, and was signed by President Roosevelt on 14 February 1938 (52 Stat. 28).[108]

With this money in hand, the Park Service could complete the purchase of land within the minimum boundary, so that development of the park could begin. Although the park commissions and the Park Service had purchased all the necessary large tracts, the new funding allowed the Park Service to file condemnation suits against several individuals who had held out for higher prices. It took more than two additional years to clear up these cases, but finally the Park Service held the official dedication of the park on 2 September 1940, with President Roosevelt giving the keynote address. Soon after the dedication, the Park Service added two additional large tracts, one in November 1940, through a friendly condemnation suit against the Aluminum Corporation of America for 16,288 acres in Tennessee near Cades Cove; and the second in 1943, through a deal made with the Tennessee Valley Authority for 45,920 acres in North Carolina between Fontana Lake and the park boundary.

No one had dreamed in 1928, at the completion of the fundraising campaign, that purchasing the land for the park would require such a battle and take so long. The attrition rate in that battle had been terrible. David Chapman had lost his job as official leader of the park movement

The financial and political support of the federal government proved decisive in completing the park. Secretary of the Interior Harold Ickes speaks at the dedication of the park at Newfound Gap on September 2, 1940, while President Franklin D. Roosevelt looks on. Photo courtesy of Great Smoky Mountains National Park.

in Tennessee, although he held on in an unofficial capacity and received his due when he stood with President Roosevelt on the podium at the dedication of the park. Anne Davis also stood on the podium for the ceremony. Others who had given so much to the park movement were not so fortunate. Horace Kephart, W. P. Davis, and Mark Squires had died well before the park was dedicated. All three did have peaks or ridges named in their honor, although, with Davis and Squires, that honor was awarded posthumously. Through their dedication and self-sacrifice to a project that few believed would succeed and that powerful enemies sought to derail, these individuals, along with countless others (including Charles Webb, Edward Meeman, Jim Thompson, George Masa, Paul Fink, Russell Hanlon, Verne Rhoades, Austin Peay, and Zebulon Weaver), had left a tremendous legacy for future generations.

Other important changes in the park movement, too, had occurred in the course of the long battle to purchase the land. Most important was the transfer of leadership from local leaders such as Chapman and Squires to the federal government—Franklin Roosevelt, Harold Ickes, Arno Cammerer, and the U.S. Congress. Indeed, in relation to the establishment of the Great Smoky Mountains National Park, perhaps no change was more important for the future of environmental protection in the United States, and particularly east of the Mississippi, than the new willingness of Congress to purchase lands for national park purposes. Undoubtedly the park could not have been completed—at least as originally envisioned—without federal intervention.

Concurrent with the purchase of the bulk of land in the Smokies from timber companies, the park commissions also were purchasing small amounts of acreage from thousands of individual landowners, most of them poor farmers. Just as the federal government began to take a more active role in the process, many individuals began to feel some ambivalence about the ultimate human cost of establishing the Great Smoky Mountains National Park. In the forced removal of thousands of individuals, and the destruction of their homes, churches, businesses, and communities, the roles were reversed. Park boosters and the National Park Service no longer could play the innocent underdog in a lopsided battle with the gigantic, grasping, evil timber companies. For the first time, the park movement itself was cast as the heavy, in one of the most dramatic and tragic scenes played out in the establishment of the Great Smoky Mountains National Park.

6.

"The Barbarism of the Huns"

Falling-down rock walls; rusted-out wash tubs; foundations of homes, barns, businesses, and churches; boxwoods and jonquils gone wild; and cemeteries. Look closely, and you will find them in almost every area of the Great Smoky Mountains National Park. They stand as legacies of a people who lived poorly by most people's standards, but who were intimately tied to their families, their communities, their churches, and their own piece of rock-strewn land. In the late 1920s and throughout the 1930s, these individuals—including many whose families had lived in the Great Smoky Mountains for generations—packed their few belongings, loaded them on a wagon or truck, said good-byes to friends and family, and headed out of the Smokies for a new life. They did not leave to find new opportunities or because they desired a change in life; rather, they were forced to go.

Although park boosters in the early days of the movement often claimed that no one would be forcibly removed from the park, it became clear early on that human beings would not inhabit the area on any permanent basis, at least if the Park Service could prevent it. Problems in western parks with what the Park Service referred to as *inholdings* made removal of the thousands of people in the Smokies, along with their homes, schools, churches, and businesses, a high priority if the park were to evince the wilderness qualities touted by park boosters.

Purchase or condemnation of farms and businesses in the Smokies and the removal of the inhabitants soon became one of the most contentious, controversial, and unpleasant aspects of the park's creation. Park boosters and the National Park Service faced a volatile situation and had to tread carefully to maintain at least some semblance of the popular support that had helped bring them so close to success. Indeed, there were no real winners in this game. Although they believed strongly in the necessity of the removal, park boosters and Park Service officials took no joy in the process. No matter how careful, sensitive, or supportive they were, the lives of most of the people who lived in the Smokies would be transformed dramatically. For those who lost their homes, churches, businesses, and communities, the experience proved wrenching. The resultant bitterness, anger, and frustration experienced by many of the inhabitants of the Smokies lingers to the present day.

In the early days of the movement, park boosters downplayed the fact that people lived within the proposed park boundary. A publication of the Great Smoky Mountains Conservation Association pointed out that, despite the wilderness character of the Smokies, "human beings exist there, although their numbers are not great and they are very much scattered in the proposed Park area."[1] Most booster publications talked about the quaint ways of the mountaineers—or, as they liked to call them, "our contemporary ancestors." They were depicted as isolated individuals, locked in the eighteenth century, their speech still reflecting the English of Shakespeare's day. Boosters never mentioned the possibility that the people living in the park area might have to move: "As inhabitants of the Park, these picturesque southern highlanders will be an asset, and so will their ancient log cabins, their foot-logs bridging streams, and their astonishing, huge water wheels."[2]

These early accounts fictionalized the lives of residents of the Smoky Mountains on a number of counts. First, although boosters spoke of the region as virtually vacant, the area inside the proposed park boundary contained an estimated twelve hundred farms, five thousand lots and summer homes, and over 4,000 people.[3] Many of these individuals lived in organized communities and townships. Cades Cove had approximately 600 residents in 1928. A school census in the mid-1920s in the Greenbriar community counted 409 individuals between the ages of six and twenty-one. The 1920 federal census listed 921 residents of Cataloochee township. Other significant concentrations of population in the Smokies included Sugarlands, Fightin' Creek, Webbs Creek, Copeland, and the logging communities of Ravensford, Tremont, Smokemont, and Elkmont. The Appalachian and Wonderland clubs near Elkmont contained almost fifty vacation cottages, with lodge and recreation facilities. These communities contained churches, general merchandise stores, schools, and post offices.[4]

The "contemporary ancestor" notion further mythologized the lives of these people. Park boosters often based their views of residents of the Smokies on contemporary popular images of the Southern Appalachian people which depicted them as "the exponents of a retarded civilization, who show the degenerate symptoms of an arrested development."[5] The portrait of Southern Appalachian life presented by Horace Kephart in *Our Southern Highlanders* played an especially powerful role in shaping the image of the mountain people among his fellow park boosters. Kephart envisioned the park as bringing tremendous benefits to a mountain people who previously had been subject "to a law of nature that dooms an isolated and impoverished people to deterioration." With the coming of the park, "the highlander, at last, is to be caught up in the current of human progress."[6]

Recent research has revealed that these accounts dramatically overstated both the isolation and the lack of change characteristic of Appalachian life and culture. In the early part of the twentieth century, the people of the Southern Appalachian region struggled to adapt to new conditions that produced an increasingly harsh and difficult economic environment. As Durwood Dunn observed, in coping with changing times, the people of Cades Cove represented "the broad mainstream of nineteenth- and

The Walker Sisters' cabin in Little Greenbriar. Images such as this helped to promote stereotypes concerning the people of the Smokies. *Jim Thompson* Photo.

twentieth-century American culture from whence they came" and not some vestigial community locked in the eighteenth century.[7] Dunn, Crandall Shifflett, and Florence Cope Bush effectively demonstrate that the people of the Smokies had a great deal of contact with the outside world, moved often in search of work, and possessed significant knowledge of life, culture, and progress outside the mountains.[8]

Most historical accounts of the establishment of the park tend to gloss over the removal of families from the Smokies. One of the first works to deal with the topic, Laura Thornborough's *The Great Smoky Mountains*, portrays removal as a great opportunity for the "land-poor farmers who sold their farms and bought valley farms nearer the larger cities." Thornborough quotes one farmer: "The Park sure helped me. I've got a farm now that I can plow and raise more and get better prices. No more hoeing. Why farming is a pure pleasure."[9] Although Michael Frome, in *Strangers in High Places*, mentions that, for some residents of the Smokies, the "park was uninvited, unwelcome, and 'plumb foolish'," he too downplays the disruption that removal from their homes may have caused the mountain people.[10] In *Birth of a National Park*, Carlos Campbell, too, dismisses any hard feelings about the displacement of people. About signs posted in Cades Cove that were hostile to David Chapman and the park movement, Campbell argues, "The attitude expressed in the grim warning sign soon passed." Summing up the removal of people from the park, Campbell concludes, "The establishment of a national park, like the building of a hydroelectric dam or other large-scale project, unavoidably imposes on a few for the benefit to the whole public."[11]

Just as these accounts trivialize the removal of individuals from the Smokies, recent observers have tended to romanticize the lives of inhabitants of the Smokies and overdramatize their removal. Some recent accounts portray residents in the late nineteenth and early twentieth centuries as living an Edenic existence, characterized by self-sufficiency, egalitarianism, independence, stability, and democracy. In this view, "familism, rather than the accumulation of material wealth, was the predominant cultural value of the region, and it sustained a lifestyle that was simple, methodical, and tranquil."[12] This view of life in the Smokies has caused observers to picture the removal of the mountain folk as the story of a people violently ejected from their tranquil, preindustrial existence and thrown into a hostile, dog-eat-dog industrialized world for which they had little preparation. Indeed, one historian recently equated the displacement of people from the Smokies with the forced removal of the Cherokee Indians from the Smokies in the 1830s.[13]

The possibility of removing people from the proposed park area first became an issue in 1926. With the passage of the park bill in Congress and talk of passing laws to allow state park commissions to condemn property for park purposes, rumors began to spread that people living in the Smokies would be forced from their homes. Gov. Austin Peay responded to these accusations at a mass meeting at Elkmont in 1926: "As long as I am a member of the Park Commission, I wish to assure these people that there will be no condemnation of their homes." Such an action, he argued, "for the pleasure and profit of the rest of the state would be a blot upon the state that the barbarism of the Huns could not match!"[14]

Despite these assurances, the issue would not go away. In 1927, when the NCPC and the Tennessee Great Smoky Mountains Park Commission (TGSMPC) began to buy small tracts of land, opponents of the park, especially in Tennessee, began to use the issue of removal against park boosters. TGSMPC Chairman David Chapman expressed his concern for the problem when he wrote to a friend that "a great deal of false propaganda has been spread along the border, with the result that quite a bit of feeling has been aroused in some places." Chapman saw the situation as one "which must be handled with great care."[15] In the summer of 1927, the park commissions and the National Park Service began to work on a plan to buy the land but then grant leases to land owners, thus allowing them to stay for a short time until they could relocate.[16] In February 1928, President Calvin Coolidge signed a bill (45 Stat. 109) that authorized the leasing of park lands to prior occupants for a period of two years.[17]

However, the Park Service contended early on that these leases served only a temporary purpose and that they intended to eliminate all private holdings inside the proposed park boundary. Secretary of the Interior Hubert Work justified this position to Sen. L. D. Tyson in an April 1928 letter. Work pointed out the difficulties that the Park Service had experienced in dealing with private holdings in western parks and firmly declared that "the policy of the Department, and the intent of Congress, is to eliminate all private holdings in our national parks." Work further explained that the Park Service had made provision through the lease process in those cases where "hardships might be imposed upon some of the old-timers who have been on their homesteads for years and who might have difficulty in orienting themselves elsewhere." Work emphasized, however, that the Park Service would not grant leases indiscriminately, but only in cases that it had "specially investigated and proven meritorious."[18]

Purchases of individual tracts began in earnest in the spring of 1928. Letters from purchasing agents indicate that many people sold willingly to the park commissions, although some priced their land much higher than commission appraisers did. Land buyer G. W. Cole wrote to David Chapman concerning his contacts with landowners in Cocke County: "The people are very nice with me in every way, the only trouble I have is the high prices they are putting on their property, lots of them."[19] Both park commissions attempted to avoid paying high prices early on, for fear of setting precedents that would prompt other landowners to raise their asking prices. David Chapman warned Blount County land buyer John Clark, "I have had many disturbing reports brought to me about the prices your men are paying for land. . . . It seems that all of the people down in the Cove [Cades Cove] know about the prices up in the hills."[20]

On other occasions, however, commission land buyers gave people higher prices if they cooperated and proved willing to help get their neighbors to sell. Land buyer John Jones urged G. W. Cole to accept an offer from a Mr. Maddron in Cocke County: "The price looks high, but when fellows act as nice as he has about his, I do not think we should 'split hairs' on a deal." Maddron got his asking price because of his willingness to help facilitate other land purchases and the fact that he knew practically everyone in the area and "stands well" in the community.[21]

Although this engendered good will from those who benefited from the practice, it also led to accusations of favoritism and partiality from those who did not. Mrs. William Hall of Cataloochee wrote to National Park Service Director Horace Albright, complaining that land buyers for the NCPC "never mentioned condemning the holdings of those they have a liking for." One well-connected family had received three thousand dollars more than the original amount offered by the park commission and a lease on their land. Mrs. Hall asked Albright to try to get the commission "to trade with us at the figures mentioned that we may not have further trouble."[22] Mrs. Hall also wrote to a Representative Jonas, accusing land buyers of political favoritism: "The park commission pays the Democrats more and gives them raises as much as three thousand dollars at once on their property. And they won't talk to a Republican."[23]

The personality of individual land buyers often had a major impact on the willingness of landowners to sell. L. Woody, who had family in Cataloochee, complained to Gov. O. Max Gardner of one land buyer who, he alleged, had "told lies after lies about the park." He argued that this individual's dishonesty, mistreatment of people in the community, and squandering of funds had resulted in a great deal of ill will against the park commission and caused people to withhold their land.[24]

The strongest opposition to attempts to purchase individual farms came from residents of Cades Cove, who possessed the richest, most fertile farm land in the Smokies. In 1927, David Chapman wrote to National Park Service Assistant Director Arno Cammerer, arguing, "I think the most difficult situation will be Cades Cove. A great many people want to sell, but quite a few do not."[25] At one point, someone erected a threatening sign in Cades Cove:

> Col. Chapman You And Hoast
> Are Notfy Let The Cove
> Peopl Alone Get Out Get
> Gone 40M Limit[26]

One cove resident sent a letter to local papers, questioning, "Our ancestors fought in the American revolution. Have we no right to life, liberty, HOME and happiness? Fresh warm blood from Cade's Cove redeemed the soil of France to make the world safe for Democracy—must Cade's Cove submit to Kaiserism?"[27]

Some cove residents wrote to prominent individuals, encouraging them to use their influence to keep the cove out of the park. Walter Gregory wrote to John D. Rockefeller Jr.: "It was the Rockefeller money that made the park a reality. Without it the park would have been a failure. We most respectfully ask, beg, and implore you to request the park people to leave us outside the park area or you will withdraw the Rockefeller donations."[28] John Oliver wrote to Hubert Work that forcing the people of Cades Cove to leave their homes "would be a crime which our national government would be ashamed of."[29]

Cove residents, especially John Oliver, who had many contacts with individuals who had stayed in his lodge in Cades Cove, encouraged influential outsiders to write letters to have the cove excluded from the park. Mary Rolfe of Champaign, Illinois, wrote to Horace Albright, saying she "was shocked that in the name of the National Park Movement such wrongs should be committed." She accused the leadership of the TGSMPC of allying themselves with Cades Cove moonshiners in buying up land outside the park boundaries, "where they felt sure that they can best ply their trade." She further threatened to tell the story to "some newspaper man who cares nothing for the National Park Service."[30] Others echoed these sentiments and encouraged the Park Service and the TGSMPC to eliminate the cove from the park.[31]

Some individuals in the park movement argued for leaving Cades Cove out of the park or for buying only from those who wanted to sell and allowing the rest to keep their land and homes for "atmosphere." David Chapman talked on several occasions about the possibility of eliminating Cades Cove from the park area.[32] The Park Service, however, insisted on keeping all of Cades Cove inside the park, as they planned to turn it into the largest developed area on the Tennessee side.[33] As for allowing individuals to keep their land inside the park, Arno Cammerer pointed out the major difficulty in such an arrangement: "Any lands they would have been permitted to hold in fee simple would within a very short time have passed into the hands of those with money who desired a homesite within the park, and the old-timers would have sold out to those who would in the first place not have been considered at all."[34]

This insistence that Cades Cove remain within the park, however, did not deter Cove resident and community leader John Oliver from seriously challenging the TGSMPC and threatening its ability to condemn land for park purposes. Oliver, a member of the cove's oldest family, owned over three hundred acres of land in the cove, owned and operated a tourist lodge and tourist cabins on his property, served as a rural mail carrier, and pastored the Primitive Baptist Church in the cove. Initially, Oliver had supported the idea of creating a national park in the Smokies as a way of creating revenue and employment for cove residents and protecting the surrounding forest. However, when it became apparent that the Park Service planned to include the cove in the proposed park, Oliver became its chief opponent.[35]

Both the Park Service and the TGSMPC knew that Oliver's opposition would cause others to resist selling their land. To break down this opposition, the TGSMPC decided to file a condemnation suit against Oliver in July 1929.[36] Oliver and his lawyer challenged the TGSMPC on a number of constitutional and technical issues. It took three years and five court proceedings, including two appeals before the Tennessee Supreme Court, before the courts decided the basic constitutional issues in favor of the TGSMPC. A decision from the Tennessee Supreme Court in July 1932 effectively closed the door on further constitutional challenges filed by homeowners in the Smokies and ended the possibility of preventing the state from condemning their homes. John Oliver's fight, however, continued for two more years and three more court appearances, as the courts determined the fair market value of his property.[37] Oliver received $17,000 for his land, plus $807.51 in interest, although earlier he had valued the property at over $30,000 and had offered to sell for $20,000. His court battles reportedly cost him $5,000 in attorney fees.[38]

Ironically, in the midst of these extended court battles, Oliver made numerous inquiries about future federal employment in the park. He seemed especially concerned that he would lose his mail route and retirement benefits from the U.S. Postal Service as cove residents moved out. No offer came from the Park Service, however, primarily due to the bitter feelings of many inside that agency who felt that Oliver had delayed the park project unnecessarily.[39]

After the conclusion of the final case, Oliver asked permission from the Park Service to remain on his land, paying rent to the Park Service. Several individuals in the Park Service and the park movement urged that Oliver be given no consideration. Park Superintendent Ross Eakin wrote to Horace Albright, "I hope he will not be given a lease even if he continues to carry the mail. The Cades Cove situation can be charged to him and he would always be a source of trouble for us."[40]

David Chapman echoed these sentiments: "It is unfortunate that those who have fought the Park hardest have gotten the most for their property. To let Oliver stay on under the circumstances will lose the respect of the natives for the Park Service and the Park Commission."[41] Despite these expressions, the Park Service granted Oliver a series of one-year leases, and he remained in Cades Cove until 25 December 1937, when he removed his belongings from the cove.[42]

Although Oliver's fight undoubtedly inspired some homeowners to resist and questions lingered concerning the legality of condemnation for park purposes, most sold their property to the park commissions in the late 1920s. By the end of 1929, the TGSMPC had purchased almost half the farms in Cades Cove.[43] In October 1929, Horace Albright reported to Secretary of the Interior Ray Lyman Wilbur that "most of the individual mountaineer holdings have been acquired."[44]

Individuals sold for a variety of reasons. Some saw a chance for a new life and new opportunities outside the mountains. Most residents, however, lived in the mountains because they liked the lifestyle and the close ties to their community. They had had earlier opportunities to leave but had adapted themselves to the difficulties of life in the mountains. Many of these individuals became resigned to the fact that the government eventually would get their land; with the lease agreements, they could stay, at least temporarily. In many cases, these individuals received generous rental terms, especially if they sold willingly, were not "antagonistic to the Park," and helped with fire protection.[45]

On the other hand, the Park Service dealt rather harshly with those whom it considered "antagonistic" or who forced the park commissions to condemn their property. The agency forced many of these individuals to vacate their homes immediately after the courts reached a judgment. In some cases, exceptions were made, especially in the case of mail carriers like John Oliver or Postmaster Beck of Smokemont, who reportedly caused "all of the North Carolina Park Commission's troubles at Smokemont." In these exceptional cases, the Park Service charged the individuals full rental value for their property.[46]

Prices paid for the land varied, and those who held out, like John Oliver, often got better prices. Cataloochee resident Lloyd Caldwell explained the situation: "Now some of 'em did get better prices 'n others but that was their own good luck by havin' sense enough to know what to do. Them that jumped to conclusions quick an' sold quick was the ones that I call it gettin' cheated. They just let them land buyers out talk 'em, some of 'em."[47]

Those who decided to stay on their land soon discovered that life as a leaseholder differed dramatically from life as a landowner. The terms of the leases prohibited leaseholders from cutting timber, digging for herbs and roots, building new structures, grazing animals, hunting, and manufacturing, selling, or possessing alcohol. Lessees agreed to fight fires and to allow Park Service personnel access to the premises at all times. If residents violated the terms of the lease, the Park Service could evict them, with no appeal allowed.[48] One resident voiced his frustration over these restrictions: "They tell me I can't break a twig, nor pull a flower, after there's a Park. Nor can I fish with bait for trout, nor kill a boomer, nor bear on land owned by my pap, and grandpap and his pap before him."[49]

Poor communication between the park commissions and the National Park Service, as well as the eagerness of both to gain good will among the mountain people, gave some of the lessees the idea that they could stay on their land for life. Once the Park Service began supervising park land in 1930, however, Superintendent Ross Eakin made it clear that lifetime leases would be given only "in part consideration of the purchase price." Eakin did qualify this statement by asserting that "for humane reasons elderly people, and perhaps others may stay in the park the remainder of their lives providing the premises are not needed for development."[50] Unfortunately, anxious park commission land buyers had assured many residents that they would be able to lease their property for life, and Arno Cammerer and Horace Albright had made speeches in the region implying the same.[51] When the Park Service unexpectedly forced them to move, some residents became embittered toward the Park Service and the park commissions.[52]

As treatment of the mountain people became an increasingly explosive political issue, especially in Tennessee, Park Service officials and members of the park commissions tried to alleviate tension as much as possible. Jim Wright and other wealthy landowners in the Smokies used the "plight of the mountain people" to gain a public relations advantage over the TGSMPC, and particularly to picture their archenemy David Chapman as a cruel and uncaring individual.[53] Bruce Keener, one such landowner, wrote a letter to the Rockefeller Foundation, pointing out that the "picturesque people of the Smoky Mountains are being driven out of their native land by the high-handed methods of the Smoky Mountain Park Commission."[54]

These attacks became especially strong when Tennessee Gov. Henry Horton began making appointments to the TGSMPC late in the summer of 1932. This criticism served to discredit Chapman and other members of the commission in some circles and provided Horton with an excuse for replacing most of the old commission. Soon after Horton appointed the new commission, the statewide newspaper chain controlled by Nashville publisher Luke Lea circulated a highly critical article by T. H. Alexander, an individual who had been evicted from the park for squatting in a cabin on Jakes Creek. Alexander condemned the "progress" which had forced the mountain people from their homes and had "swapped the log cabin of the mountain man for a filling station, the ancient tub mill for a hot dog stand and the mountain man himself for the squawking tourists of Massachusetts."[55]

To defuse this explosive issue, the Park Service and park commissions tried to exercise tolerance toward the mountain people and treat them humanely. This became an especially important issue as the Depression deepened and individuals could afford neither to move out of the park nor to pay their rent. Park Superintendent J. R. Eakin wrote to Horace Albright about such a situation involving several families in the Greenbriar section. Eakin argued, "It is unthinkable that we should eject them during this period of unemployment." He also pointed out that putting destitute individuals out of the park would give David Chapman's enemies "a real point of attack."[56]

Depression banking conditions produced a situation in which many mountain residents developed a deep hostility toward the park and the Park Service. Upon selling their land, many families put their money into local banks. In the early 1930s, practically all the banks in East Tennessee and Western North Carolina, in the words of former Park Ranger Audley Whaley, "went bursted." These unfortunate individuals now had neither land nor money. Many of these people, their families, and friends naturally blamed the coming of the park for their misfortune.[57]

Another divisive issue inherent in the removal of families and communities from the park involved the status of cemeteries in the park. Those who owned land that contained family cemeteries hesitated to sell until they had some guarantee that they would retain access to those cemeteries and that the Park Service would not disturb these sacred sites. In 1932, Horace Albright issued a statement that guaranteed families and churches the right to keep their cemeteries cleared of briars and brush, allowed them

Little Cataloochee Baptist Church and Cemetery. Dealing with church property and cemeteries proved to be one of the most controversial elements of the removal of the park's human inhabitants. Photo courtesy of Great Smoky Mountains National Park.

to continue to bury family and church members in these cemeteries, and promised the help and cooperation of the Park Service in keeping the sites as neat as possible. Albright concluded, "These cemeteries, or God's acres, are sacred places for those who have buried their loved ones there, and it will be a privilege to cooperate in safeguarding them."[58]

The purchase of church property created another highly sensitive situation. Churches were important both as places of worship and as centers of community life. As such, members often found it difficult to part with their churches. Although the Park Service offered leases to many congregations and avoided condemning church property because of the bad public relations involved, they sometimes appeared insensitive to the strong feelings of "church people." Arno Cammerer wrote to David Chapman concerning the purchase of some church property in 1931, "In all our national park contacts we find that church people are the most difficult to deal with. They have no public vision and are a most selfish crowd. I think you are most wise, however, in settling with them."[59]

Most churches disbanded as their membership moved away. The Primitive Baptist Church in Cades Cove, however, refused to disband and held regular services until the 1960s. The location of this church, in an area that the Park Service wanted to develop, forced the congregation to fight in the courts for the right to yearly leases to maintain the property.[60]

Other churches experienced difficulty in agreeing on terms to sell their property. In Greenbriar, the Friendship Baptist Church's property had been donated by the William Stinnet family, and the deed stated that the property would revert to the Stinnet family when the congregation ceased to use it for church purposes. The Park Service agreed to split the purchase price between the church trustees and Stinnet, with Stinnet getting the church building. Stinnet initially agreed but then decided he wanted the church bell and the pews. Before a deal could be signed, Stinnet became angry with the church for having meetings once a year "for the sole purpose of depriving him of his property" and demanded all the church furnishings, the building, and the entire purchase price. This action forced the Park Service to file condemnation proceedings so that the courts could clear up the problem.[61]

The Park Service practice of burning or tearing down vacant buildings also stirred the anger of many former residents. The service argued that individuals used these buildings for "moonshining and other immoral purposes" and that they presented a fire hazard.[62] However, for many former residents of the Smokies, the destruction of their homes, businesses, churches, and schools proved the final insult. As Durwood Dunn observed, "Having destroyed the community of Cades Cove by eminent domain, the community's corpse was now to be mutilated beyond recognition."[63]

The treatment accorded wealthier individuals who owned vacation and development properties in the Smokies caused more bitterness among former residents than anything else. Because the owners of the vacation properties could afford skilled attorneys, these individuals often received high prices and generous lease agreements. A special arbitration board awarded Jim Wright over $70,000 for property appraised by the State of Tennessee at $17,000.[64] These individuals also possessed the financial resources to wait out the Park Service and the park commissions, until the owners got the prices or terms they wanted. In addition, after cynically using the plight of the "mountaineers" to build up sympathy for their cause, many of these individuals collected excessive awards from local juries. The influential Whittle family of Knoxville received a jury award of $9,000 on properties appraised by the National Park Service at $2,500. To make matters worse, the land had been purchased after 1925, when everyone in East Tennessee knew that the land was to be turned into a national park.[65] In the mind of Justice Department attorney J. W. Cooper, the Whittles made the purchase solely "for the purpose of speculating on the price of lands after it was known that the Park had been established."[66]

The special privileges granted to members of the Appalachian Club and Wonderland Club in the Elkmont area especially galled many poorer residents. Wealthy Knoxvillians had formed the Appalachian Club in 1910 and the Wonderland Club in 1914 as resort communities. In 1927, when a bill to issue $1.5 million worth of bonds to buy land for the park came before the Tennessee Legislature, members of the clubs, especially attorneys James Wright and John Jennings, used their political clout to have the bill amended so that landowners in the Elkmont area would be exempt from the state's power of eminent domain. The state's inability to condemn this land forced the TGSMPC to make generous concessions to the clubs in order to gain title to the properties. As a result, club members sold their property for one-half its appraised value, in exchange for lifetime leases. With Park Service consent, many cottage owners conveyed ownership of their property, prior to selling to the TGSMPC, to their minor children, thereby appreciably extending the life of the lease. Through various means, the clubs got the Park Service to extend their leases for twenty additional years in 1950 and again in 1971. In the mean-time, many leaseholders sold their leases, using a loophole in park regu-lations that allowed transfer of leases to other club members.[67]

Finally, after sixty years, the Park Service forced residents of Elkmont to leave their cabins on 31 December 1992, despite an offer of $770,000 in cash to help build a new park visitors' center.[68] The bitterness of former residents of the Smokies toward these privileged few came out in reactions elicited by the *Knoxville News-Sentinel.* Cades Cove native Dr. Randolph Shields ar-gued that these individuals enjoyed "privileges that other people are not en-joying." He lamented the fact that he could move back into Cades Cove only as a resident of the Cades Cove Methodist Church cemetery. Carl Whaley argued, "They got money and some way the government let them live there. We had none. There isn't a thing fair about it."[69]

However, the Park Service did not force all poorer residents of the Smokies to move. Some elderly residents of the Smokies stayed on their property until their deaths. The five Walker sisters of the Little Greenbriar section provide the best example of lifelong residency in the park. The Walkers did not sell their property to the Park Service until 1941, as the Park Service hesitated to pressure them or take them to court because of the potential for adverse publicity or an extremely high jury award.[70] Over time, the Walker sisters became a tourist attraction, especially after the *Saturday Evening Post* wrote an article about them in 1946. By selling souvenirs to those curious to see people living "as mountaineers did 100 years ago," the sisters supplemented their income until 1953, when only two sisters survived. These two wrote the Park Service, requesting that rangers remove the sign directing tourists to their cabin, as "we are not able to do our Work and receive so many visi-tors, and can't make sovioners [*sic*] to sell like we once did and people will be expecting us to have them."[71]

The families forced to move from the Smokies had mixed experiences. Some moved to nearby areas, such as Pigeon Forge, Townsend, and Wears Valley, Tennessee; or to Maggie Valley, Bryson City, Waynesville, or Iron Duff, North Carolina. Others traveled farther afield. Several families moved as far away as California, Oregon, and Washington; and two fami-lies moved to Alaska.[72]

For many Smokies residents, the coming of the park proved an eco-nomic godsend. They had cash to buy new land at a time of low land prices. Despite the Depression, numerous opportunities to supplement, or even replace, farm income were provided by the economic environment of the region, with the coming of the Tennessee Valley Authority and the Civilian Conservation Corps; the expansion of industrial opportunities at Champion Fibre, Aluminum Corporation of America, and other regional industries; and the rapid development of the tourist industry.

The recent research of Crandall Shifflett demonstrates that, before the coming of the park, the economic lives of the people of the area had become increasingly precarious. According to Shifflett, the Southern Appalachian region was in the midst of a "population crisis" well before the coming of widespread industrial development. While the fertility rate in the United States as a whole dropped from 7.04 to 3.56 between 1800 and 1900, fertility rates in the Southern Appalachian region remained much higher than the national average until the 1950s.[73] Durwood Dunn observed that, in Cades Cove in the 1880s, "six to eight children per family was average; fifteen was considered large, but not unusual."[74] This high birth rate placed a tremendous strain upon the economic resources of the region. Mountain residents compounded the hardship through the custom of dividing land equally among all male heirs.[75]

To keep body and soul together and to feed their large families, farmers in the Smokies had two options. They could either adopt an itinerant lifestyle, roaming the region seeking whatever work might be available, or seek a variety of work locally to augment their often meager farm income. Heads of households and older sons sought to raise additional funds by hunting, fishing, blacksmithing, building railroads or highways, making moonshine whiskey, or working in a timber camp, mine, or textile mill. As Shifflett has argued, "Mountain farmers who lived on the margins of economic security pursued a patchwork of activities in piecing together the family economic quilt."[76]

Anecdotal evidence and population statistics bolster Shifflett's argument for the decreasing viability of life in the Great Smoky Mountains by the early twentieth century. Florence Cope Bush's mother, Dorie Cope, provides an excellent picture of the life of those mountain families who chose an itinerant lifestyle. Dorie's life involved constant moving in order to maintain family economic viability. Dorie's father moved their family from a farm near the Cherokee Indian Reservation to Spartanburg, South Carolina, to work in a textile mill, then to a farm in Tennessee near present-day Gatlinburg, and to a variety of timber camps owned by the Little River Lumber Company. When Dorie married Fred Cope, the pattern continued, with back-and-forth moves from farm to timber camp; another attempt at life in a milltown, this time in Gastonia, North Carolina; and finally a move to Knoxville, Tennessee. This constant shuttling among farm, mill, timber camp, mine, and city characterized the lives of many mountain families.[77]

Others chose to remain in the Smokies by developing a number of skills and taking on a variety of jobs to supplement farm income. In Greenbriar, Glenn Cardwell's father secured additional income by serving as a "jack leg" mechanic and even by making moonshine; reportedly, the sheriff of Sevier County was his best customer.[78] Even John Oliver, who owned some of the best farm land in Cades Cove, felt the need to supplement his farm income by carrying the mail, pastoring the Primitive Baptist Church, and running tourist cabins and a tourist lodge.[79]

The declining population of the region reveals the increasing difficulty of economic survival and the attractions of outside employment in the early twentieth century. The population of Cataloochee township, which had peaked around 1900 at 1,251, had declined to 931 by 1920.[80] Likewise, the population of Cades Cove had declined from its high of 709 in 1900 to 600 in 1928.[81]

Despite these benefits for some, however, the forced removal of the people of the Smokies, and particularly its emotional impact, had its tragic aspects. These people lost not only their homes, farms, churches, and businesses, but also their communities. When they left their homes, they became separated from many of the community, church, and kinship ties that had become so integral to their life and culture—indeed, to their very survival in the mountains. As Glenn Cardwell observed, "You can buy a farm anywhere, but tearing up your community does something to your spirit."[82]

For most former residents of the Smokies, the experience of removal remained unforgettable. Some reacted with a lifetime of bitterness towards the Park Service and the state governments that they believed had ruined their lives. Russell Whitehead expressed this view succinctly and eloquently at a special gathering in Cades Cove in 1986. Whitehead, as the last surviving individual who had owned land in Cades Cove, was the special guest of Tennessee's Gov. Lamar Alexander at the kick-off ceremonies for the year-long "Tennessee Homecoming" celebration. The introduction of Whitehead provided the climactic moment of the event. When Alexander introduced the ninety-eight-year-old man, the governor got more than he had bargained for. Whitehead stood, pointed his finger at Alexander, and in four words revealed the depth of hurt and bitterness felt by many former residents of the Smokies: "You Stole My land!"[83]

Most, however, approached the experience with resignation and eventually came to harbor merely a sentimental yearning for times past and places long since torn down or grown over. Glenn Cardwell recalls that, later in his father's life, all he wanted for his birthday was to be taken back into Greenbriar to revisit the grown-over sites where he, his family, and friends had lived, worked, worshipped, and played.[84] Florence Cope Bush expressed a similar attitude toward the changes that the coming of lumber companies and the National Park Service had brought to her family and friends: "The lumber companies had opened the door to the outside world. We became aware of 'things'—things that money could buy, things that made life easier (or harder), things to see, things to do. They had opened a door—a door we were forced to use as an exit from our ancestral homes. Then, after the exit, the door was closed to us. We were given visitors' rights to the land—to come and look, but not to stay."[85]

Many of the old communities and many of the families who once had a "home place" in the Smokies still hold their reunions in the summer.

Baptism in Cades Cove in 1915. Such events forged tight bonds among members of the communities of the Great Smoky Mountains. Photo courtesy of Great Smoky Mountains National Park.

The groups gather, usually at one of the old churches; renew acquaintances; "decorate" the graves; sing some of the old songs; and share dinner on the ground. For those who actually lived in these communities, these events are melancholy, especially when the names of those former residents who have died in the previous year are read. The number of names on this list gets smaller and smaller, as even those who lived in the Smokies as children near retirement age. Returning to the Smokies for a Cataloochee homecoming in 1950, Robert Woody reflected on an experience common to many former residents at these homecomings: "Homecoming on Cataloochee strikes a contrast between happy memories and the drab present. The Palmers and the Caldwells, the Messers and the Bennetts[,] have departed. The acres they once tilled are covered with saplings. The houses, now the abode[s] of bats and snakes, soon will be gone, [their sites] identified only by the sentinel-like chimneys brooding in stony silence over a lost land. Only when those with happy memories are gone will the present Cataloochee seem better than the old."[86]

Unfortunately, the experience of removal was to become increasingly common for residents of East Tennessee and Western North Carolina. The displacement of the residents of the Smokies by the National Park Service proved to be only the opening wave, as the presence of the federal government increased throughout the region. The Tennessee Valley Authority; construction of a top-secret military facility at Oak Ridge, Tennessee; and the coming of the Blue Ridge Parkway forced thousands of other area residents off their land. For many mountain residents, the wrenching removal experienced at Cataloochee, Cades Cove, and Greenbriar soon became the experience of Elza, Loyston, Robertsville, Scarboro, Sharp's Chapel, and Walnut Grove in Tennessee; and Almond, Bushnell, Fontana, and Proctor in North Carolina.[87]

The ordeal of one of the Whaley families of Greenbriar provides an extreme example of the federal government's impact on many area residents. Forced to move out of the Greenbriar section by the National Park Service, the family first bought land in the area around Norris, Tennessee. The building of the Tennessee Valley Authority's Norris Dam displaced them again. The Whaleys then bought a farm near Oak Ridge, Tennessee, only to be displaced for a third time when the federal government's Manhattan Project came to the region during World War II. They finally moved back to the Pigeon Forge area, where at least they could live in sight of the Smokies.[88]

Evaluating the removal of individuals from the Great Smoky Mountains leaves one ambivalent. Was the cost—in this case, the removal of thousands of individuals from their homes and communities—worth the benefits that a national park brought to the region and the nation at large? One cannot view the cabins, clapboard houses wallpapered in newspaper, pastoral settings, graveyards, churches, and jonquils and irises still blooming around long-abandoned homesites without a strong sense that we have lost something valuable: the sense of family and community that made life in the Smokies special for its residents. Try as they might, the park commissions and the National Park Service never could compensate the people of the Smokies for the loss of their communities. Nor could the people who were removed recreate them elsewhere. At the same time, viewing the scene on the edge of the park, with its neon lights, bumper-to-bumper traffic, roadside clutter, rundown trailers, and junked cars, one can't help thinking that the National Park Service and the state park commissions did us all a service in preserving at least some of the beauty and serenity of the Smokies, which made life in these mountains something to treasure.

Removal of the individuals and families who had called the Smokies home was not the only development issue that faced park boosters and the National Park Service. Once these groups had decided that the park would not contain human inhabitants, except for notable exceptions, they had to decide what it would contain. These decisions often proved as controversial and as divisive as the decision to remove the people of the Smokies.

7.

"Sounds Poetical, but It May Be an Atrocity"

"WELCOME TO MANKIND!" in neon; an avenue of flags; a lake 3.4 miles long and 1 mile wide in Cades Cove; a skyline drive from Newfound Gap to Deals Gap; an amphitheater complete with carillon organ; statues of the heroes of the park movement; huge lodges and restaurant facilities; elimination of all watersnakes, foxes, bobcats, and skunks. All these were proposed, and even seriously considered, for the Great Smoky Mountains National Park. These ideas represent serious controversies that, in the early days of development in the park, embroiled park boosters, the National Park Service, and a small but growing cadre of wilderness advocates. During the late 1930s and early 1940s, the Smokies became the focal point of a national struggle over what types of development the National Park Service would allow in its parks. This struggle not only shaped the future of the Great Smoky Mountains National Park, but also produced a legacy of wilderness preservation that impacts the use of public lands in this nation and in many parts of the world to the present day.

The battle revolved around concrete definitions of terms that park boosters and the National Park Service had thrown around for almost two decades: *set aside, natural, protection, preservation, conserve, unimpaired,* and *wilderness.* Of particular interest was the question of interpreting the Park Service's mission, dictated by Congress in the National Park Service Act of 1916: "To conserve the scenery and the natural and historic objects and the wild life therein and to provide for the enjoyment of the same in such manner as will leave them unimpaired for the enjoyment of future generations." Immediately, and continually, the tension between the twin charges of providing for the "enjoyment of future generations" and leaving the land "unimpaired" made early land use decisions in the Smokies challenging, controversial, and highly politicized.

Federal laws authorizing the creation of the Great Smoky Mountains National Park had forbidden development of the park until North Carolina and Tennessee had turned over 427,000 acres (amended in 1934 to 400,000 acres). The National Park Service, however, took over "protection and administration" of the property soon after the states presented the deeds to the first 150,000 acres in 1930. The ever-increasing number of visitors to the park soon made the Park Service's job a difficult one. An estimated 200,000 people visited the Smokies in the first year of Park Service administration, and that number quickly rose to almost 700,000 by 1938.[1] In August 1930, the Park Service sent two experienced rangers, John Needham and Phillip Hough, to make an inspection tour and determine the most pressing needs of the new park.[2] The park's new superintendent, Ross Eakin, assumed his official duties in January 1931.[3] Eakin first established the park headquarters at the Maryville post office but moved it to Gatlinburg on 1 June 1932. By 1932, Eakin had added two more rangers to the force, but the task of protecting over 300,000 acres of mountain land with a force of four proved daunting.[4]

While many of the initial land use decisions made by the Park Service received the general approval of both park boosters and proponents of wilderness, former residents of the park area and residents of neighboring communities, who traditionally had carried on a variety of activities in the Smokies, were none too pleased with the new restrictions. Implementation of Park Service regulations in the Smokies provided the first major challenge for the rangers. Enforcement of the regulation forbidding hunting in the park proved especially troublesome. Ranger Audley Whaley maintained that the people who lived in and around the park were used to "doin' as they pleased . . . they hunted and fished whenever they got ready." Some seemed determined to continue to do what they had done, despite—and even to spite—the Park Service. Whaley arrested one old coon hunter whom he had already caught hunting several times. The old man told Whaley, "I've always lived up here. Born and raised up here. An' I've hunted it an' fished it an' I'm goin' to as long as I live. You may catch me, but I'm goin' to hunt it."[5]

Despite the importance of enforcing this regulation, Park Service officials encouraged the rangers to deal with these situations with tact and sensitivity. Arno Cammerer warned John Needham to go slowly in enforcing regulations concerning carrying firearms in the park: "This is almost second nature to the mountaineers and I don't think you will be able to do much except warn them when you find them with guns on park property until we have acquired the entire interior area for the park."[6] Audley Whaley agreed with this "go slow" policy in dealing with recalcitrant individuals in the park: "I knew that you can't run over 'em. You can't tell 'em what to do. You've got to say 'let's do so an' so if we can't get by this now we've got to, it's a reglation [*sic*] now we've got to do it now.'"[7]

Another early enforcement problem for rangers concerned individuals who dug up shrubs and wildflowers in the park. In 1931, Gatlinburg hotelier Jack Huff warned Park Service officials that he had seen individuals hauling truckloads of wildflowers, rhododendron, mountain laurel, and flame azalea out of the park almost every day. Although the Park Service tried to deal severely with individuals who took these shrubs out of the park, again it went slowly in enforcing the regulations on individuals who had only a few wildflowers or plants. For one thing, in the early days of operation, a person caught with plants could always argue that he or she had taken the plants from an area not yet included in the park. Second, the Park Service had no effective way of enforcing their regulations until the federal government assigned a federal commissioner to the park to prosecute cases. Park Service employees had to depend on U.S. Commissioners in the surrounding counties or charge individuals with violating Tennessee or North Carolina laws and take the violators into state courts. Neither scenario proved totally satisfactory, as local courts and commissioners often sided with the violators over the Park Service, making convictions difficult.[8] Speaking of the plant issue, Superintendent Eakin lamented, "Our efforts along this line are mostly bluff."[9]

Fire protection became one of the chief responsibilities of the early rangers in the park. Although fires in the Smokies do not have the same explosive potential that fires in the western parks have, several local factors helped make the Smokies a high-risk area in the 1930s. The presence of huge amounts of slash and dead brush left over from logging operations made several areas of the park highly susceptible to fire.[10] The customs of people who lived, or had lived, in the Smokies exacerbated the situation. Mountain residents traditionally burned off the underbrush to improve forage for cattle, a practice known locally as "greening the grass."[11] The custom of "smoking out bee trees" in order to "rob" the honey also created fire hazards. With large amounts of slash on the ground, these fires often burned out of control.[12]

Arson, a common means of retaliation against powerful individuals or institutions in the South, became the park's most serious fire problem in the early days. Audley Whaley related that those whom he arrested for violations of park regulations often threatened, "We'll burn this place down."[13] Cases of individuals who set fires because of anger at the Park Service or at individual rangers fill several file folders. One such case in 1932 occurred because park rangers forced an individual whom they considered a "very objectionable character" to move out of the park. The man retaliated by setting fourteen separate fires along one particular trail.[14] In 1937, Lone Bales of Gatlinburg set twenty-nine separate fires, which burned over twenty-three acres, because he had a personal grudge against a ranger.[15] Later that same year, Boone Dykes entered a plea of *nolo contendere* to a charge of feloniously setting fires in the park, pleading drunkenness and loss of memory.[16]

The establishment of the Civilian Conservation Corps (CCC) greatly assisted Park Service officials in providing adequate fire protection and facilitating park development. Between 1933 and 1942, twenty-three separate CCC camps functioned in the Smokies. In 1934–35, the peak enrollment year, 4,350 young men worked in the park area, being paid at the rate of thirty dollars a month, with twenty-five of that going home to their families. Living in military-style camps, CCC workers constructed fire towers; built fire roads to improve access to the backcountry and act as fire breaks; reduced fire hazards by removing slash and tearing down and removing abandoned buildings; constructed roads, bridges, and hiking trails; built picnic areas and campgrounds; and reforested cut-over areas of the park. The CCC generally did excellent work, much of which is still evident in the park today, and few New deal programs retain such loyalty and affection on the part of their participants as this one.[17]

Although removing abandoned buildings often proved controversial, park officials believed it a necessary task. They argued that these buildings presented a fire hazard. In their view, removing them improved the overall appearance of the park and made the Smokies seem more thoroughly a wilderness. In addition, eliminating these buildings prevented people from either moving back into the park or squatting there ("Deserted houses are rallying points for the lawless element"). Many of the buildings inside the park were sold at auction by the Park Service, with the buyer guaranteeing site cleanup. Rangers burned less accessible or less desirable buildings and saved only the "best examples of pioneer architecture."[18]

Cleanup of other building sites caused the Park Service major problems. The site of Champion Fibre Company's Smokemont mill, for example, proved especially difficult. The cleanup of this site involved removing an obsolete locomotive, forty railroad cars used for hauling logs, frames and carriages used in the sawmilling process, a number of large buildings and homes, and several miles of railroad track. The sale contract did not provide for cleanup of the site by Champion, so the Park Service had to pay to have much of the metal hauled off and the buildings demolished. They buried much of the smaller debris on the site.[19]

Ironically, as the park rangers and the CCC spent much of their time trying to eliminate much of the evidence of human habitation, the Park Service discovered that the cessation of human activity had an undesirable impact on some areas. Once the farmers moved out of Cades Cove and Cataloochee, taking their cattle with them, trees began to grow in the fields. Arthur Comey, chairman of the New England Trail Conference, wrote to Arno Cammerer that the Park Service needed to do something, as "we can no longer see the scenery for the trees."[20] The solution Comey advised, and the solution adopted, was to make an exception to Park Service rules and lease land in the cove for cattle grazing, to prevent the cove from "growing up into a gigantic woodlot."[21] Today the Park Service leases rights to cut hay in Cataloochee and in Cades Cove in order to keep at least part of the land open and to create opportunities for wildlife viewing, an activity that makes both sections popular with visitors.

The same problem presented itself on the numerous grassy balds of the Smokies. When the cattle left, briars and trees began to encroach on the balds, blocking the views and crowding out the rhododendron and flame azalea that had attracted so many early visitors. As a result, most of these places today are balds in name only. In 1976, park botanist Mary Lindsay commented, "Invasion of the grassy balds by trees is continuing. Less than half of the original area of Gregory Bald is still grassy—blueberries have grown over most of its area, and the blueberry patches seem to provide shelter from severe conditions, for many trees seem to start in blueberry patches. Balds that are surrounded by beech forests, such as Thunderhead or Silers, are rapidly being taken over by beech sprouts which grow so densely that one can hardly walk between them. If no action is taken to set back and hold back their invasion by woody plants, the balds will almost certainly be no more than a memory by the end of this century."[22] In order to prevent this, the Park Service began, and currently continues, a program of mowing and controlled burning to maintain at least parts of Gregory Bald and Andrews Bald; the rest are being left to "return to a natural state" that may not have been "natural" on some of these sites for thousands of years.

The Park Service also had to deal with the problem of restoring native animal life to the Smokies. Although early promotional literature had boasted of the abundance of wild animals in the Smokies, early surveys by Park Service personnel revealed that the many years of human habitation and the destruction of habitat by logging operations had seriously depleted the animal populations of the area. A Department of the Interior official, Ernest Walker Sawyer, who made an inspection trip to the area in 1929, argued that "even song birds are not numerous." He credited the lack of animals in the Smokies to the "hundreds of mountaineers each roaming the mountains with a shot gun on his shoulder."[23] A local observer noted that "the fish have been dynamited, seined and caught in every possible way while the game has been killed in and out of season until there is scarcely any left."[24]

Although simply ending hunting and logging and replanting forests in the cut-over areas of the Smokies would aid in bringing back many species, the Park Service decided that some animals would need extra help. Restoring the deer population to the Smokies became its first priority. Superintendent Eakin argued in 1931 that years of unregulated hunting and deforestation had left the park area devoid of deer.[25] At the same time, a surplus of deer had caused serious damage to plant life in nearby Pisgah National Forest. The Forest Service and the National Park Service made an agreement to restock the Smokies gradually with deer from the Pisgah herd, beginning with twenty-five in 1933, fifty in 1934, and one hundred each subsequent year until 1940.[26]

The announcement of this restocking program in the Smokies immediately drew criticism from some circles. Most feared the damage that deer would cause to the "varied and luxurious plant life" of the area. Protest grew especially strong when an article appeared in *American Forests* magazine in March 1933, showing pictures of the plant damage caused by deer in the Pisgah National Forest. At the same time, the death by starvation of hundreds of deer in the Kaibab region of Grand Canyon National Park, due to overgrazing and the elimination of predator species, drew national attention. Eakin defended the stocking of deer by arguing that "trees and shrubs grow so prolifically the park could support a large population without damage." He also pledged that he would not institute a campaign to eliminate predators in the park, which, he argued, contributed greatly to the Kaibab disaster and the problems at Pisgah. Eakin won the battle, and the deer restocking program began.[27]

Depleted fish stocks in the park's streams and rivers also concerned Park Service officials. In an emergency measure, six streams were closed to fishing in 1932. Although Park Service Director Horace Albright initially resisted restocking as a "development measure," the Park Service soon began to re-stock streams with the help of the Bureau of Fisheries and the Izaak Walton League.[28] After several years of discussion, the Park Service constructed a fish hatchery near the confluence of Kephart Prong and the Oconoluftee River in 1936.[29] After ten years of operation, however, the Park Service closed the hatchery after poor fish harvests made it a fiscal liability. Experts called in to study the situation identified the low water temperature as the cause of the problem. After the closing of its fish hatchery, the Park Service purchased fish from other local hatcheries. The stocking program greatly improved fishing in the park and attracted fishermen from around the country. How-ever, the larger and more aggressive non-native rainbow and brown trout that the Park Service placed in area streams depleted native aquatic species, par-ticularly brook trout, and extirpated nongame species such as smoky madtom, spotfin chub, duskytail darter, and yellowfin madtom. In recent years, park biologists have attempted to reverse the process by removing rainbows and browns from some streams, forbidding the killing of brook trout, and restock-ing park streams with the nongame species.[30]

The coming of the national park also proved beneficial to the animal most associated with the Great Smoky Mountains National Park, the black bear. In 1935, Eakin reported that, ten years earlier, "bears were much depleted and rarely seen." With the end of hunting in the Smokies, they now approached "numbers which they normally should have."[31] However, Park Service officials realized the potential for trouble with a large population of bears, and Arno Cammerer advised Eakin that "there is only one satisfactory way to deal with the bear problem and that is to remove the cause of the trouble, namely, to make food inaccessible."[32] Unfortunately, the presence of garbage—reflecting the increase in human use of the park and the unwillingness of many visitors to abide by the rules not to feed the bears—created a persistent bear problem in some areas. In some CCC camps, the problem was exacerbated by the practice of dumping garbage in the open, in an attempt to attract bears so that the enrollees could be entertained by evening "bear shows." Eakin expressed his consternation at this practice but lamented the difficulty of enforcing Park Service policies in remote camps "where the wildlife furnishes the principal diversions and topic of conversation."[33]

Just as the Park Service wanted to restore stocks of "desirable" animals, some persons in the service pushed for a program to control or eliminate certain "undesirable" species. Eakin wanted to allow rangers to hunt foxes, cats, and skunks which ate the eggs of quail, grouse, and wild turkeys. Concerning foxes, Eakin argued that an "unnatural condition" existed, as fox hunters had turned several hundred foxes loose in the area so that they could hunt them down with their dogs.[34] Eakin also promoted an active program for the eradication, or at least control, of water snakes which fed on trout and other game fish. He argued that, unless the Park Service controlled these water snakes, they would "literally take our streams."[35] Eakin's attitude reflected the viewpoint of many who had served in the Park Service since its beginning, a viewpoint that considered the primary mission of the National Parks as catering to the needs and desires of visitors. The superintendent wanted to promote those species which would attract park visitors, even if it meant eradicating other less desirable species.

However, by the 1930s, the philosophy inside the Park Service had begun to change, concerning not only wildlife but also the agency's overall mission. Many in the service began to argue that its mission should encompass "complete conservation" of all native plant and animal species in the national parks. These individuals interpreted literally the Park Service's mission statement: "To conserve the scenery and the natural and historic objects and the wild life therein and to provide for the enjoyment of the same in such manner and by such means as will leave them unimpaired for the enjoyment of future generations." In denying Eakin's request to begin a program to eradicate foxes, cats, and skunks, Assistant Park Service Director Bryant quoted the mission of the service and underlined the word *unimpaired.* Bryant added that predator control could take place in national parks only in those situations "where property or life is endangered."[36] Even Arno Cammerer, a Park Service traditionalist like Eakin, responded to the request to "control" water snakes by arguing that such a policy "would be an undesirable subservience of national park purposes to the single aim of fish production."[37]

As much as the Park Service wanted to restore the Smokies to its "natural" state, its mission statement also required it to conserve "historic objects" and somehow to preserve and interpret the human history of the park. In this area, the Park Service proved selective in choosing which history was worthy of preservation. Even as people began moving out of the park, pressure began to build to perpetuate some memory of the lives of the mountain people, especially since many believed that "this interesting group is apt to undergo a radical change from their old happy, satisfied way of living."[38] As early as 1930, as people moved from the park, Park Ranger Phillip Hough began collecting from them items which he considered appropriate for a mountain culture museum. Hough encouraged the Park Service to pursue vigorously the collection of potential museum pieces, for fear that, with the "influx of tourist and relic hunters, most of the choice material will soon disappear."[39] Influential outsiders, including Waldo Leland of the American Council of Learned Societies, also advocated a program to preserve the native culture of the region. An Asheville folklorist, Bascom Lamar Lunsford, proposed that the Park Service bring together groups of mountain people to perform traditional songs, dances, and games, "both to entertain visitors interested in such matters and to perpetuate as much as possible these cultural things."[40]

Although the Park Service soon resolved to make efforts to preserve the heritage of the former inhabitants of the park, it decided to perpetuate only those aspects of mountain life that reflected a "pioneer" lifestyle. Horace Albright reflected his overall ignorance of the lives lived by the people of the Smokies when he promised that the Park Service intended to "do all it can to preserve the traditions of these sturdy people, many of whom still use spinning wheels and handlooms to weave their cloth and who grind their grain in primitive mills built by their forefathers."[41] This also meant, as Durwood Dunn put it, that "anything which might remotely suggest progress or advancement beyond the most primitive stages should be destroyed."[42]

In 1938, the Park Service commissioned H. C. Wilburn, resident landscape architect C. S. Grossman, and park naturalist Arthur Stupka to conduct a study of how best to preserve the culture of the mountain people. The group called for the construction of a museum of mountain culture and a number of field exhibits scattered throughout the park. The three men established as a basic ground rule that the Park Service should preserve and present to the public only those things representative of mountain culture prior to 1890. The trio placed great emphasis on using live demonstrations by "mountaineers" of corn milling, long rifle shooting, leather tanning, domestic textiles, honey production, and even beaten copper work, in which "material used would be mainly from confiscated still copper." The group made the remarkable proposal that the Park Service encourage some former residents to move back into the park to live as their ancestors had in the nineteenth century, but the impracticality of this plan soon became apparent.[43]

In 1941, the Park Service conducted another study of the issue, this time by Hans Huth, a German expatriate, former curator of royal palaces and parks in Prussia and Berlin, and now a special consultant on historic preservation with the Park Service. Huth recommended that the park consult such groups as the Phi Beta Phi School in Gatlinburg, the Southern Highlanders Guild, Allenstand Cottage Industry, John Campbell Folk School, Russell Sage Foundation, and Berea College for advice on effectively preserving and interpreting mountain culture. He never discussed the possibility of consulting actual residents of the Smokies in the interpretive process. Huth further suggested creating an isolated "buffer" zone on the edge of the park which "could be kept and preserved by making it inaccessible and by discouraging intercourse with the outside world." In this zone, families would live in the old way, making a living by producing high-quality handmade goods for sale in park gift shops. If the Park Service could not find individuals proficient in creating these handicrafts, then the experts at Phi Beta Phi, Berea College, or the Campbell Folk School could train them.[44]

Over time, the Park Service adopted a few of the recommendations from the two reports, all reflecting the Park Service's bias toward preserving only the "primitive." In 1945, the agency designated Cades Cove as a "historical area" and restored several of the older cabins and barns. Later the Park Service constructed a pioneer homestead at the Oconoluftee Visitors' Center, just outside of the Cherokee Indian Reservation. Concessionaires operate water-driven mills at the Cable Mill in Cades Cove and the Mingus Mill near Oconoluftee, and the Park Service sells cornmeal and stone-ground flour at each site (although the meal and flour sold actually are ground in Sevierville, Tennessee, because of health regulations). At one time, the Park Service held muzzle-loading rifle demonstrations at Oconoluftee, although Park Service employees debated whether the individual doing the demonstrations ought to wear overalls or a Confederate army uniform. The Park Service has preserved other cabins and buildings scattered around the park, while destroying or auctioning off the frame houses indicative of lives actually lived by the mountain people in the twentieth century, except for a few in the Cataloochee area.[45]

Preserving the memory of the human inhabitants of the park generally has taken a back seat to other concerns, especially in recent years of budget cutbacks. The mountain culture museum has remained in the planning stages since the establishment of the park. The hundreds of tub mills, spinning wheels, looms, long rifles, stills, and other artifacts collected by H. C. Wilburn and C. S. Grossman over the years remain in storage at various buildings scattered throughout the park, awaiting display in a museum that may never be built. The park archives has made an extensive collection of oral interviews of former residents; in the summer of 1997, it launched a project to collect interviews with all individuals who lived in the park before its establishment.

By the late 1930s, restrictions on permanent development and the growing numbers of visitors posed a dilemma concerning accommodations inside the park. The increased flow of tourists, many of whom camped on the roadside, forced the Park Service to authorize the CCC to build temporary campgrounds with pit latrines. However, the overcrowded campgrounds soon produced a serious sanitation problem. In 1937, the Park Service had to close two of these campgrounds because of contaminated wells, and rangers marked other water sources as "unsafe without boiling."[46] The situation also prompted complaints from visitors about the sanitary conditions and lack of modern "comfort stations."[47]

Although Superintendent Eakin publicly supported Park Service policy concerning development, he begged Park Service Director Cammerer to allow him to open two large permanent campgrounds which the CCC already had constructed, complete with water and sewer lines. Eakin argued that the volume of travel expected in 1937 made sanitation improvements such as the construction of flush toilets and permanent water supplies "necessary for the protection of the health of visitors and those outside the park residing along the streams which head in the park."[48] Despite Eakin's pleas, however, the Park Service did not open the campgrounds until the official opening of the park in 1940.[49]

The location of the park in the South created a unique administrative problem for the Park Service. Southern laws and customs dictated racial segregation in public accommodations. In discussing this situation with NAACP Secretary Walter White, Secretary of the Interior Harold Ickes argued that "it has long been the policy of this Department, in the administration of national parks and monuments in the west, to conform generally to the State customs with regard to the accommodation of visitors."[50] As such, in the Great Smoky Mountains National Park, the Park Service designated separate restroom and campground facilities for African-American visitors. In defense of this policy, Park Service Assistant Director A. E. Demaray stated, "We realize that there will be some criticism against segregation, but we also feel that we will be subjected to more criticism by the white as well as by the colored race if there is no segregation." Obviously, this policy later changed with changes in federal law.[51]

Perhaps the most divisive development issue within the Great Smoky Mountains National Park concerned, and still concerns, the question of roads in the park. Horace Albright expressed traditional Park Service policy on roads in the national parks in a letter to Harvey Broome in 1931: "I view my future obligations in the development of that park with a great appreciation of the serious responsibilities involved to protect and guard as much wilderness as possible, at the same time making it reasonably accessible for the motorist. We may have to concede it a fact that by far the greatest number of people will see what they are permitted to see of this glorious mountain country from their motor car, and not by horseback or hiking. At any rate we will have to plan ahead for the enjoyment of the park by those who are not as strong and agile as you and I, for they too are entitled to their inspiration and enjoyment."[52]

The Park Service received a great deal of pressure from boosters in Western North Carolina and East Tennessee to build a wide-ranging system of paved roads within the park. "Good Roads" advocates and automobile clubs in both states had helped make the park a reality, and now they insisted on expansion and improvement of the road system in the Smokies. Park boosters often had maintained that the establishment of a national park would bring good roads to these mountainous regions at last, and they looked to the federal government to fulfill what they perceived as a promise.

During the Depression, the Park Service also faced political pressure to build roads due to unemployment, especially as emergency funds became available from the federal government through the New Deal. Eakin pointed this out to Director Horace Albright in 1932, in discussing a movement launched by the Asheville Chamber of Commerce to build a skyline highway the entire length of the park. "I believe the Tennessee and North Carolina delegations in Congress will line up solidly behind this movement [for a skyline drive,] for things are in a bad plight in this country, as elsewhere."[53]

The proposed skyline drive through the park became a particularly controversial issue, as the Park Service already had begun constructing a skyline drive in Shenandoah National Park. Many local boosters argued that they deserved a similar road through the Smokies. While the Park Service made it clear that the area east of Indian Gap Highway—now Highway 441—would remain a wilderness, with no paved roads through the area, they did not oppose the idea of a skyline drive through the western end of the park.[54] Park Superintendent Eakin, in particular, remained a staunch supporter of the project. He believed that the construction of a skyline drive in Shenandoah had created a "precedent from which we cannot escape, even if we desired to do so."[55]

As Park Service plans to build the skyline drive became public, opposition from wilderness preservationists began to mount. Harris Reynolds, secretary of the Massachusetts Forestry Association, wrote to the Park Service, warning, "We must retain at all costs some real wilderness areas or our eastern parks will become merely enlarged municipal parks."[56] The executive board of the Izaak Walton League passed a resolution against any road building in the higher elevations of the Smokies.[57] Harlan Kelsey, a member of the SANP Commission, pleaded with Albright, "There are plenty of national parks and state parks where the herd instinct can be fully satisfied but for God's sake let's keep our national parks, so far as we can, in a truly wild state."[58]

The most vocal and influential opponent of the skyline drive however, was Harvey Broome, a Knoxville lawyer and clerk of the U.S. Circuit Court of Appeals. A native of the region who had made frequent hiking and camping trips into the Smokies, Broome recently had returned to Knoxville after living in Chicago. He immediately threw himself into the park movement and the activities of the Smoky Mountains Hiking Club. However, his vision of what a national park in the Smokies should look like differed dramatically from those of his compatriots in the park movement and the hiking club. In 1931, Broome wrote to Horace Albright, expressing his views on the skyline drive and on park development generally:

> Frankly, I think the automobiles rob us of our sensitivities and powers of appreciation. People (I admit there are exceptions) who expect to see the mountains from a car have no conception of the irresistible appeal to others of a leisured walk thru these fastnesses, far from the noise and impact of the machine world. Why great areas of this region should be thus seared and blighted by roads upon the demand of those who will never know what true appreciation is, and who do not know what they ask of those who *love* the mountains and who love to pit their *strength* and *emotions* and *souls* against their challenge, I do not understand. Must we yield to the cheap, when the vision of the better thing for man is clear? Many writers are of the opinion that the machine age is but a passing phase in the movement of civilization. Do those who believe that and who

> are entrusted with the exploitation of one of the grandest, most
> exquisite and spiritually refreshing areas, trust their vision and dare
> to stand out against the popular clamor?[59]

Despite Broome's passion, he remained for a number of years a lone local voice of opposition, a man whom park boosters often considered a
genial crank.

The Park Service moved quickly to answer these critics. Arno
Cammerer responded that those not thoroughly acquainted with the situation had stirred up rumors. Reflecting his bias in favor of development,
he argued that the road would not follow the crest of the mountains beyond the proposed observation area at Clingman's Dome, but would be
built from gap to gap and would not include the eastern part of the park.
He further asserted that the Park Service sought to develop the national
parks for the "health and enjoyment of the people, not only for the young
and husky . . . but also that the elderly people, the infirm and growing
children may enjoy the hidden wonders of the park."[60]

In late 1932 and early 1933, the Park Service plan received some important endorsements. Both the National Parks Association and the locally influential Smoky Mountains Hiking Club voiced approval. Harvey
Broome provided the only dissenting vote on the board of directors of the
hiking club.[61] Even Harlan Kelsey came to consider the skyline drive
project unavoidable and even necessary.[62] In early 1933, the construction
of a skyline drive through the western part of the park seemed inevitable.

In 1934, however, Harvey Broome formed an important alliance with
Benton MacKaye, the father of the Appalachian Trail, who had moved from
his home in Massachusetts to work for the Tennessee Valley Authority in
Knoxville. The two discussed development in the Smokies and began to map
a strategy for preventing the skyline drive and other "improvement" activities in the park. Later that year, the two convinced Bob Marshall, director
of forestry for the Bureau of Indian Affairs and the strongest advocate for
wilderness protection in the Department of the Interior, to join their cause.
Marshall had come to Knoxville to address a meeting of the American Forestry Association. In his speech, Marshall condemned the idea of the skyline drive: "Since the forest land in this country is very limited, it is necessary to establish recreation priorities in the use of the forests so that the most
precious values will not be wiped out by secondary or even trivial uses which
could be enjoyed in other environments."[63]

Roads in the national parks, particularly Great Smoky Mountains, became the focal issue for an important new movement that produced both local and national results. Through Marshall and MacKaye, Broome became acquainted with other like-minded men, including Aldo Leopold, Harold Anderson, and Robert Sterling Yard. In January 1935, these men and two others came together to establish the Wilderness Society, to fight in an organized manner such projects as the skyline drive.[64] In an article on the society, Broome explained its mission: "It is to preserve these remaining areas, where natural creation in its pure state [may] yet be observed and its potencies felt, that the Wilderness Society is formed. Its purposes [are] to arrest the encroachment of man's world upon the natural, and to take steps to set aside areas, variant in size and use, but alike in their freedom from intrusions such as roads, radios, overdone trails, transmission lines and other manifestations of the machine age."[65] Broome later served as the society's president from 1957 until his death in 1968. The high point of his leadership came when he stood next to President Lyndon B. Johnson in 1964 for the signing of the Wilderness Act, an event for which Broome had worked diligently for twenty-four years.[66]

Although it would take years for much of the American public to heed the call issued by the Wilderness Society, Secretary of the Interior Harold Ickes became an important early convert to the cause of wilderness protection. Even though Ickes spent most of his adult life as an urban reformer in Chicago, he quickly came to appreciate the value of wilderness. On a 1934 trip to Yosemite, Ickes mused, "One should get away once in a while as far as possible from human contacts. To contemplate nature, magnificently garbed as it is in this country, is to restore peace to the mind."[67]

Ickes sent Bob Marshall on a trip to investigate the skyline drive in the spring of 1935. In a memo to Ickes, Marshall argued that "a skyline drive, or additional fraction of it[,] would be indefensible." He further reflected the new thinking on national park development by asserting that "it will be much easier to convert a wild area into a developed one in the future than wipe out development and restore wilderness."[68]

The skyline drive idea died hard, however. Cammerer, now director of the Park Service, encouraged Ickes to visit the site of the proposed road to judge the merits of the project. Cammerer reminded Ickes that eliminating the skyline drive project would handicap the work of a number of CCC camps in the park. He further advised Ickes that the road and trail program had received the approval of the Smoky Mountains Hiking Club, the Potomac Appalachian Club, and the Appalachian Trail Conference.[69]

Cammerer's appeal went unheeded, however, as Ickes pronounced the death knell for the skyline drive venture in September 1935 at a meeting of state park authorities. At the same time, he helped usher in a new era for the National Park Service and its relationship to wilderness: "I am not in favor of building any more roads in the National Parks than we have to build. . . . This is an automobile age, but I do not have much patience with people whose idea of enjoying nature is dashing along a hard road at fifty or sixty miles per hour. I am not willing that our beautiful areas ought to be opened up to people who are either too old to walk, as I am, or too lazy to walk, as a great many young people are who ought to be ashamed of themselves. I do not happen to favor the scarring of a wonderful mountainside just so we can say we have a skyline drive. It sounds poetical, but it may be an atrocity."[70]

In the wake of Ickes's opposition to the skyline drive, a further rationale for limited development inside national parks evolved within the Park Service, based on economic considerations. In 1938, when Sen. Kenneth McKellar tried to reopen the skyline drive issue, E. K. Burlew, the Department of the Interior's acting secretary, responded, "If the park is made too accessible by roads, the tendency of tourists will be to race through it rather than to stay and enjoy it. From the standpoint of economic benefits to the surrounding communities, the Department and the National Park Service should be careful to see that it will not be possible for tourists to dash in and out and be on their way to some other resort area."[71] Roads advocates did get some consolation, in that seven miles of the skyline drive, already under construction from Newfound Gap to Clingman's Dome, were completed and opened to the public.

Construction and maintenance of trails in the park also sparked controversy between park boosters and wilderness advocates. A major portion of the work of CCC enrollees involved constructing an extensive trail system. Park Service guidelines called for the trails to be built "according to the highest standards," with grades not exceeding 15 percent at any point. The Park Service sought to "make readily accessible the most advantageous scenic points of the park."[72] However, proponents of wilderness, led by Harvey Broome, argued that the CCC made the trails too wide, that they planned too many trails, and that much of the trail construction unnecessarily destroyed surrounding vegetation. Broome's consternation over the trail construction program prompted him to write to Robert Marshall, "It was that wilderness which a half decade ago we were so eagerly seeking to bring under the protection of the Park Service, and which now some of us are just as eagerly seeking to protect from the Park Service."[73] Although the trail construction program continued, the watchdog efforts of Broome and others caused the Park Service and the CCC to consider the environmental impact of trail construction and use less intrusive methods.

The controversy between proponents of wilderness and development-minded park boosters carried over into discussions concerning the construction of lodges, hotels, and recreational facilities inside the park. Local boosters wanted the Park Service to build, or allow concessionaires to build, extensive and modern tourist accommodations. Wilderness promoters, however, focused more on keeping the park as unspoiled as possible, with a bare minimum of camping and sanitation facilities.

Splendid lodging and entertainment attractions characterized the western parks, and boosters hoped that similar features would help draw millions of visitors, as they had advertised in their promotion of the park idea. They longed for something akin to Yellowstone's "bear shows" (a boardwalk near the garbage dump, where tourists could observe the evening visits, and often fighting, of bears) and lighted eruptions of "Old Faithful," and Yosemite's firefall and Wawona Tunnel Tree. They also dreamed of grand lodges inside the park, on the order of the Old Faithful Inn in Yellowstone, the Ahwanee Inn in Yosemite, El Tovar overlooking the South Rim of the Grand Canyon, and the Glacier Park Lodge in Glacier National Park.[74]

In 1935, the Great Smoky Mountains Conservation Association sent a list of development proposals to Park Service officials. These proposals included an elaborate gateway, complete with an avenue of flags and an electric sign bridging the road emblazoned with the words "Welcome to Mankind"; a large amphitheater with carillon and mission bells; statues scattered throughout the park honoring people involved in its establishment; a museum commemorating the human history of the region; a large-scale inn, lodge, and restaurant development; and the damming of Abram's Creek, so as to flood Cades Cove and create a lake for recreational purposes.[75]

Horace Albright, now retired as Park Service director, who had often promoted tourist development within national parks, responded that "most of these proposals do not appeal to me for the reason they would detract from the wild natural features of the region. . . . The great electric sign would particularly be an inharmonious feature." However, Albright agreed that the museum and the development of hotels and restaurants were "entirely in harmony with the principles and policies of the National Park Service and would be entirely proper in the glorious mountain region that is the Great Smoky Mountains National Park."[76]

The flooding of Cades Cove to build a lake 3.4 miles long and a mile wide proved the most controversial, and most enduring, of the boosters' proposals. This project had the enthusiastic support of Arno Cammerer and Park Superintendent J. R. Eakin.[77] To get around Park Service policy against large-scale changes in the natural environment, Eakin and park boosters argued that the geologic record indicated that a lake formerly existed on the site. As David Chapman asserted, "I am told that some geologists say that you can locate the old lake line in the Cove. If this is true, it is not an artificial thing but simply a restoration of what nature did at one time."[78] This argument caused Cammerer to give his support to the project in 1934. He contended, "In that hot country in particular any small body of water would not only be a charming and attractive feature in the landscape but would be of tremendous value in bringing back native birds and animals."[79]

As in the case of the skyline drive, wilderness protectionists quickly opposed the idea. The Wilderness Society once again led the way, as Robert Sterling Yard, watchdog and frequent critic of the Park Service, weighed in with his criticisms in *Living Wilderness*, the society's chief publication. Harvey Broome also responded when Tennessee's Gov. Gordon Browning gave his support to the project: "I cannot see the wisdom of annihilating the peculiar beauty and unparalleled vegetational ecology of Cades Cove and of reducing it to the somewhat nondescript status of an artificial lake."[80]

That attitudes were changing within the Park Service and the Department of the Interior became evident when Park Service officials announced that neither the lake project nor the development of lodge facilities would go through. In 1935, Arno Cammerer changed his tune and wrote to David Chapman, "The possibility of a lake in Cades Cove is definitely out. We have found no justification for this based upon our standards." Cammerer did, however, reflect his old leanings when he told Chapman that the Park Service might build some swimming pools.[81] By 1938, Cammerer had given up on the idea of hotels within the park, too. In a bit of creative remembering that squared with the new Park Service policy of encouraging tourist development *outside* parks, Cammerer wrote to J. R. Eakin, "I have also always said that we would try to avoid placing hotels in the park, leaving that sort of installation to be supplied outside the boundaries."[82]

Even before the dedication of the Great Smoky Mountains National Park in 1940, important precedents had been set concerning development within the park. To be sure, tight Park Service budgets during the Great Depression and World War II played a role in preventing large-scale development in the park's early years. However, the changing climate of opinion within the National Park Service and the Department of the Interior made Great Smoky Mountains the first national park to emphasize preservation of wilderness over entertaining tourists.

Ironically, this new emphasis often placed the Park Service at odds with the very people who had helped make the park a reality, the regional park boosters. In the battle over development in the park, the boosters' true interest in the project—attracting tourists and their dollars to the region—came to the fore. Nevertheless, the early success of the Smokies in attracting tourists and the rapid growth and development of the gateway communities of Gatlinburg, Tennessee, and Cherokee, North Carolina, quieted their displeasure at the lack of tourist facilities inside the park.

The battle over development of the Great Smoky Mountains National Park saw the introduction of an important new type of regional booster, the wilderness advocate. While David Chapman exemplified the individuals most involved in establishing the park, the Harvey Broomes of the region would set its future course. Although few in number, their dedication to keeping the Smokies largely free of roads, lodges, and overall development created a unique national park environment. They could not have done this, of course, without the help of influential friends such as Harold Ickes and Bob Marshall.

This change in attitudes affected not only the Great Smoky Mountains but also the future of wilderness preservation generally. Perhaps the greatest product of the battles over development in the park was the formation of the Wilderness Society. For the next thirty years, this organization would stand as the most influential voice in wilderness preservation in the United States.

The influence of the Wilderness Society and other wilderness advocates produced great changes in the way that the National Park Service and other federal land management agencies administered land in their jurisdictions. Indeed, after the struggles over development in the Smokies, even Arno

Cammerer, that staunch disciple of Stephen Mather and his policy of placing highest priority on attracting tourists to the national parks, publicly would promote the philosophy of "complete conservation." As Cammerer said, "Our National Parks are wilderness preserves where true natural conditions are to be found. . . . When Americans, in years to come, wish to seek out extensive virgin forests, mountain solitudes, deep canyons, or sparsely vegetated deserts, they will be able to find them in the National Parks."[83]

Conclusion

By most measures, the establishment of the Great Smoky Mountains National Park has been a smashing success. If the park has not always fulfilled the grandest visions trumpeted by the regional boosters who led the way in the park's establishment, it has contributed greatly to the region's economy. Annually, more than eight million visitors (double the number visiting the park's closest rival, Grand Canyon National Park) and over $600 million in consumer spending are generated by the park in East Tennessee and Western North Carolina. Busy roads, crowded overlooks, bumper-to-bumper traffic with car tags from practically every state, full campgrounds and picnic areas, and "no-vacancy" signs in Cherokee, Gatlinburg, Pigeon Forge, and Townsend—all these are fitting monuments to David Chapman, Anne Davis, W. P. Davis, Mark Squires, Charles Webb, and their colleagues, attesting to the realization of their vision of the park as a regional economic powerhouse.[1]

At the same time, the wilderness character of much of the park reflects the success of John D. Rockefeller Jr., Harvey Broome, and the Wilderness Society, who had a different vision of the park as a place of solitude, quiet, and escape from the modern "machine age." All the cut-over areas have been reforested, making it hard to imagine the devastation left behind by the logging operations early in this century. Awe-inspiring old-growth forests of tulip poplar, hemlock, beech, oak, maple, basswood, silverbell, and hickory have been preserved, protecting increasingly rare forest types and crucial wildlife habitats. While fire suppression and the absence of anthropogenic fire have created a forest unlike that extant at any time in the past eight thousand years, they also have allowed less fire-resistant trees to compete more successfully with fire-resistant species, yielding an environment that, in an area known for its botanical diversity, is even more diverse than the surrounding ones.

As a result of the restoration of habitat, wildlife has returned, or been returned, to the area in significant numbers. The park harbors healthy populations of black bear, deer, turkey, and—despite the efforts of the Park Service—wild hogs. Hundreds of species of small mammals, reptiles, amphibians, and birds proliferate. In addition, the Park Service has been able to reintroduce river otters, and peregrine falcons. The smoky madtom, spotfin chub, duskytail darter, and yellowfin madtom, extirpated from the park in a losing competition with brown and rainbow trout introduced to improve sport fishing, have been successfully reintroduced, and the native brook trout are making a comeback in many of the park's streams. Park officials have even talked seriously about reintroducing elk into the park.[2]

Since the passage of the Wilderness Act in 1964, a number of bills have been introduced into Congress to designate large sections of the park as federally protected wilderness. Section 4(c) of the act prohibits the construction of new roads or structures; the use of motorized vehicles, boats, or equipment; and (except in emergencies) the landing of aircraft in wilderness areas. While all of the later bills—the first in 1966, the most recent in 1991—have been defeated, the Park Service has managed the vast majority of the park under the directives of the Wilderness Act since 1966.[3]

While much of the park may reflect our vision of wilderness, and while we would like to believe that God and Nature are now in control of what happens to this land, people still have the greatest impact—directly and indirectly, intentionally and unintentionally—in shaping and molding the landscape of the Great Smoky Mountains. To be sure, in comparison with the years of industrial logging, human impact during the national park era may seem light—something akin to that of the Indians. Nevertheless, the impact of humans since the establishment of the park has been significant. While there is no question that human action will have an impact on the Smokies, what type of impact remains to be determined.

Indeed, human impact in the park since its establishment suggests some basic paradoxes inherent in modern-day attempts to protect and preserve the places we call wilderness. One major paradox involves our desire to "see and fondle" wilderness. Aldo Leopold, one of the founders of the Wilderness Society, once observed: "All conservation of wildness is self-defeating, for to cherish we must see and fondle, and when enough have seen and fondled, there is no wildness left to cherish."[4] This human desire to "see and fondle," and the desire of regional boosters to make it easy for tourists to do so, has caused the park and its managers a good deal of consternation in recent years.

One of the best examples of a "see and fondle" issue in the park is road building. Since the dedication of the park, hardly a year has gone by without local boosters' introducing a new road project or reviving an old one. The most persistent of these ventures, the so-called "North Shore Road," had its genesis in 1943, when the National Park Service and the Tennessee Valley Authority (TVA) signed an agreement with Swain County, North Carolina, and the State of North Carolina. The federal government promised to build a thirty-seven-mile road to replace North Carolina Highway 228, which was flooded when Fontana Lake was created as TVA dammed the Little Tennessee River. The road, connecting Bryson City and Fontana Dam, was to be built in exchange for forty-four thousand acres of land between the park boundary and Fontana.[5]

For years the project lay in limbo, until, under pressure from the State of North Carolina and officials in Swain County, the Park Service finally began constructing the road in 1960. It opened a 2.5-mile section in

Organizers and participants in the "Save Our Smokies" Hike on October 23, 1966. In foreground, left to right: Stanley Murray, chairman, Appalachian Trial Conference; Ernest Dickerman, Great Smoky Mountains Hiking Club; Harvey Broome, president, Wilderness Society. Photo courtesy of Great Smoky Mountains National Park.

August 1963, completed an additional 2.1 miles in July 1963, and built one mile, complete with a 1,200-foot tunnel, in 1970.[6]

In 1965, in the midst of the project, National Park Service officials proposed a new idea. Instead of the North Shore Road, the Park Service would build a 34.7-mile transmountain highway that would climb the upper reaches of Hazel Creek, cross the divide at Buckeye Gap, and descend Miry Ridge, connecting Bryson City with Townsend, Tennessee. The people of Swain County rejoiced at the prospect of becoming a major park entrance, anticipating the same sort of tourist boom as the gateway communities of Gatlinburg, Tennessee, and Cherokee, North Carolina, on Highway 441, had experienced.[7]

Despite the support of political leaders in both Tennessee and North Carolina and the sanction of George Hartzog, director of the National Park Service, the opposition of Harvey Broome and the Wilderness Society once again helped kill a road-building project in the Smokies. The attempt to build the road came at a time when the American public and politicians in Washington, D.C., were beginning to pay attention to the concerns of environmentalists. Most important, opponents of the road got the ear of Secretary of the Interior Stewart Udall. The year before he became secretary, Udall had declared, "The one overriding principle of the conservation movement is that no work of man (save the bare minimum of roads, trails, and necessary public facilities in access areas) should intrude into the wonder places of the National Park System."[8]

In the Buckeye Gap area of the park, site of the proposed road, Broome discovered and documented such a wonder place, the southernmost stands of red spruce in North America. Armed with this information, Broome mobilized the local community and wilderness proponents nationwide to voice their opposition to the road. On 23 October 1966, 576 individuals, including eighty-one-year-old Rev. Rufus Morgan, signed in at Clingman's Dome to participate in a "Save-Our-Smokies" hike organized by Broome. Much to the dismay of Swain County residents and many in Blount County, Tennessee, Secretary Udall announced on 10 December 1967, that he would not approve construction of the transmountain road.[9]

The North Shore Road issue remains far from dead, however, and is resurrected on regular occasions. In the 1980s, a group known as the North Shore Cemetery Association intensified pressure on the Park Service to honor the 1943 commitment, arguing that construction of the road was necessary to give its members proper access to family and community cemeteries on the north shore. The group found its champion in U.S. Sen. Jesse Helms, a Republican of North Carolina. On several occasions, Helms has effectively blocked legislation that would have designated land in the park, including the north shore area, as federally protected wilderness. Such legislation would have prevented any additional road construction in the area. Although the legislation included an offer to pay Swain County up to $16 million to give up its claim to the road, the county has refused. Finding a new ally in Western North Carolina's Republican U.S. Rep. Charles Taylor, Helms has introduced several bills calling for the cash settlement plus construction of the road, even if that is only a jeep road.[10]

The bitterness of Swain County residents and their desire to get something out of the Park Service are understandable. In many ways, the establishment of the park proved more detrimental than beneficial to Swain and Haywood counties in North Carolina, and to Cocke County in Tennessee. These counties lost large areas of taxable land and were bypassed by much of the tourist traffic. Swain County alone lost 169,711 acres from its tax rolls—property valued for tax purposes at $4,242,819 when the park was established.[11] Today, among TVA, the Forest Service, and the National Park Service, over 80 percent of the land in Swain County is owned and managed by the federal government, which pays no taxes. The bitterness is compounded by the fact that this county consistently has one of the highest unemployment rates in North Carolina.

The Park Service now is determined to resist construction of the road, for both environmental and economic reasons. Environmental concerns center on the fact that road construction could expose acidic Anakeesta rock found in the north shore area. The Park Service fears that exposure of this rock would allow acid and heavy metals to leach into area streams, killing aquatic life. The agency also is concerned about the negative impact on wildlife, particularly bears, whose habitat would be divided and reduced by the road. Moreover, the cost of building such a road has become increasingly prohibitive, especially given Park Service budget cutbacks in recent years. In 1992, the Park Service estimated the cost of completing the road at $125 million.[12]

Currently, the parties are at a standoff, with neither the Park Service nor supporters of the road, such as the North Shore Cemetery Association, Citizens Against Wilderness in Western North Carolina, and Senator Helms, willing to budge on the issue. Senator Helms's latest bill died in committee, and for now the 5.6-mile road remains, in the words of Swain County residents, the "road to nowhere."

In the early 1970s, the Park Service launched another major road-building initiative, a road leading into the Cataloochee area from the Fines Creek interchange on U.S. Interstate Highway 40. The Park Service planned to turn Cataloochee into an area of concentrated development, similar to Cades Cove, complete with a 400-site picnic area, 600-site campground, 2,000-seat amphitheater, and 13.5-mile loop road. This time, much of the opposition came from within the affected county, Haywood County, North Carolina. A local group known as the Committee to Save Cataloochee Valley threatened legal action if the Park Service moved forward with its plans.[13] The combination of widespread opposition and declining park budgets eventually doomed the project, and in 1982 the Park Service deleted the road and the proposed development of Cataloochee from its long-range plan for the Smokies.[14]

The defeat of these road proposals and the increasing number of visitors have produced their own problems, as the few roads in the park are required to bear an increasingly heavy load of traffic. Because the Park Service built no lodges or hotels, only campgrounds, most of the ever more numerous visitors must be housed outside the park boundaries. Although lack of development within the park has spared the Smokies many of the concessionaire problems that have plagued the western parks, the lack of roads in the park has dictated tourist development in the surrounding areas. Gatlinburg, Tennessee, and the Cherokee Indian Reservation in North Carolina stand as "gateway communities" on Highway 441 (the one major highway that crosses the park). These areas have experienced explosive, generally uncontrolled growth as a result of the limitation on building roads and accommodations within the park. Consequently, park entrances have become increasingly congested, a condition that has been intensified by the construction of Dollywood, the most popular theme park in Tennessee; the building of countless outlet malls and country music facilities in Pigeon Forge; the opening of a 175,000-square-foot gambling casino on the Cherokee Indian Reservation; and the growth and development of Townsend, Tennessee.[15]

The thousands of tourist cars that enter the park daily from and through these gateway communities can create major traffic problems. As cars pour into the park, they can produce gridlock on the park's roads at peak times. During the summer months, especially on weekends, Highway 441 can seem more like Los Angeles at rush hour than a scenic drive through a national park. One of the most bizarre park experiences is beholding the beauties of nature on a weekend evening as you choke on exhaust fumes in bumper-to-bumper traffic on the Cades Cove loop road.[16]

Demands that the roads be kept open longer in the winter, that old roads be widened, and that new ones be built have increased in recent years. In the fall of 1996, the Cherokee Council, led by Chief Joyce Dugan, called upon the National Park Service to fire Park Superintendent Karen Wade. The tribe was angry because the Park Service had closed Highway 441 for too many days during the previous winter, limiting access to the tribe's gambling casino. In the fall of 1997, the tribe and Harrah's Casinos opened a new 175,000-square-foot facility, a move that should increase demands to convert Highway 441, a scenic highway designed to allow people access to nature in a leisurely manner, into a high-speed artery to transport gamblers to Cherokee from Pigeon Forge and Gatlinburg.

Although the vast majority of park visitors rarely ventures off the paved roads in the park, trail development and trail use remain major "see and fondle" issues. While much of the backcountry remains relatively quiet, several of the park's trails are hiked by hundreds and even thousands in a given summer. Traffic is heavy on the Alum Cave, Chimneys, Laurel Falls, Rainbow Falls, and Trillium Gap trails and the Appalachian Trail from Newfound Gap to Charlie's Bunion. This traffic, and budget shortfalls that have assigned trail maintenance a low priority, leave many of these trails muddy, heavily eroded, strewn with rocks, and covered with roots.[17]

The presence of more than eighty thousand horses annually on 517 of the park's 802 miles of trails only compounds these problems. When the park was established, the National Park Service was still under the influence of Stephen Mather, who encouraged the parks to cater to elites. With this in mind, the vast majority of trails in the park were opened to horses. As a result, low-lying trails become muddy morasses due to the constant churning of horses' hooves, while many of the higher, drier trails contain long sections of eroded ruts, in some areas waist-deep or higher. Many park visitors also complain about the smell and mess, not to mention the environmental impact, of horse manure and urine on the trails and in the streams. The popularity of horseback riding in the park and the wealth and influence of most horse owners have prevented the Park Service from limiting the number of trails available for horseback riding. In 1977, the Park Service attempted to close all of the Appalachian Trail

Three summer days in the eastern end of the park in the 1990s. Sulfate-induced haze regularly obscures views in the Smokies. Photo courtesy of Great Smoky Mountains National Park.

in the park to horse traffic, a move that virtually would have eliminated horses from the high-elevation areas of the park. The horse lobby, however, effectively blocked this move and settled for banning horse traffic on 50 percent of the trail, up from the previous 35 percent.[18]

As great an impact as "seeing and fondling" by millions of visitors have had on the park, the inability of park boundaries to truly protect the park's flora and fauna poses a relatively new but portentous paradox. Initially, park boundaries were thought to segregate, preserve, and protect the land in the park. These boundaries have come to mean less and less, however, as the surrounding world closes in on the park. While the Park Service has convinced most human beings that park boundaries have meaning and that their behavior should be different and restricted inside the park, they have not been so successful with the animals, plants, air, and water inside and outside of the park. These nonhuman elements do not recognize the boundary.

Perhaps the greatest threat to the park comes from the air. The natural haze that gives the Smokies its name traps and holds air pollution that travels over the mountains from smokestacks in Tennessee, Kentucky, Ohio, and as far away as the Great Lakes region. This haze gives the park "some of the highest exposures of air pollutants compared to any other national park in the United States." Over the years, visibility in the park has been reduced dramatically. A Park Service report recently asserted: "Visitors come to GRSM expecting clear sweeping vistas, but instead frequently have to look through a thick, white haze shrouding the scenic vistas." Indeed, studies reveal that visibility in the park was reduced 60 percent from 1948 to 1982, with an 80-percent reduction during the peak visitation period in the summer months. While visitors once could expect a visual range of 70 to 125 miles from the high peaks of the Smokies, they now have a summer view that averages only 12 miles, and in stagnant weather extends only 2 miles. The chief culprits in the reduction of visibility are sulfate particles from sulfur dioxide produced by burning coal. Ironically, another federal agency, TVA, in its electrical generating plants, burns most of the coal in the immediate vicinity.[19]

Park air in the summer also contains high levels of ozone; indeed, the air in this "wilderness" can be more damaging to breathe than the air in Los Angeles. On several occasions, ozone levels in the park have exceeded the national ambient air quality standard for safe levels of ozone. In May 1994, when ozone levels exceeded national standards for 65 hours, park employees and visitors complained of "shortness of breath, wheezing, headaches, tiredness, and scratchy eyes, nose, and throat." High ozone levels are particularly dangerous for the elderly; those with asthma, emphysema, and chronic bronchitis; and those participating in strenuous physical activity, such as hiking or backpacking. As a result of this problem, the National Park Service instituted an "Air Quality Advisory Program" in 1996, to post warning signs throughout the park when ozone levels reach or exceed dangerous levels.[20]

Air pollution has been credited with damage to plant and animal life in the Smokies as well. Ozone-sensitive plants, such as black cherry, yellow poplar, blackberry, and milkweed, have shown reduced growth and fruit productivity and dead patches on their leaves, making them less efficient at photosynthesis. Similar damage to red spruce, often attributed to acid rain, has been noted, although this species has not experienced higher-than-expected mortality. Acid rain also has been credited with causing high acidity in higher-elevation streams, resulting in damage to aquatic life, particularly salamanders and brook trout.[21]

The segregation of the Smokies as a national park has not prevented other alterations of the landscape of the mountains. Exotic pests and diseases inadvertently have been introduced into the park by human action. As in the chestnut blight of seventy years ago, the forests of the Smokies once again are undergoing dramatic change. The destruction of the Fraser fir, the signature tree of the high ridges of the Smokies, stands as the most noticeable of these. Since 1963, a tiny insect, the balsam wooly adelgid, brought from Europe to the United States around 1900, has killed almost all of the mature Fraser fir trees in the park. The Park Service periodically has sprayed small areas of accessible Fraser firs, especially along the Clingman's Dome road, with a fatty acid which prevents the infestation and maintains a small remnant population of mature trees. Even in areas of heavy infestation, the Fraser firs have regenerated themselves and generally can live twenty to thirty years before they succumb to the adelgid, thus insuring that the tree will remain part of the landscape of the Smokies, although never in an old-growth state. However, on Clingman's Dome, Mount Le Conte, Mount Guyot, and other high peaks and ridges of the park, only the ghostly white trunks of dead Fraser fir mark the grave of a formerly magnificent old-growth forest.[22]

Other exotic pests and diseases have caused extensive damage or pose potential threats as well. Stands of flowering dogwood have been decimated by the dogwood anthracnose fungus, while stem canker has attacked the butternuts, and European sawfly has wiped out much of the

Fraser firs on Clingman's Dome were killed by the balsam wooly adelgid.
Photo courtesy of Great Smoky Mountains National Park.

mountain ash. New perils lurk on the horizon, as hemlock wooly adelgid
and the gypsy moth, which already have ravaged old-growth stands of
hemlock and oak in Shenandoah National Park, rapidly make their way
southward. In many of these cases, some scientists argue, the air pollution in the park has exacerbated the situation by leaving the trees in a
weakened and vulnerable condition.[23]

To be sure, the story of the Great Smoky Mountains remains the story
of the relationship between a people and the land, as human action has
remained the chief shaping mechanism under the stewardship of the
National Park Service. Indeed, if the story of the establishment of the
Great Smoky Mountains National Park tells us anything, it is that, while
we may try to leave the land alone, try to create an illusion of wilderness,
and try to eliminate evidence of human action, we cannot. The inescap-
able conclusion we must reach when looking at the history of both the
Great Smoky Mountains and its national park is that we are going to have
an impact on this environment. The great question that looms, then, is:
what will that impact be?

On a July morning in 1998, I traveled to one of my favorite spots in
the Smokies, the Cataloochee Valley, to ponder this question of human
impact and to think about the people of this region and their relationship to the Smokies. Perhaps no place in the park speaks to me so eloquently of the people who have shaped and continue to shape these mountains. I think first of the original inhabitants of this valley. Indeed, to reach
this spot one travels over a road that follows an Indian trail carved out
hundreds, if not thousands, of years ago. The name Cataloochee itself is
the Anglicization of a Cherokee name. Look closely under the forest cover
and along the streams, and you can still find evidence of their life in this
valley in stone tools and pottery scattered around.

While the Indian presence is rather subtle, the legacy of the early white
pioneers who settled in the valley remains much in evidence. The homes of
the Woodys and Caldwells still stand, along with a few barns, the old school,
and the Palmer Chapel Methodist Church. Further evidence of these people's
lives can be found on side trails, in cemeteries scattered on nearby ridges and
in meticulously constructed, moss-covered stone walls that stand in many
adjacent areas. Many of the fields remain cleared by the Park Service, to
maintain the feeling of life in the valley seventy years ago. Come to
Cataloochee on the right summer weekend, and you may even encounter
some of the people who actually lived in "Big Catalooch," Caldwell Fork, or

Little Cataloochee. They still come back to reminisce about their life and impact in this place, and they still feel the pain of removal.

In much of the forest around the Cataloochee Valley, you also can see at least some evidence of the logging era. Most of the trees are relatively young, reflecting the activities of the Suncrest Lumber Company, Parsons Pulp and Lumber Company, and the Ravensford Lumber Company. Many of the trails in the area, particularly the Palmer Creek and Rough Fork trails, follow old railroad grades. Here occasionally one can spot coal, cinders, pieces of cable, and railroad spikes—relics of this destructive period.

While I often think about the impact that these individuals had on the land, I think most often of those individuals who helped establish the park and their impact on the Cataloochee Valley. Although David Chapman and his friends would be disappointed that the development plans of the 1970s did not go through (after all, they were "good roads" advocates), they would take heart at seeing the hundreds of people who brave the rough road and flock into the valley. I am sure they would be especially pleased to view, with me, cars sporting license tags from Florida, Indiana, Louisiana, Wisconsin, and even California, and to know that these visitors are scattering their "golden shekels" throughout the region.

The rough road into Cataloochee and the small campground speak to me of the legacy of Harvey Broome and other wilderness advocates who helped set important precedents for few roads and little development in the park. Indeed, even on busy weekends in Cataloochee, one can easily take a trail out of the valley, sit amid giant tulip poplars and hemlocks, and see or hear no other human being for hours. On this day, I'm reminded of that legacy as I look up from my reverie and find myself almost face-to-face with a young doe. Sitting in the old-growth forest reminds me of another Smokies legacy and another paradox in the Smokies story—the impact of John D. Rockefeller Jr., that lover of old-growth forests. His family has been responsible for some of the worst industrial pollution in our nation's history, but, without his help, the Smokies and many other national parks would not exist.

To me, the Cataloochee Valley and countless other "wonder places" in the Smokies stand as living monuments to the best of human action—to the heroic efforts of regional boosters like David Chapman, Ann Davis, W. P. Davis, Horace Kephart, Mark Squires, and Charles Webb; to the generosity of John D. Rockefeller Jr.; to those in the federal government like Arno Cammerer and Harold Ickes, who dearly loved the national parks; and to

Harvey Broome and other wilderness advocates, whose new vision helped turn the Smokies into something unique and wonderful. I can't help feeling gratitude for the battles they fought and the sacrifices they made to set aside this park that has brought such joy to me and my family.

Unfortunately, a trip into Cataloochee also brings me face to face with more recent evidence of human activity for which I am not so grateful. This July morning, the view from my favorite lookout at the head of the valley is obscured by a haze caused by industrial pollutants. I can barely make out the contours of nearby Mount Sterling. I know, however, that if I could see the peaks and ridges of the surrounding mountains clearly, I would see other evidence of human action in the dead and dying Fraser firs that line the ridgetops. As I hike into the backcountry along the Caldwell Fork trail, I see signs of too much "seeing and fondling" that has plagued this park. The trail, covered with horse manure and soaked with horse urine, alternates between rough, rocky sections and impassable, muddy quagmires. Although I can't see the effects of the manure, urine, and mud on the stream that follows the trail and gives it its name, I know that it cannot be positive. Indeed, after I follow the trail for a few miles, the words "environmental disaster" come to mind.

These images remind us that, just as people have the power to set aside places as wonderful as the Cataloochee Valley and the Great Smoky Mountains National Park, they also have the power to destroy it. Horace Kephart argued in a magazine article that, once established, the Great Smoky Mountains National Park would become "a joy and wonder to our people for all time."[24] To be sure, the Smokies have become a "joy and wonder" for millions of people in Western North Carolina, in East Tennessee, and around the world. Yet one must be concerned about the possibility that the Smokies may not fulfill that role "for all time." Indeed, one can't help wondering—as we praise the foresight, commitment, and wisdom of the David Chapmans, Horace Kepharts, and Harvey Broomes who helped make this park a reality—what qualities future generations will attribute to the current generation of Western North Carolinians and East Tennesseans when they read the landscape of the Great Smoky Mountains.

Notes

Introduction

1. Michael Frome, *Strangers in High Places* (Garden City, N.Y.: Doubleday, 1966), 11.

2. Rose Houk, *A Natural History Guide: Great Smoky Mountains National Park* (Boston: Houghton Mifflin Company, 1993).

3. Quentin R. Bass, "Prehistoric Settlement and Subsistence Patterns in the Great Smoky Mountains," May 1977, box—Archeology I, folder—Archeology I-7, file no. 108, GSMNP Archives.

4. William Cronon, "The Trouble with Wilderness; or, Getting Back to the Wrong Nature," in *Uncommon Ground: Toward Reinventing Nature,* ed. William Cronon (New York: Norton, 1995), 69–70.

5. The phrase "wonderment of mountains" comes from a book on the Smokies by Carson Brewer, *A Wonderment of Mountains* (Knoxville: Tenpenny Press, 1981).

Chapter 1

1. William Cronon and Richard White, "Indians in the Land," *American Heritage* 37, no. 5 (Aug.-Sept. 1986): 20.

2. Stephen Fox, *John Muir and His Legacy: The American Conservation Movement* (Boston: Little, Brown, 1981), 350.

3. Bass, "Prehistoric Settlement," 108.

4. Bennie Keel, *Cherokee Archaeology: A Study of the Appalachian Summit* (Knoxville: Univ. of Tennessee Press, 1976), 9–10, 206.

5. William Cronon, *Changes in the Land: Indians, Colonists, and the Ecology of New England* (New York: Hill and Wang, 1983), 37–40.

6. Keel, *Cherokee Archaeology,* 226.

7. Charles Faulkner, "First Interim Report on the Archeological Survey of Great Smoky Mountains National Park," box—Archeology I, folder—Archeology I-3, GSMNP Archives.

8. Quentin Bass, "Second Interim Report on the Archeological Survey of Great Smoky Mountains National Park," box—Archeology I, folder—Archeology I-3, file no. 91, GSMNP Archives; and Charles Hudson, *Southeastern Indians* (Knoxville: Univ. of Tennessee Press, 1976), 269.

9. James Mooney, *Myths of the Cherokee and Sacred Formulas of the Cherokees* (rpt. Nashville: Charles Elder Bookseller, 1972), 319–22.

10. Ibid., 325–27.

11. Timothy Silver, *A New Face on the Countryside: Indians, Colonists, and Slaves in South Atlantic Forests, 1500–1800* (Cambridge, England: Cambridge Univ. Press, 1990), 37; Keel, *Cherokee Archaeology,* 206.

12. Bass, "Second Interim Report," 72–80.

13. Silver, *New Face,* 37.

14. Hudson, *Southeastern Indians,* 291.

15. Ibid., 292–94.

16. Cronon and White, "Indians in the Land," 21.

17. Silver, *New Face*, 40–41 and 65–66.

18. Keel, *Cherokee Archeology*, 216.

19. Stephen Pyne, Patricia Andrews, and Richard Laven, *Introduction to Wildland Fire*, 2d ed. (New York: John Wiley and Sons, 1996), 236.

20. Silver, *New Face*, 50.

21. Indians' use of fire as a way of manipulating their environment has drawn belated but increased attention in recent years. Source material for this section comes from Pyne, Andrews, and Laven, *Introduction to Wildland Fire*, 235–40; Cronon, *Changes in the Land*, 48–51; Silver, *New Face*, 59–65; Gary Goodwin, *The Cherokees in Transition: A Study of Changing Culture and Environment Prior to 1775* (Chicago: Dept. of Geography, Univ. of Chicago, 1977), 63–65; Michael Williams, *Americans and Their Forests: A Historical Geography* (Cambridge, England: Cambridge Univ. Press, 1989), 33–49.

22. Goodwin, *Cherokees in Transition*, 64

23. Mooney, *Myths of the Cherokee*, 405–6.

24. Garrett A. Smathers, "The Anthropic Factor in Southern Appalachian Bald Formation," in *Status and Management of Southern Appalachian Mountain Balds*, ed. Richard Sanders (proceedings of a workshop sponsored by the Southern Appalachian Research/Resource Management Cooperative [Cullowhee, N.C.: Western Carolina Univ., 1981]), 31–32.

25. Bass, "Second Interim Report," 89–90.

26. This hypothesis is one that I arrived at through reading and interpreting the literature on bald formation, particularly Mary Lindsay, "History of the Grassy Balds of the Great Smoky Mountains National Park," vertical file, GSMNP Library; Sanders, ed., *Status and Management of Southern Appalachian Balds;* and the archeological reports on the Smokies by Quentin Bass, C. R. McCollough, and Charles Faulkner, housed in the GSMNP Archives.

27. Williams, *Americans and Their Forests*, 49.

28. Charles Hudson, *The Forgotten Centuries: Indians and Europeans in the American South* (Athens: Univ. of Georgia Press, 1994).

29. William Bartram, *Travels Through North and South Carolina, Georgia, East and West Florida* (Philadelphia: James and Johnson, 1791; rpt. Savannah, Ga.: Beehive Press, 1973), 357–62.

30. Cronon, *Changes in the Land*, 51.

31. Bartram, *Travels*, 357–62.

32. Grace Steele Woodward, *The Cherokees* (Norman: Univ. of Oklahoma Press, 1963), 57–138; John R. Finger, *The Eastern Band of the Cherokees, 1819–1900* (Knoxville: Univ. of Tennessee Press, 1984), 3–19.

33. Finger, *Eastern Band*, 10–11.

34. Frome, *Strangers*, 68–69.

35. Durwood Dunn, *Cades Cove: The Life and Death of a Southern Appalachian Community, 1818–1937* (Knoxville: Univ. of Tennessee Press, 1988), 1–21.

36. W. Clark Medford, *The Early History of Haywood County* (Asheville, N.C.: Miller Printing Co., 1961), 81–82.

37. Jerry Wear, Mary Alice Teague, and Lynn Alexander, *Lost Communities of Sevier County, Tennessee: Greenbriar* (Sevierville, Tenn.: Sevier County Heritage Committee, 1985); Jerry Wear, Mary Alice Teague, and Lynn Alexander, *Lost Communities of Sevier County, Tennessee: Sugarlands* (Sevierville, Tenn.: Sevier County Heritage Committee, 1985); Edward Hunt, "Little Greenbriar Cove," paper in vertical file, GSMNP Library; Hazel Jenkins, coordinator, *The Heritage of Swain County, North Carolina* (Winston-Salem, N.C.: Hunter Publishing Co., 1988), 12 and 18.

38. Tyler Blethen and Curtis Wood, *From Ulster to Carolina: The Migration of the Scotch-Irish to Southwestern North Carolina* (Cullowhee, N.C.: Western Carolina Univ. Mountain Heritage Center, 1983).

39. Florence Cope Bush, *Dorie: Woman of the Mountains* (Knoxville: Univ. of Tennessee Press, 1992), 24.

40. Dunn, *Cades Cove,* 30.

41. For general descriptions of upland grazing in the South and the connection between Scotch-Irish culture and land use practices, see Blethen and Wood, *From Ulster to Carolina,* 36–37; Forrest McDonald and Grady McWhiney, "The South from Self-Sufficiency to Peonage," *American Historical Review* 85, no. 5 (Dec. 1980): 1095–1118; and Grady McWhiney, *Cracker Culture: Celtic Ways in the Old South* (Tuscaloosa: Univ. of Alabama Press, 1988), 51–79. On upland grazing in the Smokies, see Dunn, *Cades Cove,* 32–34 and 76–77; Lindsay, "History of the Grassy Balds"; and Medford, *Early History,* 85–86.

42. Arnold Guyot, "Notes on the Geography of the Mountain District of Western North Carolina," *North Carolina Historical Review* 15 (1938): 281.

43. Ibid.

44. Dunn, *Cades Cove,* 44.

45. Lindsay, "History of the Grassy Balds," 14–15.

46. E. Stanley Godbold Jr. and Mattie U. Russell, *Confederate Colonel and Cherokee Chief: The Life of William Holland Thomas* (Knoxville: Univ. of Tennessee Press, 1990), 29–30.

47. Lindsay, "The History of the Grassy Balds," 16–17. A fictionalized yet highly accurate account of the herder experience on the mountain balds of the Smokies can be found in Charles Frazier, *Cold Mountain* (New York: Atlantic Monthly Press, 1997), 13–15.

48. McWhiney, *Cracker Culture,* 64–69.

49. Lindsay, "History of the Grassy Balds," 14–17.

50. Ibid., 8.

51. Ibid., 7–21.

52. Silver, *New Face,* 179–80.

53. Mark Edward Harmon, "The Influence of Fire and Site Factors on Vegetation Pattern and Process: A Case Study of the Western Portion of Great Smoky Mountains National Park" (Master's. thesis, Univ. of Tennessee, 1980), 121.

54. Pyne, Andrews, and Laven, *Introduction to Wildland Fire,* 280.

55. Dunn, *Cades Cove,* 30; and *Friends' Weekly Intelligencer* 6 (1849), copy found in William Holland Thomas Papers, folder 73, WCUSC.

56. Alicia V. Linzey and Donald W. Linzey, *Mammals of the Great Smoky Mountains National Park* (Knoxville: Univ. of Tennessee Press, 1971), 53.

57. Ibid., 69.

58. Jeff Rennicke, *Black Bear: Spirit of the Smokies* (Gatlinburg, Tenn.: Great Smoky Mountains Natural History Association, 1991).

59. Silver, *New Face*, 91–94.

60. Mattie Russell, "William Holland Thomas, White Chief of the North Carolina Cherokee" (Ph.D. diss., Duke Univ., 1956), 152–91; and William Holland Thomas Papers, folders 73, 74, and 78, WCUSC.

61. Silver, *New Face*, 83–84.

62. Russell, "William Holland Thomas," 189–91; Dunn, *Cades Cove*, 30–32.

63. Russell, "William Holland Thomas," 189–91.

64. Dunn, *Cades Cove*, 82.

65. *Knoxville Journal*, 8 Mar. 1988.

66. Gary C. Jenkins, "The Mining of Alum Cave," paper in file titled "Geology—Copper Deposits + Mining and Prospecting," vertical file, GSMNP Library.

67. Robert D. O'Brien, "Evaluation of the Fontana Mine–Great Smoky Mountains National Park, Tennessee and North Carolina"; C. H. Epenshade, M. H. Stantz, and E. A. Brown, "Preliminary Report: Hazel Creek Mine, Swain County, N.C., April–June, 1943"; "Copper Deposits in Swain County"; John Parris, articles on the Everett Mine, *Asheville Citizen-Times*, 25 and 30 June 1989; all in file titled "Geology," vertical file, GSMNP Library.

68. Dunn, *Cades Cove*, 83–85.

69. Medford, *Early History*, 99–101.

70. Frome, *Strangers*, 97.

71. Guyot, "Notes on Geography," 264–65, 284.

72. Finger, *Eastern Band*, 20–29.

73. Dunn, *Cades Cove*, 123–41.

74. Finger, *Eastern Band*, 87–88.

75. Medford, *Early History*, 150–51. Frazier, *Cold Mountain*, fictionalizes this incident.

76. Kephart, *Our Southern Highlanders* (New York: Outing Publishing Co., 1913; rpt. Knoxville: Univ. of Tennessee Press, 1976), 122–23.

77. William H. Thomas Papers, folders 73 and 74, WCUSC.

78. Dunn, *Cades Cove*, 77–78.

79. Wilbur R. Miller, *Revenuers and Moonshiners: Enforcing Federal Liquor Law in the Mountain South, 1865–1900* (Chapel Hill: Univ. of North Carolina Press, 1991), 40–60; Kephart, *Our Southern Highlanders*, 122–37; Dunn, *Cades Cove*, 77–78 and 232–35.

80. Kephart, *Our Southern Highlanders*, 138.

81. Dunn, *Cades Cove*, 199.

82. The problems of population growth in the Southern Appalachian region in the late 19th and early 20th centuries have received a great deal of attention recently. Two of the best sources on this subject are: Crandall A. Shifflett, *Coal Towns: Life, Work, and Culture in Company Towns of Southern Appalachia, 1880–*

1960 (Knoxville: Univ. of Tennessee Press, 1991); and Dwight Billings and Kathleen Blee, "Agriculture and Poverty in the Kentucky Mountains: Beech Creek, 1850–1910," in *Appalachia in the Making: The Mountain South in the Nineteenth Century*, ed. Mary Beth Pudup, Dwight Billings, and Altina Waller, 233–69 (Chapel Hill: Univ. of North Carolina Press, 1995).

83. Kephart, *Our Southern Highlanders*, 36.

84. There is an extensive literature on this process, but one of the best sources, especially regarding the Smokies, is Bush, *Dorie.*

85. Kephart, *Our Southern Highlanders*, 68–69.

86. Dunn, *Cades Cove*, 81.

87. Robert S. Lambert, "Logging in the Great Smoky Mountains: A Report to the Superintendent—October 1, 1958," copy in GSMNP Library.

88. Ibid.

89. A board foot equals 12 x 12 x 1 inches.

90. Lambert, "Logging in the Great Smokies," 25–28.

91. Ibid., 10–60. Bush, *Dorie,* gives an excellent account of life in the timber camps of the Smokies.

92. Lambert, "Logging in the Great Smokies," 7–12.

93. Ibid., 17–18.

94. Ibid., 20–23.

95. Ibid.

96. Ibid.

97. Ibid., 34–35.

98. Arthur Stupka, *Trees, Shrubs, and Woody Vines of Great Smoky Mountains National Park* (Knoxville: Univ. of Tennessee Press, 1964), 44–46.

99. Ibid.; Dunn, *Cades Cove,* 25–26.

100. Map of areas still containing old-growth forests, in GSMNP Archives; Lambert, "Logging in the Great Smokies."

101. Charles Lanman, *Letters from the Allegheny Mountains* (New York: Geo. P. Putnam, 1849), 87.

102. Dunn, *Cades Cove,* 84 and 159–60.

103. Advertising brochure for Little River Railroad, in vertical file, GSMNP Library. The railroad bed of the Little River Railroad was converted into the Little River Road that now runs through the park.

104. John Ogden Morrell, "A Brief History of the Appalachian Club and Wonderland Club Within the Great Smoky Mountains National Park," in John Ogden Morrell Papers, GSMNP Archives.

105. Ed Trout, *Gatlinburg: Cinderella City* (Sevierville, Tenn.: Griffin Graphics, 1984), 81; Dunn, *Cades Cove,* 243.

Chapter 2

1. Alfred Runte, "Promoting Wonderland: Western Railroads and the Evolution of National Park Advertising," *Journal of the West* 31 (1992): 48.

2. U.S. Dept. of the Interior, NPS, *Report of the Director of the NPS to the Secretary of the Interior for the Fiscal Year Ended June 30, 1923, and the Travel Season, 1923* (Washington, D.C.: Government Printing Office, 1923), 5.

3. Alfred Runte, *National Parks: The American Experience* (Lincoln: Univ. of Nebraska Press, 1987), 6–7.

4. Ibid., 19–21, 37–38, 112.

5. Ibid., 28–30.

6. Ibid., 45.

7. Ibid., 42–47.

8. Henry O. Marcy, "The Climatic Treatment of Disease: Western North Carolina as a Health Resort," *Journal of the American Medical Association* 5 (1885): 707.

9. Runte, *National Parks*, 26.

10. George W. McCoy, *A Brief History of the Great Smoky Mountains National Park Movement in North Carolina* (Asheville: Inland Press, 1940), 6.

11. Ibid., 6–8.

12. Ibid., 58–63.

13. Samuel P. Hays, *Conservation and the Gospel of Efficiency* (Cambridge, Mass.: Harvard Univ. Press, 1959).

14. Fox, *John Muir*, 129.

15 Runte, *National Parks*, 69.

16. Ibid., 76–77.

17. Charles Dennis Smith, "The Appalachian National Park Movement, 1885–1901," *North Carolina Historical Review* 37 (1960): 46.

18. Ibid., 13–14.

19. Ibid., 15.

20. McCoy, *Brief History*, 23–24.

21. Ibid.

22. Ibid.

23. Ibid., 30; Charles Smith, "Appalachian National Park Movement," 54–65.

24. Frome, *Strangers*, 177–78.

25. Fox, *John Muir*, 111 and 139–47; Ernest Morrison, *J. Horace McFarland: A Thorn for Beauty* (Harrisburg: Pennsylvania Historical and Museum Commission, 1995), 153–72.

26. Morrison, *J. Horace McFarland*, 156.

27. Fox, *John Muir*, 144.

28. Ibid., 77–81.

29. Morrison, *J. Horace McFarland*, 166.

30. Ibid., 166–68.

31. Ibid., 173.

32. Runte, *National Parks*, 71–72, 97–98.

33. Ibid.; Morrison, *J. Horace McFarland*, 173–74.

34. Fox, *John Muir*, 132.

35. Morrison, *J. Horace McFarland*, 188.

36. Ibid., 177 and 184.

37. Runte, *National Parks,* 90.

38. Ibid., 92.

39. Morrison, *J. Horace McFarland,* 187.

40. Donald Swain, "The Passage of the National Park Service Act of 1916," *Wisconsin Magazine of History* 50 (1966): 4–17.

41. Ibid., 17.

42. Ibid., 4–17.

43. Runte, *National Parks,* 103.

44. Ibid., 103.

45. Ibid., 109–10.

46. Runte, "Promoting Wonderland," 48.

47. Runte, *National Parks,* 104.

48. Swain, "Passage of the NPS Act," 17.

49. U.S. Dept. of the Interior, NPS, *Report of Director of NPS, 1923,* 5.

50. Runte, *National Parks,* 105.

51. V. O. Key, *Southern Politics in State and Nation* (New York: Alfred A. Knopf, 1949; rpt. Knoxville: Univ. of Tennessee Press, 1984), 345.

52. Ibid., 349–55 and 370–73.

53. U.S. Congress, House Committee on the Judiciary, *Hearing on House Resolution 208* (60th Cong., 2d sess.), 33.

54. U.S. Congress, House Committee on Agriculture, *Hearings Before the Committee on Agriculture on Bills Having for Their Object the Acquisition of Forest and Other Lands for the Protection of Watersheds and Conservation of Navigable Streams* (60th Cong., 2d sess.), 131. The five dissenting members of the committee were Charles F. Scott (R-Kansas), William Lorimer (R-Illinois), George W. Cook (R-Colorado), Jack Beall (D-Texas), and W. W. Rucker (D-Missouri).

55. Roderick Nash, *Wilderness and the American Mind* (New Haven, Conn.: Yale Univ. Press, 1967), 175–80.

56. *Congressional Record,* 6 Dec. 1913 (63rd Cong., 2d sess.), 362.

57. Ibid., 84.

58. Robert Shankland, *Steve Mather of the National Parks* (New York: Alfred A. Knopf, 1970), 172.

59. Ibid., 167.

60. Robert Sterling Yard, "Gift-Parks the Coming National Park Danger," *National Parks Bulletin* 4 (1923): 4–5.

61. Runte, *National Parks,* 218–20.

62. U.S. Dept. of the Interior, NPS, *Report of Director of NPS, 1923,* 14.

63. Runte, *National Parks,* 114–15.

64. "Department of the Interior Memorandum for the Press," 2 Jan. 1924, in box 1147, file 870-1, RG 79, NA. During research for this book, both RG 48 (records of the U.S. Dept. of the Interior) and RG 79 (records of the NPS) were transferred to Archives II, College Park, Md.

65. Hubert Work to William J. Harris, 18 Mar. 1924, in box 24, file 0-32, RG 79, NA.

66. Stephen Mather, "Memorandum for the Secretary of the Interior," 9 Feb. 1924, in box 1147, file 870-1, RG 79, NA.

67. U.S. Dept. of the Interior, *Final Report of the Southern Appalachian National Park Commission to the Secretary of the Interior, June 30, 1931* (Washington, D.C.: Government Printing Office, 1931), 1.

68. "Department of the Interior Memorandum for the Press," 26 Mar. 1924, in box 1147, file 870-1, RG 79, NA.

69. "Minutes of the Preliminary Meeting of the Southern Appalachian National Park Committee," 26–27 Mar. 1924, in box 1147, file 870-1, RG 79, NA.

70. Henry C. Wallace to George Norris, 24 Apr. 1924, in Peay Papers, box 84, file 1.

71. Ibid.

72. U.S. Congress, "Memorandum for the Press," 27 Mar. 1924, in box 1147, file 870-1, RG 79, NA.

Chapter 3

1. Sinclair Lewis, *Babbitt* (New York: Harcourt, Brace and Company, 1922), 188.

2. Milton Ready, *Asheville: Land of the Sky* (Northridge, Calif.: Windsor Publications, 1986), 73–93; Michael J. McDonald and William Bruce Wheeler, *Knoxville, Tennessee: Continuity and Change in an Appalachian City* (Knoxville: Univ. of Tennessee Press, 1983), 48–60; Lucille Deaderick, ed., *Heart of the Valley: A History of Knoxville, Tennessee* (Knoxville: East Tennessee Historical Society, 1976), 361–482.

3. Ready, *Asheville*, 83.

4. The phrase "God's good out-o'-doors" comes from Lewis, *Babbitt*, 181.

5. George Ellison, introduction to Horace Kephart, *Our Southern Highlanders* (rpt. ed. Knoxville: Univ. of Tennessee Press, 1984), xliv. Unfortunately, information on Kephart is relatively limited. The best account of Kephart's life is in Ellison's introduction. Additional information on Kephart can be found in Special Collections, Hunter Library, Western Carolina Univ., Cullowhee, N.C.; and in the North Carolina Collection, Pack Memorial Library, Asheville, N.C. Many of Kephart's papers and much of his correspondence, including a good deal of material on his involvement in the park project, have disappeared.

6. Paul Fink, *Backpacking Was the Only Way: A Chronicle of Camping Experiences in the Southern Appalachian Mountains* (Johnson City, Tenn.: Research Advisory Council, East Tennessee State Univ., 1975), 65.

7. On Paul Fink, see Paul Fink Papers, MHC.

8. Ellison, introduction to Kephart, *Our Southern Highlanders*, xlv.

9. Correspondence between Kephart and Fink concerning their early interest in the park can be found in a file marked "Horace Kephart," box 6, Paul Fink Papers, MHC.

10. Horace Kephart to Paul Fink, 28 Jan. 1920, in "Horace Kephart" file, box 6, Paul Fink Papers, MHC.

11. Mrs. Davis's words are reported in most accounts of the park's establishment, including Carlos Campbell, *Birth of a National Park in the Great Smoky Mountains,* rev. ed. (Knoxville: Univ. of Tennessee Press, 1969), 13; and Frome, *Strangers,* 182. The quotation used here was taken from "Excerpts of Directors' Meetings of the Knoxville Automobile Club: History of the Creation of the Great Smoky Mountains National Park," in GSMCA Papers, box 12, file 12. The most thorough assessment of Knoxville's role in the establishment of the park can be found in John Thomas Whaley, "A Timely Idea at an Ideal Time: Knoxville's Role in Establishing the Great Smoky Mountains National Park" (Master's thesis, Univ. of Tennessee, 1984).

12. Deaderick, *Heart of the Valley,* 514–16.

13. Hubert Work to W. P. Davis, 28 Sept. 1923, in box 2012, file 12–22, Records of the Dept. of the Interior, RG 48, NA.

14. The name change is reflected in a change in letterhead on letters in box 305, file 601, RG 79, NA.

15. *Knoxville Sentinel,* 10 Oct. 1923.

16. Ibid.

17. Francis Butler Simkins, *The South, Old and New: A History, 1820–1947* (New York: Alfred A. Knopf, 1947), 374.

18. Howard Lawrence Preston, *Dirt Roads to Dixie: Accessibility and Modernization in the South, 1885–1935* (Knoxville: Univ. of Tennessee Press, 1991), 41 and 164.

19. George Tindall, "Business Progressivism: Southern Politics in the Twenties," *South Atlantic Quarterly* 62 (1963): 99–101.

20. Preston, *Dirt Roads,* 25; *Asheville Citizen,* 4 Aug. 1924.

21. Campbell, *Birth of a National Park,* 17.

22. Wiley Brownlee to W. P. Davis, 27 Oct. 1923, in W. P. Davis Papers, GSMNP Archives.

23. "Excerpts from Directors' Meetings of the Knoxville Automobile Club," GSMNP Archives.

24. *Knoxville Men and Women of Affairs* (Knoxville, Tenn.: GSM Publishing Co., 1928).

25. *Knoxville Journal and Tribune,* 1 Feb. 1924.

26. *Knoxville Sentinel,* 24 May 1924.

27. *New York Times,* 27 July 1924, p. 4–E.

28. *Asheville Citizen,* 13 Jan. 1924.

29. *Asheville Citizen,* 30 July 1924.

30. Shankland, *Steve Mather,* 172.

31. U.S. Dept. of the Interior, *Final Report of the SANPC, 1931,* 2.

32. Joseph Hyde Pratt to Glenn S. Smith, 19 July 1924, in box 1147, file 870-1, RG 79, NA; *Asheville Citizen,* 28 and 30 July 1924.

33. *Asheville Citizen,* 30 July 1924.

34. U.S. Dept. of the Interior, *Final Report of the SANPC, 1931,* 2–3.

35. *Asheville Citizen,* 2 and 3 Aug. 1924.

36. *Asheville Citizen,* 30 July and 2 and 3 Aug. 1924.

37. *Knoxville Sentinel,* 27 July 1924.

38. Campbell, *Birth of a National Park,* 25.

39. Harlan Kelsey to Henry Temple, 18 Aug. 1924, in box 1147, file 870-1, RG 79, NA.

40. David Chapman to Austin Peay, undated, in Peay Papers, box 13, file 8.

41. "Excerpts from the Directors' Meetings of the Knoxville Automobile Club," GSMCA Papers, box 12, file 12.

42. Runte, *National Parks,* 116.

43. Harlan Kelsey to Henry Temple, 18 Aug. 1924, in box 1147, file 870-1, RG 79, NA.

44. Henry Temple to Harlan Kelsey, 25 Aug. 1924, in box 1147, file 870-1, RG 79, NA.

45. Ibid.

46. General Assembly of North Carolina, Resolution Nos. 16 and 29, 23 Aug. 1924; Willard B. Gatewood, "North Carolina's Role in the Establishment of the Great Smoky Mountains National Park," *North Carolina Historical Review* 37 (1960): 167–68.

47. Gatewood, "North Carolina's Role," 167–68.

48. "Minutes of Former North Carolina Park Commission," in Parks ORC Papers, file 136, NCSA.

49. Ibid.

50. Williston Cox to Austin Peay, 25 Sept. 1924, in Peay Papers, box 13, file 11.

51. Campbell, *Birth of a National Park,* 31.

52. W. P. Davis to Hubert Work, 1 Feb. 1924, in box 305, file 601, RG 79, NA; W. P. Davis to Austin Peay, 16 Aug. 1924 and 23 Aug. 1924, in Peay Papers, box 13, file 11; and Court Document, "Charles E. Malone et al. v. Austin Peay et al.," in GSMCA Papers, box 7, file 5.

53. "Charles E. Malone et al. v. Austin Peay et al."

54. W. P. Davis to Austin Peay, 31 Dec. 1924, in Peay Papers, box 13, file 11.

55. U.S. Dept. of the Interior, *Final Report of the SANPC, 1931,* 4–6.

56. Ibid., 7.

57. Ibid.

58. Ibid.

59. *Knoxville Sentinel,* 14 Dec. 1924.

60. *Asheville Citizen,* 14 and 15 Dec. 1924.

61. Key, *Southern Politics,* 212–13.

62. *Asheville Citizen,* 7 Jan. 1925.

63. *Knoxville Sentinel,* 6 Jan. 1925.

64. "Department of the Interior Memorandum for the Press," 11 Jan. 1925, in box 24, file 0-32, RG 79, NA.

65. Horace Kephart to Zebulon Weaver, 9 Jan. 1925, in Horace Kephart Papers, WCUSC.

66. Horace Kephart to Zebulon Weaver, 13 Jan. 1925, in Horace Kephart Papers, WCUSC.

67. *Asheville Citizen,* 18 Jan. 1925.

68. *Knoxville Sentinel*, 24, 25, and 28 Jan. 1925; John Thomas Whaley, "Timely Idea," 33–34.

69. "Acts of Congress Relating to Great Smoky Mountains National Park," box 1079, file 120, RG 79, NA.

70. *Asheville Citizen*, 27 Jan. 1925.

71. "Acts of Congress Relating to Great Smoky Mountains National Park."

72. "Department of the Interior Memorandum for the Press," 27 Feb. 1925, in box 24, file 0-32, RG 79, NA.

73. *Knoxville Journal*, 23 Feb. and 8 Mar. 1925; John Thomas Whaley, "Timely Idea," 37–38.

74. *Knoxville Journal*, 16 Mar. 1925.

75. *Knoxville News*, 16 Mar. 1925.

76. W. P. Davis to Ann Davis, 28 Mar. 1925, in W. P. Davis Papers, GSMNP Archives.

77. *Knoxville News*, 1 Apr. 1925.

78. *Knoxville Journal*, 9 Mar. 1925.

79. *Knoxville News*, 9 Apr. 1925.

80. *Knoxville Journal*, 11 Apr. 1925.

81. Chapter 57, *State of Tennessee Public Acts of 1925*.

82. *Knoxville Journal*, 31 Mar. 1926.

83. "Minutes of the Third Meeting of the Southern Appalachian National Park Commission, July 18, 1925," in box 24, file 0-32, RG 79, NA.

84. *Knoxville Journal*, 5 and 6 June 1925.

85. *Knoxville News*, 5 and 6 June 1925.

86. *Knoxville Journal*, 19 June 1925.

87. Ibid.; *Knoxville News*, 19 June 1925.

88. W. J. Damtoft to Harlan P. Kelsey, 18 May 1925, in box 25, file 0-32, RG 79, NA.

89. Ibid.; William Gregg to H. W. Temple, 2 June 1925, box 25, file 0-32, RG 79, NA.

90. *Asheville Citizen*, 26 July 1925.

91. Harlan P. Kelsey to Henry W. Temple, 22 Sept. 1925, in box 24, file 0-32, RG 79, NA.

92. Ibid.

93. Ibid.

94. William Gregg to H. W. Temple and Other Park Commissioners, 4 July 1925, in box 204, file 0-32, RG 79, NA.

95. Ibid.

96. Glenn S. Smith to H. W. Temple, 14 July 1925, in box 24, file 0-32, RG 79, NA.

97. Ibid.

98. "Minutes of the Third Meeting of the SANPC."

99. Ibid.

100. *Asheville Citizen*, 27 July 1925.

101. Ibid., 12 Aug. 1925.

102. Ibid., 16 Aug. 1925.

103. Ibid.

104. Ibid.

105. Charles A. Webb to William A. Jardine, 22 Aug. 1925, in box 305, file 601, RG 79, NA.

106. "Minutes of National Park Conference held at the Battery Park Hotel, Asheville, N.C., September 2, 1925," in NCPC Papers, box 5, file 13, GSMNP Archives; *Asheville Citizen,* 3 Sept. 1925.

107. *Asheville Citizen,* 3 and 4 Sept. 1925.

108. *Knoxville News,* 27 July 1925.

109. William Gregg to Horace Kephart, 29 July 1925, in Horace Kephart Papers, WCUSC.

110. Arno Cammerer to Stephen Mather, 19 Aug. 1925, in box 302, file 204-020, RG 79, NA.

111. Ibid.

112. Robert Sterling Yard, "A National Park in the Great Smoky Mountains," *National Parks Bulletin* 46 (1925): 3–6.

Chapter 4

1. *Knoxville News,* 25 Sept. 1925; "From the Interstate Executive Committee of the Great Smoky Mountain Conservation Association of Tennessee and the North Carolina Park Commission," undated, press release in NCPC Papers, box 5, file 15, GSMNP Archives.

2. *Asheville Citizen,* 3 Oct. 1925.

3. A copy of the contract is in GSMCA Papers, box 1, file 2.

4. Charles Trimmer to George M. Tamblyn, 6 Oct. 1925, in GSMCA Papers, box 1, file 3.

5. Charles Trimmer to George O. Tamblyn, 9 Oct. 1925, in GSMCA Papers, box 1, file 3.

6. Charles Trimmer to George O. Tamblyn, 12 Oct. 1925, in GSMCA Papers, box 1, file 3.

7. Contract by Great Smoky Mountains Conservation Association, Inc., Great Smoky Mountains, Inc., and Tamblyn and Brown, in GSMCA Papers, box 1, file 2.

8. *Knoxville Journal,* 5 Nov. 1925; *Asheville Citizen,* 5 Nov. 1925.

9. "Plan of Campaign: Great Smoky Mountain National Park Purchase Fund, Tennessee and North Carolina," in GSMCA Papers, box 1, file 5.

10. "Great Smoky Mountain National Park Campaign: Memoranda on Women's Part in the Campaign," in GSMCA Papers, box 1, file 7.

11. "Great Smoky Mountains," in GSMCA Papers, box 12, file 32.

12. "A National Park in the Great Smoky Mountains," in Horace Kephart Collection, WCUSC.

13. "Suggestions for Speakers," in GSMCA Papers, box 1, file 6.

14. "Suggested Slogans for Use in Advancing the Great Smoky Mountains

National Park Purchase Fund During Weeks of November 30th and December 6th," in GSMCA Papers, box 1, file 7.

15. "Great Smoky Mountains National Park Campaign Song Sheet," in GSMCA Papers, box 1, file 7.

16. *Asheville Citizen,* 11–16 Nov. 1925.

17. W. A. Welch to H. W. Temple, 11 Nov. 1925, in box 24, file 0-32, RG 79, NA.

18. *Knoxville Journal,* 22–24 Nov. 1925.

19. *Knoxville Journal,* 1 Nov. 1925.

20. *Asheville Citizen,* 9 Nov. 1925.

21. *Asheville Citizen,* 13 Sept. 1925.

22. *Asheville Citizen,* 23 Nov. 1925.

23. *Knoxville Journal,* 7 Nov. 1925.

24. William Gregg to H. W. Temple, 27 Nov. 1925, in box 24, file 0-32, RG 79, NA.

25. *Asheville Citizen,* 24 Nov. 1925.

26. *Knoxville Journal,* 8 Dec. 1925. John Thomas Whaley, "Timely Idea," 46–55, contains additional details concerning Knoxville's fundraising efforts.

27. *Asheville Citizen,* 25, 27, and 29 Nov. 1925.

28. Ibid.

29. *Knoxville Journal,* 6 Dec. 1925; "An Industrial Argument for the Smoky Mountain Forest Area," *Manufacturers Record,* 17 Dec. 1925.

30. "Forestry—The National Park and Western North Carolina Prosperity," full-page ad in *Asheville Citizen,* 6 Dec. 1925.

31. *Knoxville Journal,* 1 Dec. 1925.

32. *Asheville Citizen,* 29 Nov. 1925.

33. Ibid.

34. *Asheville Citizen,* 3 Dec. 1925.

35. *Asheville Citizen,* 8 Dec. 1925.

36. *Asheville Citizen,* 9 Dec. 1925.

37. *Knoxville Journal,* 10 Dec. 1925.

38. *Asheville Citizen,* 29 Nov. 1925.

39. *Asheville Citizen,* 19 Dec. 1925.

40. *Knoxville Journal,* 10 and 20 Dec. 1925.

41. *Knoxville Journal,* 6 Dec. 1925; *Asheville Citizen,* 7 Dec. 1925.

42. *Asheville Citizen,* 13, 14, and 7 Dec. 1925.

43. *Asheville Citizen,* 8 Jan. 1926; *Knoxville Journal,* 13 Jan. 1926.

44. *Asheville Citizen,* 28 Jan. 1926.

45. Ibid.

46. *Asheville Citizen,* 6 Feb. 1926.

47. *Asheville Citizen,* 5 Mar. 1926.

48. *Knoxville Journal,* 1 Feb. 1926.

49. *Knoxville Journal,* 1–7 Feb. 1926.

50. *Asheville Citizen,* 14 Feb. 1926.

51. *Asheville Citizen,* 23 Mar. 1925.

52. *Asheville Citizen,* 13 Mar. 1926.

53. *Knoxville Journal,* 5 Mar. 1926.

54. *Knoxville Journal,* 9 Mar. 1926.

55. *Knoxville Journal,* 21 Feb. 1926.

56. *Knoxville Journal,* 10 Mar. 1926.

57. *Knoxville Journal,* 7 Mar. 1926.

58. *Knoxville Journal,* 13 Mar. 1926; "Great Smoky Mountain National Park Day: A Proclamation," in GSMCA Papers, box 1, file 7.

59. *Knoxville Journal,* 12 Mar. 1926.

60. *Knoxville Journal,* 18 and 21 Mar. 1926.

61. *Knoxville Journal,* 19 Mar. 1926.

62. *Knoxville Journal,* 24 Mar. 1926.

63. *Knoxville Journal,* 20 Mar. 1926, p. 4–A.

64. *Knoxville Journal,* 26 Mar. 1926.

65. *Knoxville Journal,* 28, 30, and 31 Mar. 1926.

66. *Knoxville Journal,* 3 Apr. 1926.

67. *Asheville Citizen,* 2 and 6 Apr. 1926.

68. William Gregg, "Two New National Parks?" *The Outlook* 131 (Dec. 1925): 662–66.

69. Horace Kephart, "The Last of the Eastern Wilderness," *World's Work* 53 (Apr. 1926): 617–32.

70. *New York Times,* 25 Jan. and 28 Mar. 1926.

71. *Asheville Citizen,* 15 Apr. 1926.

72. U.S. Congress, House, Committee on the Public Lands, *Hearings Before the Committee on the Public Lands, House of Representatives, on H.R. 11287* (69th Cong., 1st sess.), 11 May 1926.

73. U.S. Congress, Senate, Committee on Public Lands and Surveys, *Hearings Before the Committee on Public Lands and Surveys, United States Senate, on S. 3176, S. 3427, S. 3428, S. 3433, S. 4073, S. 4209, S. 4258, and H.R. 9387* (69th Cong., 1st sess.), 27, 29 and 30 Apr., 11 and 12 May, and 2 June 1926.

74. U.S. Congress, Senate, *A Bill to Provide for the Establishment of the Shenandoah National Park in the State of Virginia and the Great Smoky Mountain National Park in the States of North Carolina and Tennessee, and for Other Purposes* (69th Cong., 1st sess., S. 4073).

75. David Chapman to Glenn S. Smith, 20 Apr. 1926, in box 25, file 0-32, RG 79, NA.

76. Ibid.

77. *Asheville Citizen,* 29 Apr. 1926.

78. *Asheville Citizen,* 30 Apr. 1926.

79. U.S. Congress, House, Committee on the Public Lands, *Hearings Before the Committee,* 11 May 1926, pp. 4–9.

80. Ibid., 9–33.

81. U.S. Congress, Senate, Committee on Public Lands and Surveys, *Hearings Before the Senate Public Lands Committee,* 11–12 May 1926, pp. 107–33.

82. Ibid.

83. Ibid., 142.

84. Ibid., 142–44.

85. *Asheville Citizen,* 16 May 1926.

86. *Knoxville Journal,* 27 Mar. 1926.

87. *Biographical Directory of the United States Congress, 1774–1989* (Washington, D.C.: U.S. Government Printing Office, 1989).

88. *Knoxville Journal,* 29 May 1926.

89. Ibid.; John Thomas Whaley, "Timely Idea," 56–57.

90. *Asheville Citizen,* 22 July 1926.

91. *Knoxville Journal,* 8 Aug. 1926.

92. *Knoxville News,* 7 Sept. 1926.

93. *Knoxville Journal,* 9 Sept. 1926.

94. *Knoxville News,* 7 Sept. 1926.

95. Ibid.

96. Wright's views on the park movement are contained in a self-published book, *Great Smoky Mountains National Park: Statement of Jas. B. Wright of Knoxville, Tennessee, Elicited by the Park Investigating Committee Appointed by the 66th General Assembly (1929) Under House Resolution No. 21, the Senate Concurring,* in box 307, file 608, RG 79, NA. Also see Joseph T. MacPherson, "Democratic Progressivism in Tennessee: The Administration of Governor Austin Peay" (Ph.D. diss., Vanderbilt Univ., 1969), note on p. 333.

97. MacPherson, "Democratic Progressivism in Tennessee," note on p. 333.

98. Campbell, *Birth of a National Park,* 45.

99. David D. Lee, *Tennessee in Turmoil: Politics in the Volunteer State, 1920–1932* (Memphis: Memphis State Univ. Press, 1979), 64–75.

100. Ibid.

101. Austin Peay to W. B. Townsend, 7 Sept. 1926, in LRLC Papers, box 1, file 17.

102. *Knoxville Journal,* 10 Sept. 1926.

103. Frank Maloney to Arno Cammerer, 11 Sept. 1926, in GSMCA Papers, box 11, file 7.

104. *Knoxville Journal,* 9 Sept. 1926, 13 Nov. 1926, 16 and 26 Feb. 1927.

105. *Knoxville Journal,* 19, 22, and 23 Mar. 1927.

106. L. D. Smith, Attorney General, "In the Supreme Court of Tennessee at Nashville, December Term, 1928, Charles E. Malone et al., Appellants v. Austin Peay et al., Appellees, Reply Brief in Behalf of the Governor, Secretary of State, and Treasurer of Tennessee, Appellees," in LRLC Papers, box 1, file 19, GSMNP Archives.

107. *Knoxville Journal,* 22 and 27 Mar. 1927.

108. Gatewood, "North Carolina's Role," 174.

109. *Asheville Citizen,* 27 Jan. 1927.

110. J. D. Murphy to E. C. Brooks, 19 Jan. 1927, in E. C. Brooks Collection, NCPC Papers, box 9, file D, Special Collections Library, Duke Univ., Durham, N.C.

111. A. M. Kistler to Angus McLean, 3 Feb. 1927, in Gov. Angus McLean Papers, NCSA.

112. Reuben Robertson to Angus McLean, undated, in McLean Papers, NCSA.

113. Charles Webb to Angus McLean, 31 Jan. 1927, in McLean Papers, NCSA.

114. *Asheville Citizen,* 3 Feb. 1927.

115. *Asheville Citizen,* 4, 5, and 8 Feb. 1927.

116. Telegram, J. D. Murphy to Angus McLean, 8 Feb. 1927, in McLean Papers, NCSA.

117. Telegram, Charles Webb to Angus McLean, 8 Feb. 1927, in McLean Papers, NCSA.

118. *Asheville Citizen,* 9 and 10 Feb. 1927.

119. *Asheville Citizen,* 13 Feb. 1927; Angus McLean to Charles Webb, 4 Feb. 1927, in McLean Papers, NCSA.

120. Hubert Work to Angus McLean and Austin Peay, 12 Feb. 1927, in McLean Papers, NCSA.

121. *Asheville Citizen,* 16 Feb. 1927.

122. *Asheville Citizen,* 17, 23 Feb. 1927.

123. Gatewood, "North Carolina's Role," 174–75.

124. "Minutes of Meeting of N.C. Park Commission," 18 Mar. 1927, Parks ORC, file 136, NCSA.

125. MacPherson, "Democratic Progressivism," 337–40; Lee, *Tennessee in Turmoil,* 76–78.

126. David Chapman to Henry Colton, 1 Apr. 1927, in GSMCA Papers, box 7, file 11.

127. Ibid.

128. *Knoxville Journal,* 30 Mar. 1927.

129. *Knoxville Journal,* 3 Apr. 1927.

130. MacPherson, "Democratic Progressivism," 338–41.

131. *Knoxville Journal,* 15 Apr. 1927.

132. *Knoxville Journal,* 17 Apr. 1927; John Thomas Whaley, "Timely Idea," 63–64.

133. *Knoxville Journal,* 17 Apr. 1927.

134. Campbell, *Birth of a National Park,* 52.

135. *Knoxville Journal,* 18 Apr. 1927.

136. *Knoxville Journal,* 20 Apr. 1927.

137. Ibid.

138. *Knoxville Journal,* 23 Apr. 1927.

139. *Knoxville Journal,* 25 Apr. 1927.

140. *Knoxville Journal,* 27 Apr. 1927.

141. Lee, *Tennessee in Turmoil,* 76–114.

142. William D. Miller, *Mr. Crump of Memphis* (Baton Rouge: Louisiana State Univ. Press, 1964), 160.

143. Stephen Mather to George Eastman, 20 Feb. 1925, in box 306, file 604, RG 79, NA.

144. Annie Florence Brown to Stephen Mather, 1 June 1926, in box 306, file 604, RG 79, NA.

145. W. P. Davis to Arthur Davis, 28 May 1928, in W. P. Davis Papers, box 1, file 13, GSMNP Archives.

146. Russell Hanlon to W. P. Davis, 27 July 1925, in W. P. Davis Papers, box 1, file 13, GSMNP Archives.

147. W. P. Davis to Mark Squires, 27 Oct. 1925, in W. P. Davis Papers, box 1, file 13, GSMNP Archives.

148. Campbell, *Birth of a National Park,* 59–60; John Thomas Whaley, "Timely Idea," 60.

149. Copy of the incorporation papers for Appalachian National Parks Association, Inc., in box 24, file 0-32, RG 79, NA.

150. Arno Cammerer to David Chapman, 14 Sept. 1927, in GSMCA Papers, box 11, file 10.

151. W. A. Welch to Hubert Work, 10 Jan. 1928, in box 24, file 0-32, RG 79, NA.

152. Arno Cammerer to David Chapman, undated, in GSMCA Papers, box 11, file 10.

153. Cammerer to Chapman, 14 Sept. 1927.

154. Chapman to Cammerer, 10 Jan. 1928, in GSMCA Papers, box 11, file 10.

155. Arno Cammerer to Mark Squires, 5 Aug. 1927, in GSMCA Papers, box 11, file 8.

156. John D. Rockefeller Jr. to W. A. Welch, 26 Sept. 1927, in RFA, folder 853.

157. Ibid.

158. Chronology entitled "Great Smoky Mountains National Park," 5 June 1963, in RFA, folder 853.

159. Arno Cammerer to David Chapman, 12 Jan. 1928, in GSMCA Papers, box 11, file 10.

160. John D. Rockefeller Jr. to Arno Cammerer, 23 Jan. 1928, in LSRM, folder 143.

161. Raymond B. Fosdick, *John D. Rockefeller, Jr.: A Portrait* (New York: Harper, 1956), 302.

162. Ibid.

163. John Ettling, *The Germ of Laziness: Rockefeller Philanthropy and Public Health in the New South* (Cambridge, Mass.: Harvard Univ. Press, 1981), 77–93, 222–23.

164. Arno Cammerer to Mark Squires, 28 Jan. 1928, in LSRM, folder 143.

165. Trustees of the Great Smoky Mountains Memorial Fund to Laura Spelman Rockefeller Memorial, 11 Feb. 1928, in LSRM, folder 143.

166. Kenneth Chorley to Arthur Woods, 9 Mar. 1928, in LSRM, folder 143.

167. Ibid.

168. Ibid.

169. Ibid.

170. Ibid.

171. Ibid.

172. Ibid.

173. *Asheville Citizen,* 8 Mar. 1928.

174. *Asheville Citizen,* 9 Mar. 1928, p. 4.

175. Chorley to Woods, 9 Mar. 1928.

176. John Ensor Harr and Peter J. Johnson, *The Rockefeller Conscience: An American Family in Public and Private* (New York: Charles Scribner's Sons, 1991), 7–8.

Chapter 5

1. *Knoxville News-Sentinel,* 10 Jan. 1933.

2. The other sizable timber tract, more than 76,000 acres owned by the Little River Lumber Company, already had been purchased by the State of Tennessee in 1926, although Little River retained timber rights to 16,000 acres.

3. *Asheville Citizen,* 22 June 1927.

4. David Chapman to Austin Peay, in Peay Papers, box 13, file 15; and *Knoxville Journal,* 6 Aug. 1927. Other members of the commission included E. E. Conner, a Sevier County banker; John Clark, a Blount County banker; Nashville attorney Henry Colton; and Tiptonville businessman A. E. Markham.

5. *Knoxville Journal,* 6 Aug. 1927.

6. "Data of Messrs. Rhoades and Chapman of Investigations Conducted at Rhinelander, Wisconsin; Madison, Wisconsin; and Erie, Pennsylvania," in Champion Fibre Company Papers, box 1, file 15, GSMNP Archives; and Verne Rhoades, "Report on the Activities of the North Carolina Park Commission to January 31, 1929," Gov. O. Max Gardner Papers, box 82, NCSA.

7. Campbell, *Birth of a National Park,* 12; Mark Squires to Arno Cammerer, 20 Nov. 1928, in GSMCA Papers, box 11, file 10.

8. Arno Cammerer to Kenneth Chorley, 25 July 1928, in LSRM, folder 144.

9. Arno Cammerer to Mark Squires, 21 Apr. 1928, in LSRM, folder 144.

10. Mark Squires to Arno Cammerer, 23 Apr. 1928, and L. R. Varser to Angus McLean, 15 Nov. 1928, both in LSRM, folder 144.

11. Francis Christy to Kenneth Chorley, 7 Dec. 1928, in LSRM, folder 144.

12. *Asheville Citizen,* 15, 16, 18, and 22 Jan. 1929.

13. *Asheville Citizen,* 15 Jan. 1929.

14. *Knoxville News-Sentinel,* 29 Jan. 1929; Francis Christy, "The Great Smoky Mountain Park: An Episode in Its Creation," Apr. 1973, in RFA, folder 854.

15. Christy, "Great Smoky Mountain Park," 2–8.

16. Wright, *Great Smoky Mountains National Park.*

17. Arno Cammerer to Kenneth Chorley, 4 Apr. 1929, in LSRM, folder 145.

18. Ibid.; Campbell, *Birth of a National Park,* 73.

19. *Knoxville News-Sentinel,* 7 Apr. 1929.

20. Christy, "Great Smoky Mountain Park," 9.

21. *Knoxville News-Sentinel,* 9 Apr. 1929.

22. *Knoxville News-Sentinel,* 14 Apr. 1929.

23. Ibid.

24. Memo from David Chapman, 10 Feb. 1929, in LRLC Papers, box 1, file 17, GSMNP Archives.

25. Lambert, "Logging on Little River, 1890–1940," East Tennessee Historical Society *Publications* 33 (1961): 41.

26. *Asheville Citizen*, 5 Feb. 1930; *Knoxville News-Sentinel*, 5 and 6 Feb. 1930.

27. Governor Gardner's speech at the presentation of deeds to the Secretary of the Interior, 6 Feb. 1930, in Gardner Papers, box 82, NCSA.

28. National Park Press Release, 29 Apr. 1931, in LSRM, folder 146.

29. Reuben Robertson to Mark Squires, 5 Oct. 1925, in box 25, file 0-32, RG 79, NA.

30. "Notes on Conference Between Mr. Reuben Robertson of the Champion Fibre Company and Mr. Verne Rhoades and Mr. S. F. Chapman of the Park Commission in the Forenoon of the Above Dated," 11 June 1928, in Papers of the North Carolina National Park, Parkway and Forest Development Commission (1927–37), box 17, NCSA.

31. Reuben Robertson to Mark Squires and David Chapman, 11 July 1929, in Reuben Robertson Papers, UNCASC.

32. Ibid.; Verne Rhoades to Arno Cammerer, 26 Apr. 1930, in box 306, file 604, RG 79, NA.

33. "Data of Messrs. Rhoades and Chapman of Investigations conducted at Rhinelander, Wisconsin; Madison, Wisconsin; and Erie, Pennsylvania," 21 Sept. 1929, in Champion Papers, box 1, file 15, GSMNP Archives.

34. Verne Rhoades to Arno Cammerer, 21 Aug. 1929, in box 306, file 604, RG 79, NA.

35. Reuben Robertson to Mark Squires and David Chapman, 6 Dec. 1929, in Robertson Papers, UNCASC.

36. George Smathers to Felix Alley, 1 July 1930, in Champion Papers, box 3, file 11, GSMNP Archives; Campbell, *Birth of a National Park,* 82.

37. Kenneth Chorley to A.W. [Arthur Woods], 30 Oct. 1929, in LSRM, folder 146.

38. David Chapman to Reuben Robertson, 29 Jan. 1931, in Gardner Papers, box 82, NCSA.

39. "The Champion Fibre Company a Good Taxpayer," in box 309, file 610, RG 79, NA.

40. Arno Cammerer to Horace Albright, 10 Jan. 1931, in box 309, file 610, RG 79, NA; *Asheville Citizen,* 16 Jan. 1931; *Knoxville News-Sentinel,* 16 Jan. 1931.

41. W. J. Damtoft, "Memorandum for Mr. R. B. Robertson," in Robertson Papers, UNCASC.

42. *Knoxville News-Sentinel,* 16 Jan. 1931; *Asheville Citizen,* 16 Jan. 1931; David Chapman to Reuben Robertson, 29 Jan. 1931, in Robertson Papers, UNCASC.

43. Arno Cammerer, "Confidential Report for the Director," 22 Jan. 1931, in LSRM, folder 146.

44. *Knoxville News-Sentinel,* 2 May 1935; David Chapman to Arno Cammerer, 3 July 1935, in GSMCA Papers, box 11, file 17.

45. Cammerer, "Confidential Report for the Director."

46. Reuben Robertson to David Chapman, 21 Jan. 1931; and John Davis to Arthur Woods, 27 Jan. 1931; both in LSRM, folder 146.

47. David Chapman to Horace Albright, 30 Jan. 1931, in box 309, file 610, RG 79, NA; Kenneth Chorley, "Memo for New York Files—Re. Great Smoky Mts.," in LSRM, folder 146.

48. Reuben Robertson to Horace Albright, 13 Apr. 1931, in box 309, file 610, RG 79, NA.

49. Horace Albright to Reuben Robertson, 14 Apr. 1931, in box 309, file 610, RG 79, NA.

50. Horace Albright to Kenneth Chorley, 30 Apr. 1931, in LSRM, folder 146.

51. Reuben Robertson to Horace Albright, 7 May 1931, in box 309, file 610, RG 79, NA.

52. *Knoxville News-Sentinel,* 29 Apr. 1931.

53. *Asheville Citizen,* 30 Apr. 1931.

54. *Knoxville News-Sentinel,* 29 Apr. 1931.

55. *Knoxville News-Sentinel,*., 30 Apr. 1931.

56. *Knoxville News-Sentinel,* 1 May 1931.

57. Reuben Robertson, "A New Machine," in "A History of the Champion Fibre Company," Robertson Papers, UNCASC; Thomas D. Clark, *The Greening of the South: The Recovery of Land and Forest* (Lexington: Univ. Press of Kentucky, 1984), 118.

58. *Asheville Citizen,* 3 May 1931.

59. Verne Rhoades, "Report of Executive Secretary," 1 Oct. 1931, in Brooks Collection, NCPC Papers, box 9, file D, Special Collections Library, Duke Univ., Durham, N.C.

60. *Asheville Citizen,* 25 and 29 Sept., and 1 Oct. 1932.

61. *Asheville Citizen,* 1 May 1934.

62. Verne Rhoades to Arno Cammerer, 30 Sept. 1931, in Papers of the North Carolina National Park, Parkway and Forest Development Commission (1927–37), box 16, NCSA.

63. David Chapman to Arno Cammerer, 26 Sept. 1933, in GSMCA Papers, box 11, file 15.

64. Rhoades to Cammerer, 30 Sept. 1931.

65. Harold Ickes to Kenneth McKellar, 28 Sept. 1940, in box 1078, file 101, RG 79, NA.

66. Chapman to Cammerer, 26 Sept. 1933.

67. "North Carolina Park Commission: Report on Audit, October 31, 1925, to June 30, 1933," in Gov. J. C. B. Ehringhaus Papers, box 160, NCSA.

68. Arno Cammerer to Kenneth Chorley, 3 Oct. 1931, in LSRM, folder 147. On Depression conditions, especially bank closings, in Asheville and Knoxville, see Ready, *Asheville,* 85–91; and McDonald and Wheeler, *Knoxville, Tennessee,* 62–63.

69. Lee, *Tennessee in Turmoil,* 76–149; Key, *Southern Politics,* 58–81.

70. Key, *Southern Politics,* 205–15.

71. David Chapman to John Clark, 22 Sept. 1932, in box 313, file 870.1, RG 79, NA; *Knoxville News-Sentinel,* 29 Aug. 1932.

72. A. E. Demaray to Frank Bond, n.d., in box 312, file 731-01, RG 79, NA.

73. Arno Cammerer to Kenneth Chorley, 17 Jan. 1933, in LSRM, folder 148, contains a brief summary of the chaotic conditions within the Tennessee Park Commission from Aug. 1932 to Jan. 1933. Also see the *Knoxville News-Sentinel's* thorough coverage during this period.

74. Dempster later achieved lasting fame as the inventor of the "Dempster Dumpster." Deaderick, *Heart of the Valley,* 520.

75. Harold Wimberly to Hill McAlister, 8 Feb. 1933, in Gov. Hill McAlister Papers, box 74, file 15, TSLA.

76. Thurman Ailor to Hill McAlister, 8 Feb. 1933, in McAlister Papers, box 74, file 15, TSLA.

77. Horace Albright to Hill McAlister, 10 Apr. 1933, in GSMCA Papers, box 11, file 2; Steve Whaley to Hill McAlister, 20 Apr. 1933, in McAlister Papers, box 74, file 15, TSLA; *Knoxville News-Sentinel,* 6, 7, 8, and 11 Apr. 1933.

78. *Knoxville News-Sentinel,* 11 Apr. 1933; Hill McAlister to Kenneth McKellar, 12 Sept. 1933, in McAlister Papers, box 78, file 5, TSLA.

79. *Knoxville News-Sentinel,* 8 Apr. 1933.

80. Robert Lindsay Mason to Horace Albright, 18 May 1931, in box 312, file 731-01, RG 79, NA.

81. Hill McAlister to Kenneth McKellar, 12 Sept. 1934, in McAlister Papers, box 78, file 5, TSLA; David Chapman to Arno Cammerer, 19 May 1933, in GSMCA Papers, box 11, file 15.

82. Arno Cammerer to David Chapman, 27 Sept. 1933, in GSMCA Papers, box 11, file 15.

83. *Asheville Citizen,* 19 July 1933.

84. "North Carolina Park Commission: Report on Audit, October 31, 1925, to June 30, 1933."

85. *Asheville Citizen,* 19 July 1933.

86. Ibid. The new members of the North Carolina Park Commission were Will W. Neal, chairman; C. A. Cannon; Thomas Raoul; John Aiken; and Foster Hankins.

87. Mark Squires to E. C. Brooks, 10 Aug. 1933, in Brooks Collection, NCPC Papers, box 9, file D, Special Collections Library, Duke Univ., Durham, N.C.

88. E. C. Brooks to Mark Squires, 15 Sept. 1933, in Brooks Collection, NCPC Papers, box 9, file D, Special Collections Library, Duke Univ., Durham, N.C.

89. On Franklin D. Roosevelt and his interest in conservation projects, see Fox, *John Muir,* 183–217; Edgar B. Nixon, ed., *Franklin D. Roosevelt and Conservation, 1911–1945* (Hyde Park, N.Y.: Franklin D. Roosevelt Library, 1957)

90. Harold Ickes to Franklin Roosevelt, 28 July 1933, in LSRM, folder 148.

91. *Asheville Citizen,* 4 Jan. 1934.

92. Max Mason to John D. Rockefeller Jr., 19 Jan. 1934, in RFA, folder 855.

93. Memorandum, Arno Cammerer to Harold Ickes, 17 Apr. 1937, in box 3816, file 12–22, RG 48, NA.

94. "Acts of Congress Relating to Great Smoky Mountains National Park." Despite this change, the NPS maintained the requirement that Tennessee and North Carolina turn over 427,000 acres before development would begin; note that the act mentions "administration, protection and maintenance" but not "development."

95. Campbell, *Birth of a National Park,* 138.

96. *Asheville Citizen,* 15 Nov. 1933; A. Hall Johnston to J. C. B. Ehringhaus, 23 Aug. 1933, in Ehringhaus Papers, box 160, NCSA.

97. Arno Cammerer to David Chapman, 14 Dec. 1933, in GSMCA Papers, box 11, file 15.

98. *Asheville Citizen,* 13 Jan. 1934.

99. *Asheville Citizen,* 29 Apr., 1 May, and 16 June 1934.

100. Report on Morton Butler Timber Company negotiations sent by Edward Ryerson to Kenneth Chorley, in LSRM, folder 146.

101. Arno Cammerer to Ross Eakin, 20 May 1932; and Ross Eakin to Arno Cammerer, 23 May 1932; both in box 305, file 602, RG 79, NA.

102. Harold Ickes to Hill McAlister, 29 June 1935, in McAlister Papers, box 66, file 7, TSLA.

103. *Knoxville News-Sentinel,* 5 May 1935.

104. J. W. Cooper to Hill McAlister, 17 July 1935, in McAlister Papers, box 66, file 7, TSLA.

105. *Knoxville Journal,* 7 Aug. 1935.

106. Memorandum, Arno Cammerer to Harold Ickes, 24 Mar. 1936, in Land Acquisition Papers, box 15, file 6, GSMNP Archives.

107. Memorandum, Arno Cammerer to Harold Ickes, 17 Apr. 1937, in box 3816, file 12-22, RG 48, NA.

108. Ibid.; *Asheville Citizen,* 3 and 15 Feb. 1938; and "Acts of Congress Relating to Great Smoky Mountains National Park."

Chapter 6

1. Great Smoky Mountains Conservation Association, "Great Smoky Mountains," in GSMNP Archives.

2. Ibid.

3. Campbell, *Birth of a National Park,* 12; Margaret Lynn Brown, "Power, Privilege, and Tourism: A Revision of the Great Smoky Mountains National Park Story" (Master's thesis, Univ. of Kentucky, 1990), 40.

4. Estimates for Cades Cove come from Dunn, *Cades Cove,* 251. For Greenbriar, see Wear, Teague, and Alexander, *Lost Communities: Greenbriar,* 41. For Cataloochee, see Peter Shelburne Givens, "Cataloochee and the Establishment of the Great Smoky Mountains National Park" (Master's thesis, Western Carolina Univ., 1978), 59. On the logging communities of the Smokies, see Vic Weals, *Last Train to Elkmont: A Look Back at Life on Little River in the Great Smoky Mountains* (Knoxville: Olden

Press, 1993); and Bush, *Dorie*. On the vacation cabins at Elkmont, see Morrell, "Brief History of the Appalachian and Wonderland Clubs."

5. Ellen Semple Churchill, "The Anglo-Saxons of the Kentucky Mountains: A Study in Anthrogeography," *Geographical Journal* 17 (1901): 592.

6. Kephart, *Our Southern Highlanders*, 445, 450–51.

7. Dunn, *Cades Cove*, 256.

8. Ibid.; Shifflett, *Coal Towns*; Bush, *Dorie*.

9. Laura Thornborough, *The Great Smoky Mountains* (New York: Thomas Crowell Co., 1937; rpt. Knoxville: Univ. of Tennessee, 1962), 154–55.

10. Frome, *Strangers*, 195.

11. Campbell, *Birth of a National Park*, 92–99.

12. Ronald D Eller, *Miners, Millhands, and Mountaineers: Industrialization of the Appalachian South, 1880–1930* (Knoxville: Univ. of Tennessee Press, 1982), 38.

13. Margaret Lynn Brown, "Power, Privilege, and Tourism."

14. Dunn, *Cades Cove*, 247.

15. David Chapman to Glenn Smith, 11 July 1927, in box 25, file 0-32, RG 79, NA.

16. Mark Squires to Plato Ebbs, 3 Aug. 1927, in North Carolina National Park, Parkway, and Forest Development Commission Papers, 1927–37, box 18, North Carolina State Archives, Raleigh; Arno Cammerer to David Chapman, 28 Dec. 1927, in GSMCA Papers, box 11, file 8.

17. "Acts of Congress Relating to Great Smoky Mountains National Park," NA.

18. Hubert Work to L. D. Tyson, 19 Apr. 1928, in box 306, file 604, RG 79, NA.

19. G. W. Cole to David Chapman, 23 June 1928, in GSMCA Papers, box 7, file 10.

20. David Chapman to John Clark, 18 May 1928, in GSMCA Papers, box 7, file 9.

21. John Jones to G. W. Cole, 16 July 1928, in GSMCA Papers, box 7, file 10.

22. Mrs. William Hall to Horace Albright, 4 Jan. 1930, in box 306, file 604, RG 79, NA.

23. Mrs. William Hall to Representative Jonas, 16 Dec. 1929, in box 308, file 609, RG 79, NA.

24. L. Woody to O. Max Gardner, 12 Mar. 1931, in Gov. O. Max Gardner Papers, box 82, NCSA.

25. David Chapman to Arno Cammerer, 3 May 1927, in box 1100, file 601, RG 79, NA.

26. For a photograph of this sign, see Campbell, *Birth of a National Park*, facing p. 92.

27. Wright, *Great Smoky Mountains National Park*, 57.

28. G. Walter Gregory to John D. Rockefeller Jr., 18 June 1928, in box 306, file 604, RG 79, NA. Mrs. R. D. Burchfield sent an identical letter to Rockefeller, in the same file.

29. John Oliver to Hubert Work, 20 Apr. 1928, in box 306, file 604, RG 79, NA.

30. Mary A. Rolfe to Horace Albright, 19 Apr. 1929, in box 305, file 501-04, RG 79, NA.

31. Other writers included George H. Browne and Mrs. H. T. Bailie, both of Cambridge, Mass. See box 308, file 609, RG 79, NA, and Condemnation: Tennessee, box 3, file 2, GSMNP Archives.

32. Acting Secretary of the Interior to David Chapman, n.d. [late summer of 1927], in box 306, file 604, RG 79, NA; and David Chapman to Ben Hooper, 17 July 1928, in GSMCA Papers, box 8, file 2.

33. Arno Cammerer to George H. Browne, n.d. [Mar. 1930?], in box 308, file 609, RG 79, NA.

34. Arno Cammerer to Mary Rolfe, 4 May 1929, in box 305, file 501-04, RG 79, NA.

35. Dunn, *Cades Cove*, 221–54.

36. David Chapman to A. E. Demaray, 19 Sept. 1929, in box 306, file 604, RG 79, NA; and Dunn, *Cades Cove*, 349.

37. Dunn, *Cades Cove*, 249–50.

38. J. W. Cooper to Arno Cammerer, 30 July 1936; and J. R. Eakin to Horace Albright, 29 Aug. 1931; both in Condemnation: Tennessee Papers, box 3, file 3, GSMNP Archives.

39. Arno Cammerer, "Confidential Memorandum for Director Albright," 11 Mar. 1931, in box 306, file 603, RG 79, NA.

40. J. R. Eakin to Horace Albright, 17 Oct. 1931, in Condemnation: Tennessee Papers, box 3, file 3, GSMNP Archives.

41. David Chapman to Arno Cammerer, 23 June 1934, in GSMCA Papers, box 11, file 16.

42. Dunn, *Cades Cove*, 254.

43. Ibid., 251.

44. Horace Albright, "Memorandum for Secretary Wilbur," 31 Oct. 1929, in box 302, file 204-020, RG 79, NA.

45. David Chapman to J. R. Eakin, 26 Dec. 1930, in box 308, file 609, RG 79, NA; and J. R. Eakin to Horace Albright, 14 Aug. 1931, in box 307, file 604, RG 79, NA.

46. Eakin to Albright, 14 Aug. 1931.

47. Lloyd Caldwell, interview by Sam Easterly, July 24, 1973, transcript in GSMNP Archives.

48. Lease agreement, in box 308, file 609, RG 79, NA.

49. Thornborough, *Great Smoky Mountains*, 154.

50. J. R. Eakin to David Chapman, 15 Oct. 1931, in Land Acquisition Papers, box 15, file 1, GSMNP Archives.

51. W. R. Mize to David Chapman, 13 Oct. 1931, in Land Acquisition Papers, box 15, file 1, GSMNP Archives.

52. Dunn, *Cades Cove*, 251.

53. The best example of this tactic is Wright, *Great Smoky Mountains National Park*.

54. Bruce Keener Jr. to John A. Ferrell, 25 Aug. 1931, in LSRM, folder 147.

55. J. R. Eakin to Arno Cammerer, 3 Sept. 1932, in box 313, file 870.1, RG 79, NA.

56. J. R. Eakin to Horace Albright, 9 Feb. 1932, in box 308, file 609, RG 79, NA.

57. Audley Whaley, interview by William Alston, 30 July 1975, transcript in GSMNP Archives; Dunn, *Cades Cove,* 252.

58. Horace Albright to W. H. Woodbury, 16 Apr. 1932, in Land Acquisition Papers, box 15, file 2, GSMNP Archives.

59. Arno Cammerer to David Chapman, 21 May 1931, in box 1100, file 601, RG 79, NA.

60. Dunn, *Cades Cove,* 253–54.

61. John O. Morrell, "Big Greenbriar Cove, Sevier County, Tennessee: Showing Necessity for Condemnation Proceedings," in Land Acquisition Papers, box 6, file 5, GSMNP Archives.

62. J. R. Eakin to Luther Flynn, 14 Sept. 1931, in box 308, file 609, RG 79, NA.

63. Dunn, *Cades Cove,* 256.

64. Arno Cammerer, "Memorandum for Secretary Ickes," 14 May 1935, in box 2012, file 12-22, RG 48, NA.

65. A. E. Demaray, "Memorandum for the Acting Secretary," 30 Dec. 1938, in box 3816, file 12-22, RG 48, NA.

66. J. W. Cooper to the Attorney General, 3 May 1939, in box 1079, file 120, RG 79, NA.

67. Morrell, "Brief History of the Appalachian Club and Wonderland Club"; Arno Cammerer, "Memorandum for Colonel Chapman," 10 Mar. 1930, in box 313, file 901, RG 79, NA.

68. "Cabin Fervor: Elkmont Debate Pits Family vs. Public Use," *Knoxville News-Sentinel,* 19 Apr. 1992, p. 1.

69. "Ex-residents Want Special Deal Ended," *Knoxville News-Sentinel,* 3 May 1992, p. B2.

70. Newton Drury, "Memorandum for the First Assistant Secretary," 23 Nov. 1940, in box 1128, file 610, RG 79, NA.

71. Wilma Dykeman and Jim Stokely, *Highland Homeland: The People of the Great Smokies* (Washington, D.C.: National Park Service, 1978), 153–57.

72. Map "Where They Went," in GSMNP Archives.

73. Shifflett, *Coal Towns,* 13–15.

74. Dunn, *Cades Cove,* 79.

75. Shifflett, *Coal Towns,* 13–15.

76. Ibid., 15–16.

77. Bush, *Dorie.*

78. Glenn Cardwell, interview by Daniel S. Pierce, Gatlinburg, Tenn., 21 Mar. 1995. Records in author's possession.

79. Dunn, *Cades Cove,* 221–40.

80. Givens, "Cataloochee and the Establishment of the GSMNP," 59.

81. Dunn, *Cades Cove,* 179 and 251.

82. *Asheville Citizen-Times,* 28 Aug. 1995.

83. Bruce Wheeler, interview by Daniel S. Pierce, Knoxville, Tenn., 9 Apr. 1992. Records in author's possession.

84. Cardwell, interview by Pierce, 21 Mar. 1995.

85. Bush, *Dorie,* 220–21.

86. Robert H. Woody, "Cataloochee Homecoming," *South Atlantic Quarterly* 49 (1950): 8–17.

87. The best accounts of removal are in Michael J. McDonald and John Muldowney, *TVA and the Dispossessed: The Resettlement of Population in the Norris Dam Area* (Knoxville: Univ. of Tennessee Press, 1982); and Stephen Taylor, "Building the Back of Beyond: Government Authority, Community Life, and Economic Development in the Upper Little Tennessee, 1880–1992" (Ph.D. diss., Univ. of Tennessee, 1996). On Oak Ridge, see Charles W. Johnson and Charles O. Jackson, *City Behind a Fence: Oak Ridge, Tennessee, 1942–1946* (Knoxville: Univ. of Tennessee Press, 1981). On the Blue Ridge Parkway, see Harley E. Jolley, *The Blue Ridge Parkway* (Knoxville: Univ. of Tennessee Press, 1969).

88. Cardwell, interview by Pierce, 21 Mar. 1995.

Chapter 7

1. J. R. Eakin, "Memorandum for the Director," 23 Dec. 1930, in box 1081, file 201-006, RG 79, NA; *Nashville Banner,* 15 Oct. 1938.

2. Arno Cammerer, "Memorandum for Mr. Needham and Mr. Hough," in box 302, file 204-010, RG 79, NA.

3. Campbell, *Birth of a National Park,* 96–97.

4. J. R. Eakin, "Proposed Great Smoky Mountains National Park," in box 302, file 207-001.2, RG 79, NA.

5. Audley Whaley, interview by Alston, 30 July 1975.

6. Arno Cammerer to John Needham, 17 Sept. 1930, in box 302, file 204-020, RG 79, NA.

7. Audley Whaley, interview by Alston, 30 July 1975.

8. Arno Cammerer to Mrs. C. W. Edge, 22 Oct. 1938, in box 3815, file 12-22, RG 48, NA.

9. J. R. Eakin to David Chapman, 7 May 1931, in box 312, file 715-04, RG 79, NA.

10. J. R. Eakin to J. D. Coffman, 11 June 1931, in box 313, file 871, RG 79, NA.

11. Eakin, "Proposed GSMNP"; Frome, *Strangers,* 164.

12. Cammerer to Needham, 17 Sept. 1930.

13. Audley Whaley, interview by Alston, 30 July 1975.

14. J. R. Eakin to Horace Albright, 27 Jan. 1932, in box 303, file 302, RG 79, NA.

15. B. B. Smith, "Memorandum for the Solicitor," 29 Jan. 1937, in box 3816, file 12-22, RG 48, NA.

16. B. B. Smith, "Memorandum for the Secretary," 18 Dec. 1937, in box 3816, file 12-22, RG 48, NA.

17. Charlotte Pyle, "CCC Camps in the Great Smoky Mountains National

Park" (Apr. 1979); and Walter Miller, "The Civilian Conservation Corps in East Tennessee and the Great Smoky Mountains National Park, 1933–1942" (Dec. 1974); both papers in GSMNP Library. *Asheville Citizen-Times*, 19 Aug. 1984, p. 7a; Program for "Park Homecoming and CCC Reunion," 18 Aug. 1984, in collection of Bernice McClure, Asheville, N.C.

18. Eakin, "Proposed GSMNP"; Arno Cammerer to David Chapman, n.d., in box 302, file 204-020, RG 79, NA.

19. Eakin, "Proposed GSMNP"; J. R. Eakin to Horace Albright, 9 July 1931, in box 311, file 631-1, RG 79, NA.

20. Arthur Comey to Arno Cammerer, 21 Aug. 1931, in box 306, file 602.1, RG 79, NA.

21. Ibid.; Dunn, *Cades Cove*, 255.

22. Lindsay, "History of the Grassy Balds," 23.

23. Ernest Walker Sawyer, "General Memorandum on Trip to the Smokies," undated, in box 2012, file 12-22, RG 48, NA.

24. Clifford Bogle to H. P. Sheldon, 28 May 1930, in box 303, file 208-06, RG 79, NA.

25. J. R. Eakin to Albert Ganier, 13 July 1931, in box 312, file 715-04, RG 79, NA.

26. J. R. Eakin to Horace Albright, 30 Mar. 1931, in box 312, file 715-04, RG 79, NA.

27. Eakin to Ganier, 13 July 1931; J. R. Eakin to Horace Albright, undated, in box 1139, file 715-04, RG 79, NA.

28. J. R. Eakin to Horace Albright, 8 Aug. 1931, in box 303, file 208.06, RG 79, NA; and Eakin, "Proposed GSMNP."

29. J. R. Eakin to Horace Albright, 30 Jan. 1932, in box 310, file 620-30, RG 79, NA. J. R. Eakin to Arno Cammerer, 19 Feb. 1934; and David Madsen to Conrad Wirth, 12 Dec. 1935, in box 1132, file 620-30, RG 79, NA.

30. Thomas J. Allen, "Memorandum of the Director," in box 1132, file 620-30, RG 79, NA.

31. J. R. Eakin to Victor Cahalane, 24 July 1935, in box 1138, file 715-02, RG 79, NA.

32. Arno Cammerer to J. R. Eakin, 1 July 1935, in box 1138, file 715-02, RG 79, NA.

33. Eakin to Cahalane, 24 July 1935.

34. J. R. Eakin to Horace Albright, 21 Jan. 1932, in box 303, file 208-06, RG 79, NA.

35. J. R. Eakin to Arno Cammerer, 15 Oct. 1934, in box 1137, file 710, RG 79, NA.

36. Assistant Director Bryant to J. R. Eakin, 19 Jan. 1932, in box 303, file 208-06, RG 79, NA.

37. Arno Cammerer to J. R. Eakin, 11 Sept. 1934, in box 1137, file 710, RG 79, NA.

38. George Smith, "Report of Trip to the Great Smoky Mountain National Park," 1931, in box 302, file 204-020, RG 79, NA.

39. Ibid.; Phillip Hough to Horace Albright, 17 Sept. 1930, in box 302, file 204-010, RG 79, NA.

40. Waldo Leland to Arno Cammerer, 7 Mar. 1935; and Bascom Lamar Lunsford to Waldo Leland, 6 Mar. 1935; both in box 1077, file 101, RG 79, NA.

41. Horace Albright, "The South's First National Park," in box 305, file 501-04, RG 79, NA.

42. Dunn, *Cades Cove,* 256.

43. H. C. Wilburn, C. S. Grossman, and Arthur Stupka, "Report on the Proposed Mountain Culture Program for the Great Smoky Mountains National Park," undated, in GSMNP Library.

44. Hans Huth, "Report on the Preservation of Mountain Culture in Great Smoky Mountains National Park," Aug. 1941, in GSMNP Library.

45. V. Ross Bender, "Living History in the Great Smoky Mountains National Park," 1967, in GSMNP Library; Dunn, *Cades Cove,* 256.

46. J. R. Eakin to Arno Cammerer, 27 July 1937, in box 1135, file 640, RG 79, NA.

47. J. R. Eakin to John S. Beck, 28 Sept. 1937, in box 3816, file 12-22, RG 48, NA.

48. J. R. Eakin to Arno Cammerer, 17 Sept. 1937, in Land Acquisition Papers, box 15, file 7, GSMNP Archives.

49. "Accommodations for Visitors Summary Sheet," 3 Mar. 1939, in box 3791, file 12-0, RG 48, NA.

50. Harold Ickes to Walter White, 4 Feb. 1937, in box 3791, file 12-0, RG 48, NA.

51. A. E. Demaray, "Memorandum for Superintendent Eakin," 9 Sept. 1938, in box 3791, file 12-0, RG 48, NA; and "Accommodations for Visitors Summary Sheet."

52. Horace Albright to Harvey Broome, Oct. 1931, in box 310, file 630, RG 79, NA.

53. J. R. Eakin to Horace Albright, 16 Feb. 1932, in box 310, file 630, RG 79, NA.

54. Horace Albright to Fred L. Weede, 18 Feb. 1932, in box 310, file 630, RG 79, NA.

55. J. R. Eakin to Horace Albright, 16 Feb. 1932, in box 310, file 630, RG 79, NA.

56. Harris Reynolds to Arno Cammerer, 6 Sept. 1932, in box 311, file 631-1, RG 79, NA.

57. Horace Albright, "Memorandum for the Staff," 14 Nov. 1932, in box 310, file 630, RG 79, NA.

58. Harlan Kelsey to Horace Albright, 19 Nov. 1932, in box 311, file 630, RG 79, NA.

59. Harvey Broome to Horace Albright, 14 Oct. 1931, in Harvey Broome Papers, MHC.

60. Arno Cammerer to Phillip Ayres, 6 Dec. 1932, in box 311, file 630, RG 79, NA.

61. Lorne W. Barclay to Horace Albright, 27 Dec. 1932, in box 311, file 630, RG 79, NA; E. G. Frizzell to Arno Cammerer, 20 Jan. 1933, in box 1135, file 630, RG 79, NA.

62. Harlan Kelsey to Horace Albright, 30 Nov. 1932, in box 311, file 630, RG 79, NA.

63. *Knoxville News-Sentinel,* 20 Oct. 1934.

64. Fox, *John Muir,* 209–12; Nash, *Wilderness and American Mind,* 203–8.

65. Copy of charter with Broome's handwritten corrections, in Harvey Broome Papers, MHC.

66. Obituary for Harvey Broome, *Living Wilderness* 31, no. 99 (Winter 1967–68): 4–6.

67. Fox, *John Muir,* 209.

68. Robert Marshall, "Memorandum for the Secretary," 9 June 1935, in box 1081, file 201, RG 79, NA.

69. Arno Cammerer, "Memorandum for the Secretary," 15 July 1935, in box 2012, file 12-22, RG 48, NA.

70. T. H. Watkins, *Righteous Pilgrim: The Life and Times of Harold Ickes, 1874–1952* (New York: Henry Holt and Co.), 471–72.

71. E. K. Burlew to Kenneth McKellar, 3 June 1938, in box 3816, file 12-22, RG 48, NA.

72. Albright, "South's First National Park."

73. Fox, *John Muir,* 210.

74. Runte, *National Parks,* 163–70.

75. Horace Albright to David Chapman, 3 Apr. 1935, in GSMCA Papers, box 11, file 2.

76. Ibid.

77. J. R. Eakin to Arno Cammerer, 15 Aug. 1932, in box 312, file 650-01, RG 79, NA.

78. David Chapman to Arno Cammerer, 2 Dec. 1935, in GSMCA Papers, box 11, file 17.

79. Arno Cammerer to Orpheus Schantz, 17 Nov. 1934, in box 1135, file 650-01, RG 79, NA.

80. Harvey Broome to Gov. Gordon Browning, 31 May 1937, in Gov. Gordon Browning Papers, box 8, file 7, TSLA.

81. Arno Cammerer to David Chapman, 4 Dec. 1935, in GSMCA Papers, box 11, file 17.

82. Arno Cammerer to J. R. Eakin, 9 May 1938, in box 1093, file 501-04, RG 79, NA.

83. Runte, *National Parks,* 170.

Conclusion

1. Michael Satchell, "Trouble in Paradise," *U.S. News and World Report,* 19 June 1995, pp. 30–31.

2. Great Smoky Mountains Natural History Association, "Smokies Guide," Summer 1997, p. 7.

3. U.S. Dept. of the Interior, National Park Service, "A Strategic Plan for Managing Backcountry Recreation in Great Smoky Mountains National Park," Sept. 1995, p. 33, in GSMNP Library.

4. Aldo Leopold, *A Sand County Almanac* (New York: Oxford Univ. Press, 1966), 101.

5. U.S. Dept. of the Interior, National Park Service, "Transportation Concepts: Great Smoky Mountains National Park," 1971, in vertical file, GSMNP Library.

6. Ibid.; *Asheville Citizen*, 2 and 4 Oct. 1965.

7. U.S. Dept. of the Interior, "Transportation Concepts."

8. Fox, *John Muir*, 319.

9. Harvey Broome, *Out Under the Sky of the Great Smokies* (Knoxville, Tenn.: Greenbriar Press, 1975), 282–85; U.S. Dept. of the Interior, NPS, "Transportation Concepts," 57–58.

10. U.S. Dept. of the Interior, National Park Service, "Briefing Statement: North Shore Road Issue Settlement," 11 Jan. 1995, in vertical file, GSMNP Library.

11. Edward P. Moses to Mr. Horton, 12 July 1940, in E. P. Moses Papers, Southern Historical Collection, Univ. of North Carolina–Chapel Hill.

12. U.S. Dept. of the Interior, NPS, "Briefing Statement"; and U.S. Dept. of the Interior, NPS, "Transportation Concepts."

13. *Asheville Citizen*, 30 July 1974.

14. *Asheville Citizen*, 26 Jan. 1982.

15. John Mitchell, "Legacy at Risk," *National Geographic* 186, no. 4 (Oct. 1994): 20–55; and David Nevin, "Tranquillity, Tourism—and Trouble: The Great Smokies Have It All," *Smithsonian* 24 (Aug. 1993): 21–30.

16. Mitchell, "Legacy at Risk," 35–36.

17. U.S. Dept. of the Interior, NPS, "Strategic Plan for Managing Backcountry Recreation," 33; Jeffrey Marion, "An Assessment of Trail Conditions in Great Smoky Mountains National Park," NPS Research Report, July 1994, pp. 1–7, in GSMNP Library.

18. Marion, "An Assessment of Trail Conditions."

19. James Renfro, "Air Quality Advisory Program at Great Smoky Mountains National Park: Standard Operating Procedures," 27 Feb. 1996, pp. 1–5, in vertical file, GSMNP Library.

20. Ibid.

21. Ibid.; Christopher Eagar, "Forest Damage on Clingman's Dome, Great Smoky Mountains National Park," in vertical file, GSMNP Library.

22. U.S. Dept. of Agriculture, "Evaluation of Spruce and Fir Mortality in the Southern Appalachian Mountains," Protection Report R8-PR 13, 13 Oct. 1988, in GSMNP Library.

23. Mitchell, "Legacy at Risk," 27–29.

24. Kephart, "Last of the Eastern Wilderness," 632.

Bibliography

Primary Sources

Newspapers

Asheville (N.C.) Citizen, 1923–40.
Knoxville (Tenn.) Journal and Tribune, 1923–24.
Knoxville (Tenn.) Journal, 1924–40.
Knoxville (Tenn.) News, 1923–26.
Knoxville (Tenn.) News-Sentinel, 1926–40.

Manuscript Collections

Duke Univ., Special Collections Library. Durham, North Carolina.
———. Brooks, Eugene Clyde. Papers
———. Simmons, Sen. Furnifold M. Papers.
Great Smoky Mountains National Park Archives. Gatlinburg, Tenn.
———. Appalachian Club Collection.
———. Champion Fibre Company. Papers.
———. Chapman, David. Papers.
———. Condemnation: Tennessee. Records.
———. Davis, Willis P. Papers.
———. Great Smoky Mountains Conservation Association. Papers.
———. Knoxville Automobile Club. Papers.
———. Land Acquisition Records.
———. Little River Lumber Company. Papers.
———. Morrell, John C. Papers.
———. North Carolina Park Commission. Papers.
McClung Historical Collection, Lawson McGhee Library. Knoxville, Tenn.
———. Broome, Harvey. Papers.
———. Fink, Paul. Papers.
National Archives. Washington, D.C.
———. U.S. Dept. of the Interior. Records (RG 48).
———. U.S. National Park Service. Records (RG 79).
North Carolina State Archives. Raleigh, North Carolina.
———. Ehringhaus, Gov. J. C. B. Papers.

————. Gardner, Gov. O. Max. Papers.

————. McLean, Gov. Angus. Papers.

————. North Carolina National Park, Parkway and Forest Development Commission. Papers.

————. North Carolina Park Commission. Records.

————. Parks ORC. Papers.

Rockefeller Archive Center. Pocantico Hills, New York.

————. Rockefeller Family Archives.

————. Laura Spelman Rockefeller Memorial Archives.

Southern Historical Collection. Univ. of North Carolina, Chapel Hill.

————. Moses, Edward Pearson. Papers.

Tennessee State Archives and Library. Nashville.

————. Browning, Gov. Gordon. Papers.

————. Horton, Gov. Henry. Papers.

————. McAlister, Gov. Hill. Papers.

————. Peay, Gov. Austin. Papers.

Western Carolina Univ., Special Collections. Cullowhee, North Carolina.

————. Kephart, Horace. Papers.

————. Masa, George. Papers.

————. Weaver, Zebulon. Papers.

Secondary Sources

Books

Albright, Horace M., as told to Robert Cahn. *The Birth of the National Park Service: The Founding Years, 1913–1933.* Salt Lake City, Utah: Howe Brothers, 1985.

Bartram, William. *Travels Through North and South Carolina, Georgia, East and West Florida.* Philadelphia: James and Johnson, 1791; rpt. Savannah: Beehive Press, 1973.

Biographical Directory of the United States Congress, 1774–1989. Washington, D.C.: Government Printing Office, 1989.

Blethen, Tyler, and Curtis Wood. *From Ulster to Carolina: The Migration of the Scotch-Irish to Southwestern North Carolina.* Cullowhee, North Carolina: Western Carolina Univ. Mountain Heritage Center, 1983.

Brewer, Carson. *A Wonderment of Mountains.* Knoxville: Tenpenny Press, 1981.

Broome, Harvey. *Out Under the Sky of the Great Smokies.* Knoxville: Greenbriar Press, 1975.

Bucholtz, C. W. *Rocky Mountain National Park: A History.* Boulder: Colorado Associated Univ. Press, 1983.

Bush, Florence Cope. *Dorie: Woman of the Mountains.* Knoxville: Univ. of Tennessee Press, 1992.

Campbell, Carlos C. *Birth of a National Park in the Great Smoky Mountains.* Rev. ed. Knoxville: Univ. of Tennessee Press, 1969.

Corbitt, David Leroy, ed. *The Papers and Public Letters of Angus Wilton McLean, Governor of North Carolina, 1925–1929.* Raleigh: Council of State, State of North Carolina, 1931.

————. *The Public Papers and Letters of Oliver Max Gardner, Governor of North Carolina, 1929–1933.* Raleigh: Council of State, State of North Carolina, 1937.

Cronon, William. *Changes in the Land: Indians, Colonists, and the Ecology of New England.* New York: Hill & Wang, 1983.

————, ed. *Uncommon Ground: Toward Reinventing Nature.* New York: W. W. Norton & Co., 1995.

Deaderick, Lucille, ed. *Heart of the Valley: A History of Knoxville, Tennessee.* Knoxville: East Tennessee Historical Society, 1976.

Dunn, Durwood. *Cades Cove: The Life and Death of a Southern Appalachian Community, 1818–1937.* Knoxville: Univ. of Tennessee Press, 1988.

Eller, Ronald D. *Miners, Millhands, and Mountaineers: Industrialization of the Appalachian South, 1880–1930.* Knoxville: Univ. of Tennessee Press, 1982.

Ettling, John. *The Germ of Laziness: Rockefeller Philanthropy and Public Health in the New South.* Cambridge, Mass.: Harvard Univ. Press, 1981.

Everhart, William. *The National Park Service.* 2d ed. Boulder, Colorado: Westview Press, 1983.

Finger, John R. *The Eastern Band of the Cherokees, 1819–1900.* Knoxville: Univ. of Tennessee Press, 1984.

Fosdick, Raymond B. *John D. Rockefeller, Jr.: A Portrait.* New York: Harper, 1956.

Fox, Stephen. *John Muir and His Legacy: The American Conservation Movement.* Boston: Little, Brown, 1981.

Frazier, Charles. *Cold Mountain.* New York: Atlantic Monthly Press, 1997.

Frome, Michael. *Strangers in High Places: The Story of the Great Smoky Mountains.* Garden City, New York: Doubleday, 1966.

Gatewood, Willard B. *Eugene Clyde Brooks: Educator and Public Servant.* Durham, N.C.: Duke Univ. Press, 1960.

Godbold, Stanley, and Mattie U. Russell. *Confederate Colonel and Cherokee Chief: The Life of William Holland Thomas.* Knoxville: Univ. of Tennessee Press, 1990.

Goodwin, Gary. *The Cherokees in Transition: A Study of Changing Culture and Environment Prior to 1775.* Chicago: Dept. of Geography, Univ. of Chicago, 1977.

Grantham, Dewey. *Southern Progressivism: The Reconciliation of Progress and Tradition.* Knoxville: Univ. of Tennessee Press, 1983.

Harr, John Ensor, and Peter J. Johnson. *The Rockefeller Conscience: An American Family in Public and Private.* New York: Charles Scribner's Sons, 1991.

Hays, Samuel P. *Conservation and the Gospel of Efficiency.* Cambridge, Mass.: Harvard Univ. Press, 1959.

Houk, Rose. *A Natural History Guide: Great Smoky Mountains National Park.* Boston: Houghton Mifflin Company, 1993.

Hudson, Charles. *The Forgotten Centuries: Indians and Europeans in the American South.* Athens: Univ. of Georgia Press, 1994.

————. *Southeastern Indians.* Knoxville: Univ. of Tennessee Press, 1976.

Ise, John. *Our National Park Policy: A Critical History.* Baltimore, Maryland: Johns Hopkins Univ. Press, 1961.

Jenkins, Hazel, coordinator. *The Heritage of Swain County, North Carolina.* Winston-Salem, N.C.: Hunter Publishing Co., 1988.

Jolley, Harley E. *The Blue Ridge Parkway.* Knoxville: Univ. of Tennessee Press, 1969.

Keel, Bennie. *Cherokee Archaeology: A Study of the Appalachian Summit.* Knoxville: Univ. of Tennessee Press, 1976.

Kephart, Horace. *Our Southern Highlanders.* New York: Outing Publishing Company, 1913; rpt. Knoxville: Univ. of Tennessee Press, 1976.

Key, V. O. *Southern Politics in State and Nation.* New York: Alfred A. Knopf, 1949; rpt. Knoxville: Univ. of Tennessee Press, 1984.

Lanman, Charles. *Letters From the Allegheny Mountains.* New York: Geo. P. Putnam, 1849.

Lee, David D. *Tennessee in Turmoil: Politics in the Volunteer State, 1920–1932.* Memphis: Memphis State Univ. Press, 1979.

Leopold, Aldo. *A Sand County Almanac.* New York: Sierra Club/Ballantine Books, 1970.

Linzey, Alicia V., and Donald W. Linzey. *Mammals of the Great Smoky Mountains National Park.* Knoxville: Univ. of Tennessee Press, 1971.

McCoy, George W. *A Brief History of the Great Smoky Mountains National Park Movement in North Carolina.* Asheville, North Carolina: Inland Press, 1940.

McDonald, Michael J., and William Bruce Wheeler. *Knoxville, Tennessee: Continuity and Change in an Appalachian City.* Knoxville: Univ. of Tennessee Press, 1983.

McWhiney, Grady. *Cracker Culture: Celtic Ways in the Old South.* Tuscaloosa: Univ. of Alabama Press, 1988.

Medford, Clark W. *The Early History of Haywood County.* Asheville, North Carolina: Miller Printing Company, 1961.

Miller, Wilbur R. *Revenuers and Moonshiners: Enforcing Federal Liquor Law in the Mountain South, 1865–1900.* Chapel Hill: Univ. of North Carolina Press, 1991.

Miller, William D. *Mr. Crump of Memphis.* Baton Rouge: Louisiana State Univ. Press, 1964.

Mooney, James. *Myths of the Cherokee and Sacred Formulas of the Cherokees.* 1900. Rpt. Nashville: Charles Elder Bookseller, 1972.

Morrison, Ernest. *J. Horace McFarland: A Thorn for Beauty.* Harrisburg: Pennsylvania Historical and Museum commission, 1995.

Nash, Roderick. *Wilderness and the American Mind.* New Haven, Connecticut: Yale Univ. Press, 1967.

———, ed. *The American Environment: Readings in the History of Conservation.* Reading, Massachusetts: Addison-Wesley, 1968.

Nixon, Edgar B., ed. *Franklin D. Roosevelt and Conservation, 1911–1945.* 2 vols. Hyde Park, New York: Franklin D. Roosevelt Library, 1957.

Powers, Elizabeth, with Mark Hannah. *Cataloochee, Lost Settlement of the Smokies: The History, Social Customs, and Natural History.* Charleston, South Carolina: Powers-Hannah Publishers, 1982.

Preston, Howard Lawrence. *Dirt Roads to Dixie: Accessibility and Modernization in the South, 1885–1935.* Knoxville: Univ. of Tennessee Press, 1991.

Pudup, Mary Beth; Dwight Billings; and Altina Waller, eds. *Appalachia in the Making: The Mountain South in the Nineteenth Century.* Chapel Hill: Univ. of North Carolina Press, 1995.

Pyne, Stephen; Patricia Andrews; and Richard Laven. *Introduction to Wildland Fire.* 2d ed. New York: John Wiley and Sons, 1996.

Ready, Milton. *Asheville: Land of the Sky.* Northridge, California: Windsor Publications, 1986.

Rennicke, Jeff. *Black Bear: Spirit of the Smokies.* Gatlinburg, Tennessee: Great Smoky Mountains Natural History Association, 1991.

Righter, Robert. *Crucible for Conservation: The Creation of Grand Teton National Park.* Boulder: Colorado Associated Univ. Press, 1982.

Runte, Alfred. *National Parks: The American Experience.* Lincoln: Univ. of Nebraska Press, 1987.

Sandborn, Margaret. *Yosemite: Its Discovery, Its Wonders, and Its People.* New York: Random House, 1981.

Schrepfer, Susan R. *The Fight to Save the Redwoods: A History of Environmental Reform, 1917–1978.* Madison: Univ. of Wisconsin Press, 1983.

Shankland, Robert. *Steve Mather of the National Parks.* New York: Knopf, 1970.

Shapiro, Henry D. *Appalachia on Our Mind: The Southern Mountains and Mountaineers in the American Consciousness, 1870–1920.* Chapel Hill: Univ. of North Carolina Press, 1978.

Shifflett, Crandall. *Coal Towns: Life, Work, and Culture in Company Towns of Southern Appalachia, 1880–1960.* Knoxville: Univ. of Tennessee Press, 1991.

Silver, Timothy. *A New Face on the Countryside: Indians, Colonists, and Slaves in South Atlantic Forests, 1500–1800.* Cambridge, England: Cambridge Univ. Press, 1990.

Simkins, Francis Butler. *The South, Old and New: A History, 1820–1947.* New York: Alfred A. Knopf, 1947.

Strong, Douglas. *Tahoe: An Environmental History.* Lincoln: Univ. of Nebraska Press, 1984.

Stupka, Arthur. *Trees, Shrubs, and Woody Vines of Great Smoky Mountains National Park.* Knoxville: Univ. of Tennessee Press, 1964.

Swain, Donald C. *Wilderness Defender: Horace M. Albright and Conservation.* Chicago: Univ. of Chicago Press, 1970.

Thornborough, Laura. *The Great Smoky Mountains.* New York: Thomas Crowell Company, 1937. Rpt. Knoxville: Univ. of Tennessee Press, 1962.

Tindall, George B. *The Emergence of the New South, 1913–1945.* Baton Rouge: Louisiana State Univ. Press. 1967.

Trout, Ed. *Gatlinburg: Cinderella City.* Sevierville, Tennessee: Griffin Graphics, 1984.

U.S. Dept. of the Interior, National Park Service, Division of Publications. *At Home in the Smokies: A History Handbook for the Great Smoky Mountains National Park, North Carolina and Tennessee.* Washington, D.C.: U.S. Dept. of the Interior, 1984.

Van Noppen, Ina W., and John J. Van Noppen. *Western North Carolina Since the Civil War.* Boone, North Carolina: Appalachian Consortium Press, 1973.

Watkins, T. H. *Righteous Pilgrim: The Life and Times of Harold Ickes, 1874–1952.* New York: Henry Holt and Company, 1990.

Weals, Vic. *Last Train to Elkmont: A Look Back at Life on Little River in the Great Smoky Mountains.* Knoxville, Tennessee: Olden Press, 1993.

Wear, Jerry; Mary Alice Teague; and Lynn Alexander. *Lost Communities of Sevier County, Tennessee: Greenbriar.* Sevierville, Tennessee: Sevier County Heritage Committee, 1985.

————. *Lost Communities of Sevier County, Tennessee: Sugarlands* (Sevierville, Tenn.: Sevier County Heritage Committee, 1985).

Whisnant, David E. *All That Is Native and Fine: The Politics of Culture in an American Region.* Chapel Hill: Univ. of North Carolina Press, 1983.

White, Robert H., and Stephen V. Ash. *Messages of the Governors of Tennessee.* 10 vols. to date. Nashville: Tennessee Historical Commission, 1952– .

Williams, Michael. *Americans and Their Forests: A Historical Geography.* Cambridge, England: Cambridge Univ. Press, 1989.

Wirth, Conrad L. *Parks, Politics, and the People.* Norman: Univ. of Oklahoma Press, 1980.

Woodward, Grace Steele. *The Cherokees.* Norman: Univ. of Oklahoma Press, 1963.

Articles

Cronon, William, and Richard White. "Indians in the Land." *American Heritage* 37 (1986): 18–25.

Gatewood, Willard B. "North Carolina's Role in the Establishment of the Great Smoky Mountains National Park." *North Carolina Historical Review* 37 (1960): 165–84.

Gregg, William C. "Two New National Parks?" *Outlook* 141 (1925): 667.

Guyot, Arnold. "Notes on the Geography of the Mountain District of Western North Carolina." Rpt. in *North Carolina Historical Review* 15 (1938): 275–86.

Kephart, Horace. "The Last of the Eastern Wilderness." *World's Work* 53 (Apr. 1926): 617–32.

Lambert, Robert S. "Logging in the Great Smokies, 1880–1930." *Tennessee Historical Quarterly* 21 (1961): 350–63.

————. "Logging on Little River, 1890–1940." East Tennessee Historical Society's *Publications* 33 (1961): 32–43.

MacPherson, Joseph T. "Democratic Progressivism in Tennessee: The Administrations of Governor Austin Peay, 1923–1927." East Tennessee Historical Society's *Publications* 40 (1968): 50–61.

Marcy, Dr. Henry O. "The Climatic Treatment of Disease: Western North Carolina as a Health Resort." *Journal of the American Medical Association* 5 (1885): 704–8.

McDonald, Forrest, and Grady McWhiney. "The South from Self-Sufficiency to Peonage." *American Historical Review* 85 (1980): 1095–1118.

Mitchell, John G. "Legacy at Risk." *National Geographic* 186 (Oct. 1994): 20–55.

Nevin, David. "Tranquillity, Tourism—and Trouble: The Great Smokies Have It All." *Smithsonian* 24 (Aug. 1993): 20–32.

Powers, Charles L., Jr. "A National Park in Our Southern Highlands." *Manufacturers Record,* 6 Mar. 1924, pp. 101–4.

Runte, Alfred. "Promoting Wonderland: Western Railroads and the Evolution of National Park Advertising." *Journal of the West* 31 (1992): 43–48.

Satchell, Michael. "Trouble in Paradise." *U.S. News and World Report,* 19 June 1995, pp. 30–32.

Semple, Ellen Churchill. "The Anglo-Saxons of the Kentucky Mountains: A Study in Anthrogeography." *Geographical Journal* 17 (1901): 592–95.

Shields, A. Randolph. "Cades Cove in the Great Smoky Mountains National Park." *Tennessee Historical Quarterly* 24 (1965): 3–20.

Smith, Charles Dennis. "The Appalachian Park Movement, 1885–1901." *North Carolina Historical Review* 37 (1960): 38–65.

Swain, Donald. "The Passage of the National Park Service Act of 1916." *Wisconsin Magazine of History* 50 (1966): 4–17.

Tindall, George B. "Business Progressivism: Southern Politics in the Twenties." *South Atlantic Quarterly* 62 (1963): 92–106.

Woody, Robert H. "Cataloochee Homecoming." *South Atlantic Quarterly* 49 (1950): 8–17.

Yard, Robert Sterling. "Gift-Parks the Coming National Park Danger." *National Parks Bulletin* 4 (1923): 4–5.

———. "A National Park in the Great Smoky Mountains." *National Parks Bulletin* 46 (1925): 3–6.

Theses and Dissertations

Brown, Margaret Lynn. "Power, Privilege, and Tourism: A Revision of the Great Smoky Mountains National Park Story." Master's thesis, Univ. of Kentucky, 1990.

Dickinson, Joel Ray. "The Creation of Redwood National Park: A Case Study in the Politics of Conservation." Ph.D. diss., Univ. of Missouri–Columbia, 1974.

Givens, Peter Shelburne. "Cataloochee and the Establishment of the Great Smoky Mountains National Park." Master's thesis, Western Carolina Univ., 1978.

Lankford, Jesse R. "The Campaign for a National Park in Western North Carolina." Master's thesis, Western Carolina Univ., 1973.

MacPherson, Joseph T. "Democratic Progressivism in Tennessee: The Administration of Governor Austin Peay." Ph.D. diss., Vanderbilt Univ., 1969.

Pope, Robert Dean. "Senatorial Baron: The Long Political Career of Kenneth D. McKellar." Ph.D. diss., Yale Univ., 1976.

Russell, Mattie. "William Holland Thomas, White Chief of the North Carolina Cherokee." Ph.D. diss., Duke Univ., 1956.

Simmons, Dennis Elwood. "The Creation of Shenandoah National Park and the Skyline Drive, 1924–1936." Ph.D. diss., Univ. of Virginia, 1978.

Whaley, John Thomas. "A Timely Idea at an Ideal Time: Knoxville's Role in Establishing the Great Smoky Mountains National Park." Master's thesis, Univ. of Tennessee, Knoxville, 1984.

Index

The Great Smokies was designed and typeset on a Macintosh computer system using PageMaker software. The text is set in Caslon, and the chapter openings are set in Caslon Antique. This book was designed by Sheila Hart, typeset by Kimberly Scarbrough, and manufactured by Thomson-Shore, Inc. The recycled paper used in this book is designed for an effective life of at least three hundred years.